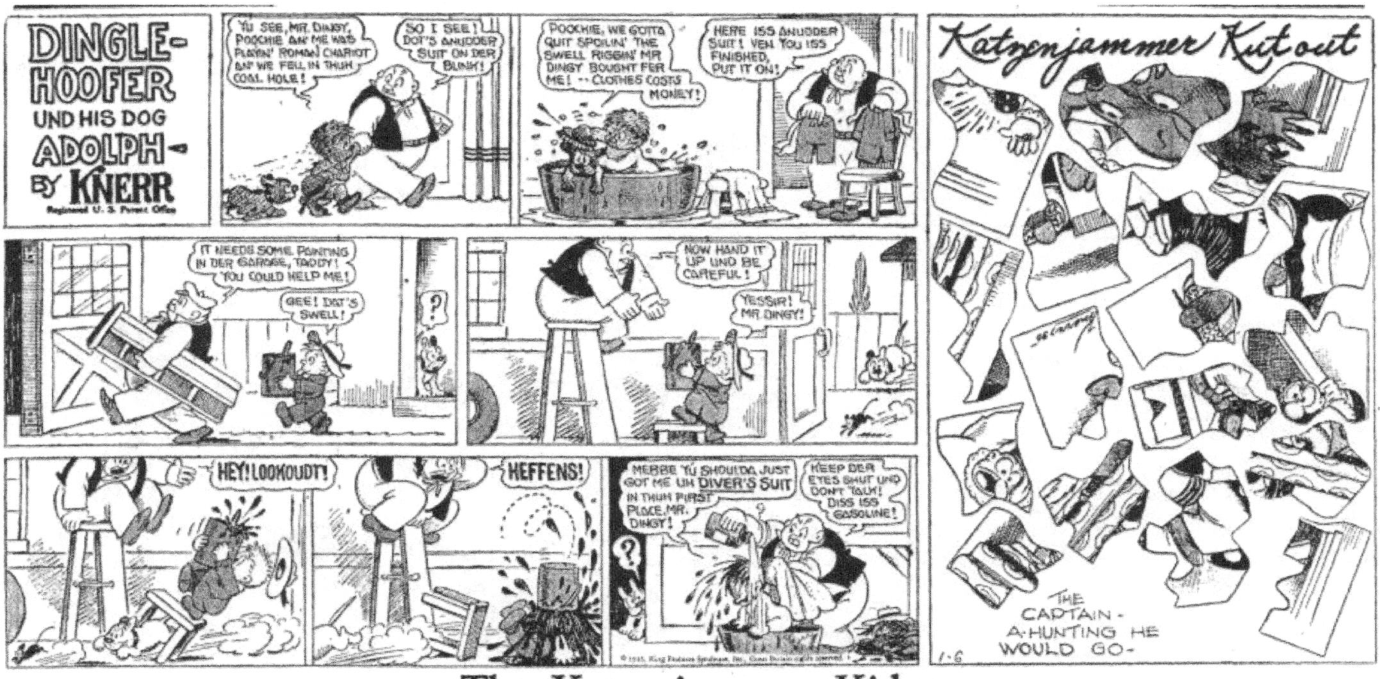
DINGLE-HOOFER UND HIS DOG ADOLPH
BY KNERR
Registered U. S. Patent Office
YU SEE, MR. DINGY, POOCHIE AN' ME WAS PLAYIN' ROMAN CHARIOT AN' WE FELL IN THUH COAL HOLE!
SO I SEE! DOT'S ANUDDER SUIT ON DER BUNK!
POOCHIE, WE GOTTA QUIT SPOILIN' THE SWELL RIGGIN' MR DINGY BOUGHT FER ME! -- CLOTHES COSTS MONEY!
HERE ISS ANUDDER SUIT! VEN YOU ISS FINISHED, PUT IT ON!
IT NEEDS SOME PAINTING IN DER GARAGE, TADDY! YOU COULD HELP ME!
GEE! DAT'S SWELL!
?
NOW HAND IT UP UND BE CAREFUL!
YESSIR! MR. DINGY!
HEY! LOOKOUDT!
HEFFENS!
MEBBE YU SHOULDA JUST GOT ME UH DIVER'S SUIT IN THUH FIRST PLACE, MR. DINGY!
KEEP DER EYES SHUT UND DON'T TALK! DISS ISS GASOLINE!
?
Katzenjammer Kut out
THE CAPTAIN - A-HUNTING HE WOULD GO-
1-6

The Katzenjammer Kids

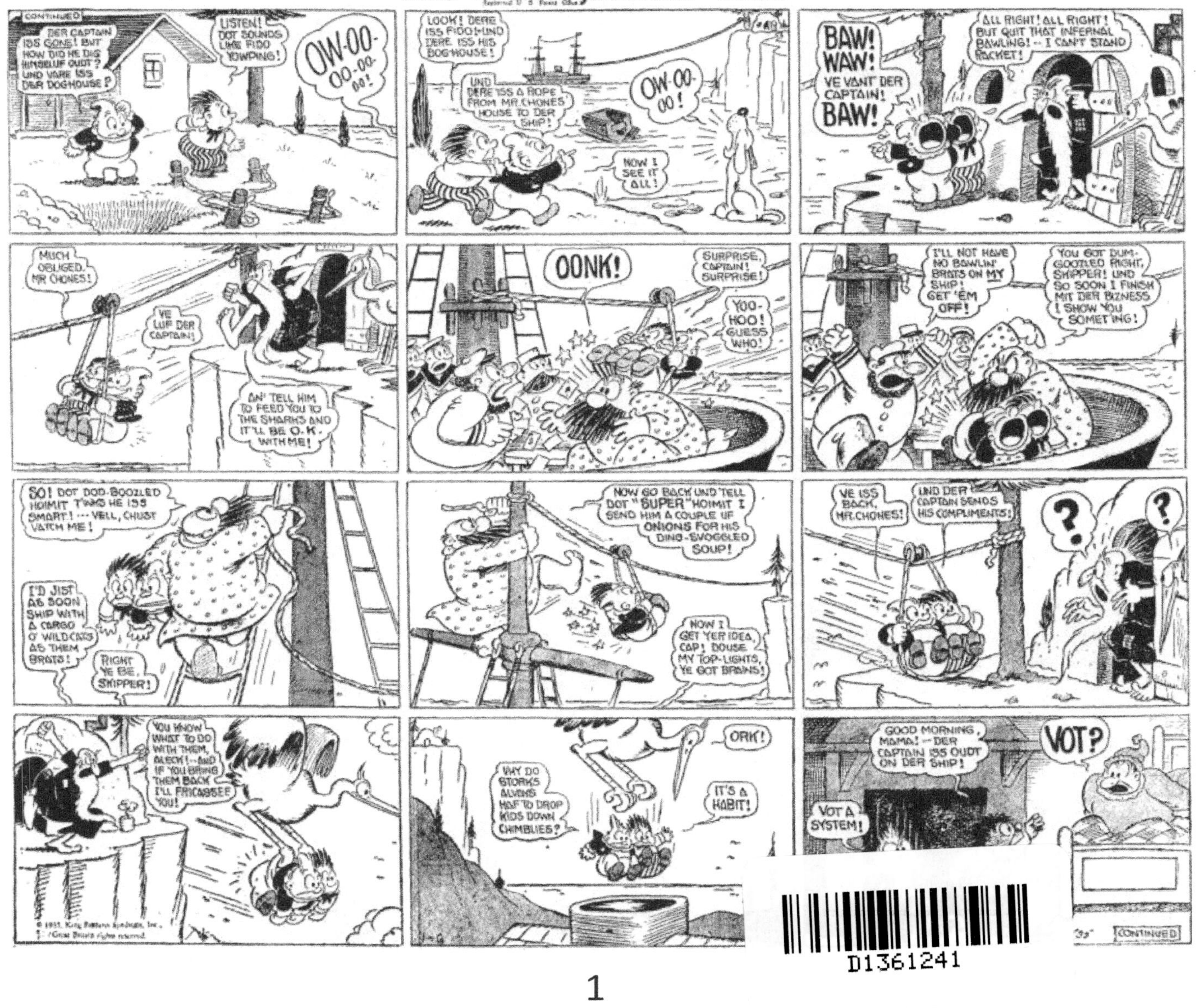
CONTINUED
DER CAPTAIN ISS GONE! BUT HOW DID HE DIG HIMSELUF OUDT? UND VARE ISS DER DOGHOUSE?
LISTEN! DOT SOUNDS LIKE FIDO YOWPING!
OW-OO-OO-OO-OO!
LOOK! DERE ISS FIDO!-UND DERE ISS HIS DOG-HOUSE!
UND DERE ISS A ROPE FROM MR. CHONES' HOUSE TO DER SHIP!
OW-OO-OO!
NOW I SEE IT ALL!
BAW! WAW! VE VANT DER CAPTAIN! BAW!
ALL RIGHT! ALL RIGHT! BUT QUIT THAT INFERNAL BAWLING! -- I CAN'T STAND RACKET!
MUCH OBLIGED, MR CHONES!
VE LUF DER CAPTAIN!
AN' TELL HIM TO FEED YOU TO THE SHARKS AND IT'LL BE O.K. WITH ME!
OONK!
SURPRISE, CAPTAIN! SURPRISE!
YOO-HOO! GUESS WHO!
I'LL NOT HAVE NO BAWLIN' BRATS ON MY SHIP! GET 'EM OFF!
YOU GOT DUM-GOOZLED RIGHT, SKIPPER! UND SO SOON I FINISH MIT DER BIZNESS I SHOW YOU SOMETING!
SO! DOT DOD-BOOZLED HOIMIT TINKS HE ISS SMART! --- VELL, CHUST VATCH ME!
I'D JIST AS SOON SHIP WITH A CARGO O' WILDCATS AS THEM BRATS!
RIGHT YE BE, SKIPPER!
NOW GO BACK UND TELL DOT "SUPER" HOIMIT I SEND HIM A COUPLE UF ONIONS FOR HIS DING-SWOGGLED SOUP!
NOW I GET YER IDEA, CAP! DOUSE MY TOP-LIGHTS, YE GOT BRAINS!
VE ISS BACK, MR. CHONES!
UND DER CAPTAIN SENDS HIS COMPLIMENTS!
?
?
YOU KNOW WHAT TO DO WITH THEM, ALECK! -- AND IF YOU BRING THEM BACK I'LL FRICASSEE YOU!
ORK!
WHY DO STORKS ALWAYS HAF TO DROP KIDS DOWN CHIMBLIES?
IT'S A HABIT!
GOOD MORNING, MAMA! -- DER CAPTAIN ISS OUDT ON DER SHIP!
VOT?
VOT A SYSTEM!
1-6
CONTINUED

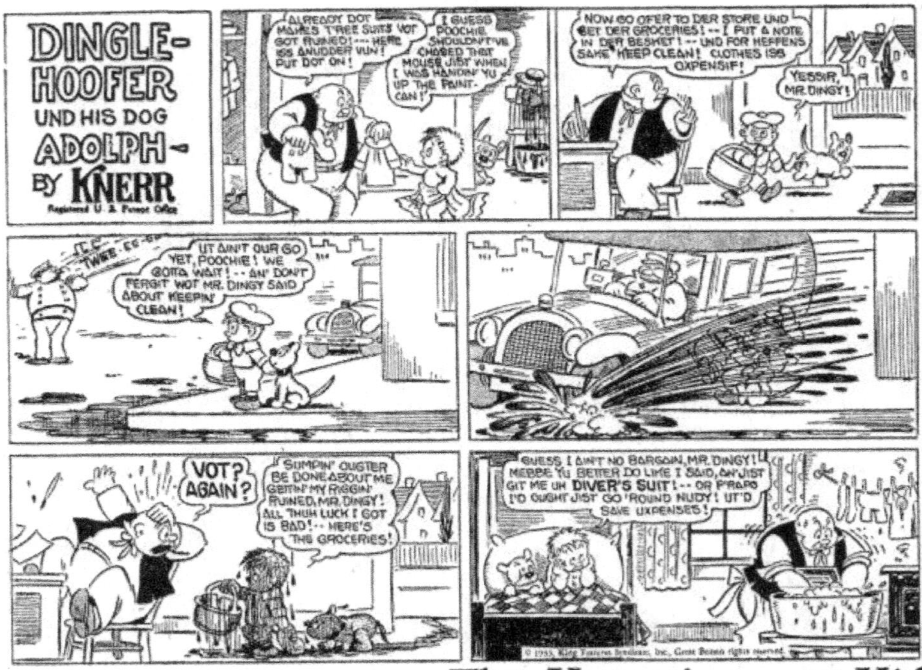
DINGLE-HOOFER UND HIS DOG ADOLPH - BY KNERR
Registered U. S. Patent Office
ALREADY DOT MAKES T'REE SUITS VOT GOT RUINED! --- HERE ISS ANUDDER VUN! PUT DOT ON!
I GUESS POOCHIE SHOULDN'T'VE CHASED THAT MOUSE JIST WHEN I WAS HANDIN' YU UP THE PAINT-CAN!
NOW GO OFER TO DER STORE UND GET DER GROCERIES! -- I PUT A NOTE IN DER BESKET! -- UND FOR HEFFENS SAKE KEEP CLEAN! CLOTHES ISS OXPENSIF!
YESSIR, MR. DINGY!
TWEE-EE-EE
UT AIN'T OUR GO YET, POOCHIE! WE GOTTA WAIT! -- AN' DON'T FERGIT WOT MR. DINGY SAID ABOUT KEEPIN' CLEAN!
VOT? AGAIN?
SUMPIN' OUGHTER BE DONE ABOUT ME GETTIN' MY RIGGIN' RUINED, MR. DINGY! ALL THUH LUCK I GOT IS BAD! -- HERE'S THE GROCERIES!
GUESS I AIN'T NO BARGAIN, MR. DINGY! MEBBE YU BETTER DO LIKE I SAID, AN' JIST GIT ME UH DIVER'S SUIT! -- OR P'RAPS I'D OUGHT JIST GO 'ROUND NUDY! UT'D SAVE UXPENSES!
© 1935, King Features Syndicate, Inc., Great Britain rights reserved.

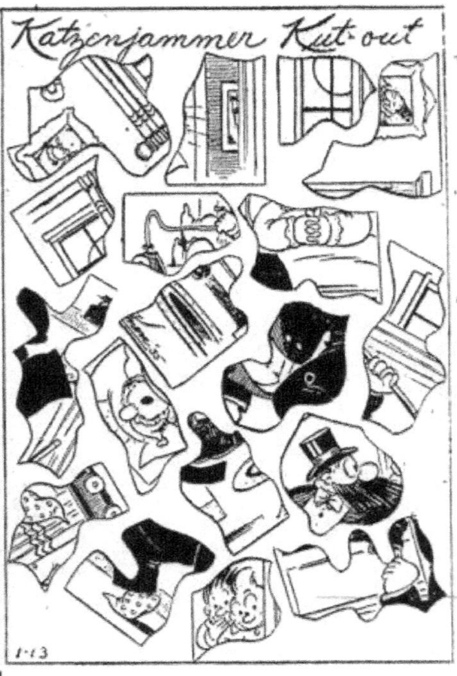
Katzenjammer Kut-out
1-13

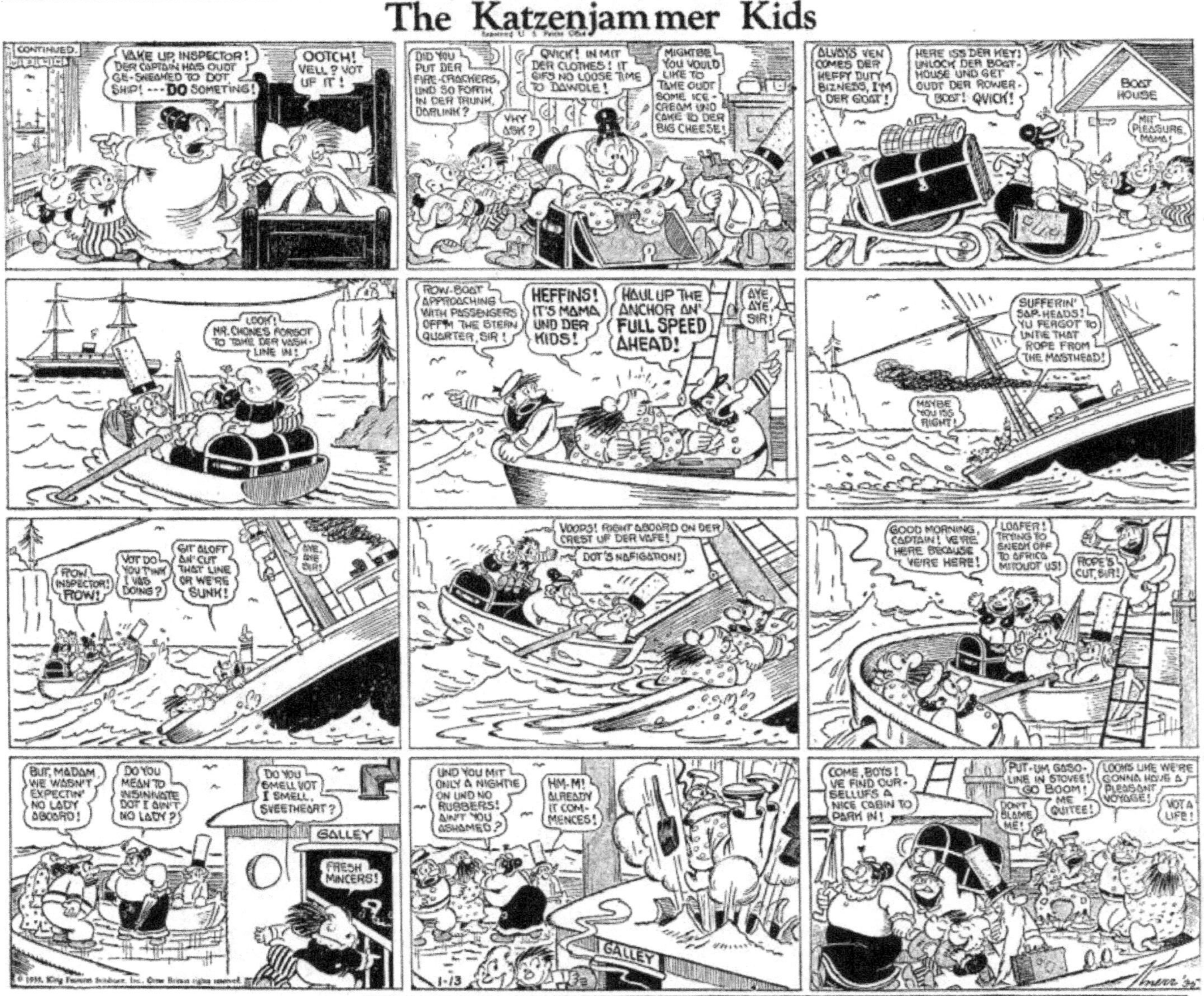
The Katzenjammer Kids
Registered U. S. Patent Office
CONTINUED.
VAKE UP, INSPECTOR! DER CAPTAIN HAS OUDT GE-SHEAKED TO DOT SHIP! --- DO SOMETING!
OOTCH! VELL? VOT UF IT!
DID YOU PUT DER FIRE-CRACKERS, UND SO FORTH IN DER TRUNK, DORLINK?
VHY ASK?
QVICK! IN MIT DER CLOTHES! IT GIFS NO LOOSE TIME TO DAWDLE!
MIGHTBE YOU VOULD LIKE TO TAKE OUDT SOME ICE-CREAM UND CAKE TO DER BIG CHEESE!
ALVAYS VEN COMES DER HEFFY DUTY BIZNESS, I'M DER GOAT!
HERE ISS DER KEY! UNLOCK DER BOAT-HOUSE UND GET OUDT DER ROWER-BOAT! QVICK!
BOAT HOUSE
MIT PLEASURE, MAMA!
LOOK! MR. CHONES FORGOT TO TAKE DER VASH-LINE IN!
ROW-BOAT APPROACHING WITH PASSENGERS OFF'M THE STERN QUARTER, SIR!
HEFFINS! IT'S MAMA UND DER KIDS!
HAUL UP THE ANCHOR AN' FULL SPEED AHEAD!
AYE, AYE, SIR!
SUFFERIN' SAP-HEADS! YU FERGOT TO UNTIE THAT ROPE FROM THE MASTHEAD!
MAYBE YOU ISS RIGHT!
ROW! INSPECTOR! ROW!
VOT DO YOU T'INK I VAS DOING?
GIT ALOFT AN' CUT THAT LINE OR WE'RE SUNK!
AYE, AYE SIR!
VOOPS! RIGHT ABOARD ON DER CREST UF DER VAFE!
DOT'S NAFIGATION!
GOOD MORNING, CAPTAIN! VE'RE HERE BECAUSE VE'RE HERE!
LOAFER! TRYING TO SNEAK OFF TO AFRICA MITOUDT US!
ROPE'S CUT, SIR!
BUT, MADAM, WE WASN'T EXPECTIN' NO LADY ABOARD!
DO YOU MEAN TO INSINUATE DOT I AIN'T NO LADY?
DO YOU SMELL VOT I SMELL, SWEETHEART?
GALLEY
FRESH MINCERS!
UND YOU MIT ONLY A NIGHTIE ON UND NO RUBBERS! AIN'T YOU ASHAMED?
HM-M! ALREADY IT COM-MENCES!
GALLEY
1-13
COME, BOYS! VE FIND OUR-SELLUFS A NICE CABIN TO PARK IN!
PUT-UM GASO-LINE IN STOVEE! GO BOOM! ME QUITEE!
DON'T BLAME ME!
LOOKS LIKE WE'RE GONNA HAVE A PLEASANT VOYAGE!
VOT A LIFE!
© 1935, King Features Syndicate, Inc., Great Britain rights reserved.

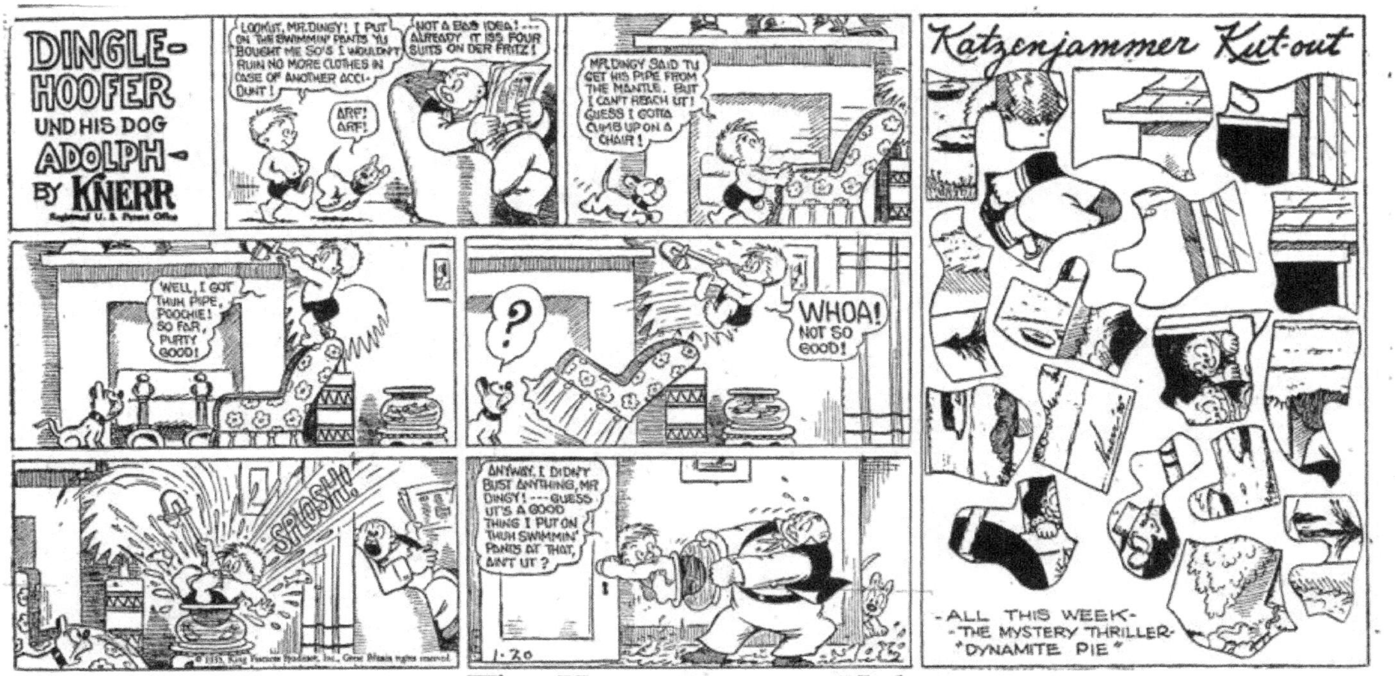
DINGLE-HOOFER UND HIS DOG ADOLPH BY KNERR
Registered U. S. Patent Office
LOOKUT, MR. DINGY! I PUT ON THE SWIMMIN' PANTS YU BOUGHT ME SO'S I WOULDN'T RUIN NO MORE CLOTHES IN CASE OF ANOTHER ACCI-DUNT!
ARF! ARF!
NOT A BAD IDEA! --- ALREADY IT ISS FOUR SUITS ON DER FRITZ!
MR. DINGY SAID TU GET HIS PIPE FROM THE MANTLE. BUT I CAN'T REACH UT! GUESS I GOTTA CLIMB UP ON A CHAIR!
WELL, I GOT THUH PIPE, POOCHIE! SO FAR, PURTY GOOD!
?
WHOA! NOT SO GOOD!
SPLOSH!
ANYWAY, I DIDN'T BUST ANYTHING, MR DINGY! --- GUESS UT'S A GOOD THING I PUT ON THUH SWIMMIN' PANTS AT THAT, AIN'T UT?
1-20
Katzenjammer Kut-out
-ALL THIS WEEK-
-THE MYSTERY THRILLER-
"DYNAMITE PIE"

The Katzenjammer Kids

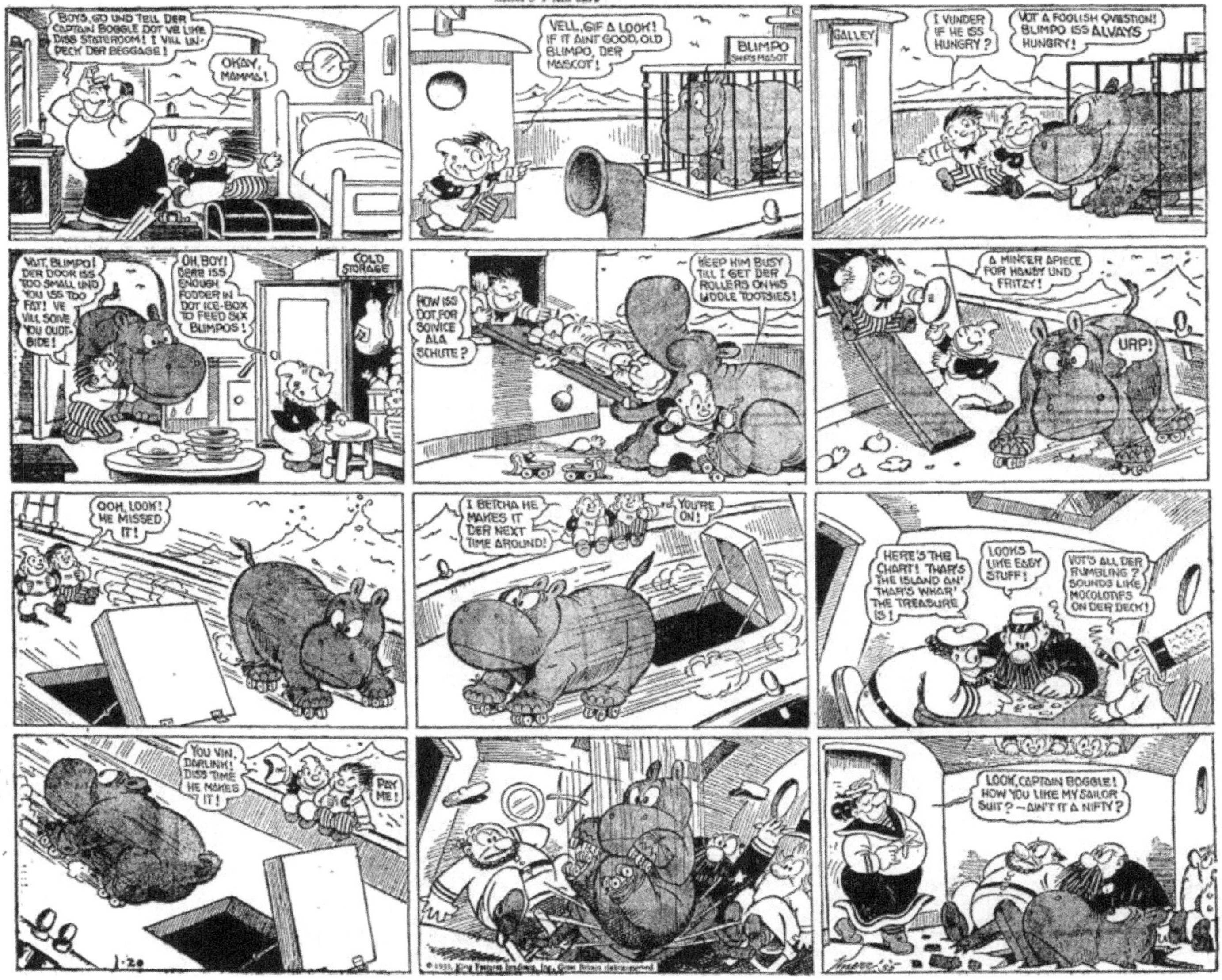
BOYS, GO UND TELL DER CAPTAIN BOGGLE DOT VE LIKE DISS STATEROOM! I VILL UN-PECK DER BEGGAGE!
OKAY, MAMMA!
VELL, GIF A LOOK! IF IT AINT GOOD, OLD BLIMPO, DER MASCOT!
BLIMPO SHIP'S MASCOT
GALLEY
I VUNDER IF HE ISS HUNGRY?
VOT A FOOLISH QVESTION! BLIMPO ISS ALVAYS HUNGRY!
VAIT, BLIMPO! DER DOOR ISS TOO SMALL UND YOU ISS TOO FAT! VE VILL SOIVE YOU OUDT-SIDE!
OH, BOY! DERE ISS ENOUGH FOODER IN DOT ICE-BOX TO FEED SIX BLIMPOS!
COLD STORAGE
HOW ISS DOT FOR SOIVICE ALA SCHUTE?
KEEP HIM BUSY TILL I GET DER ROLLERS ON HIS WIDDLE TOOTSIES!
A MINCER APIECE FOR HANSY UND FRITZY!
URP!
OOH, LOOK! HE MISSED IT!
I BETCHA HE MAKES IT DER NEXT TIME AROUND!
YOU'RE ON!
HERE'S THE CHART! THAR'S THE ISLAND AN' THAR'S WHAR' THE TREASURE IS!
LOOKS LIKE EASY STUFF!
VOT'S ALL DER RUMBLING? SOUNDS LIKE MOCOLOTIFS ON DER DECK!
YOU VIN, DARLINK! DISS TIME HE MAKES IT!
PAY ME!
LOOK, CAPTAIN BOGGLE! HOW YOU LIKE MY SAILOR SUIT? — AIN'T IT A NIFTY?
1-20

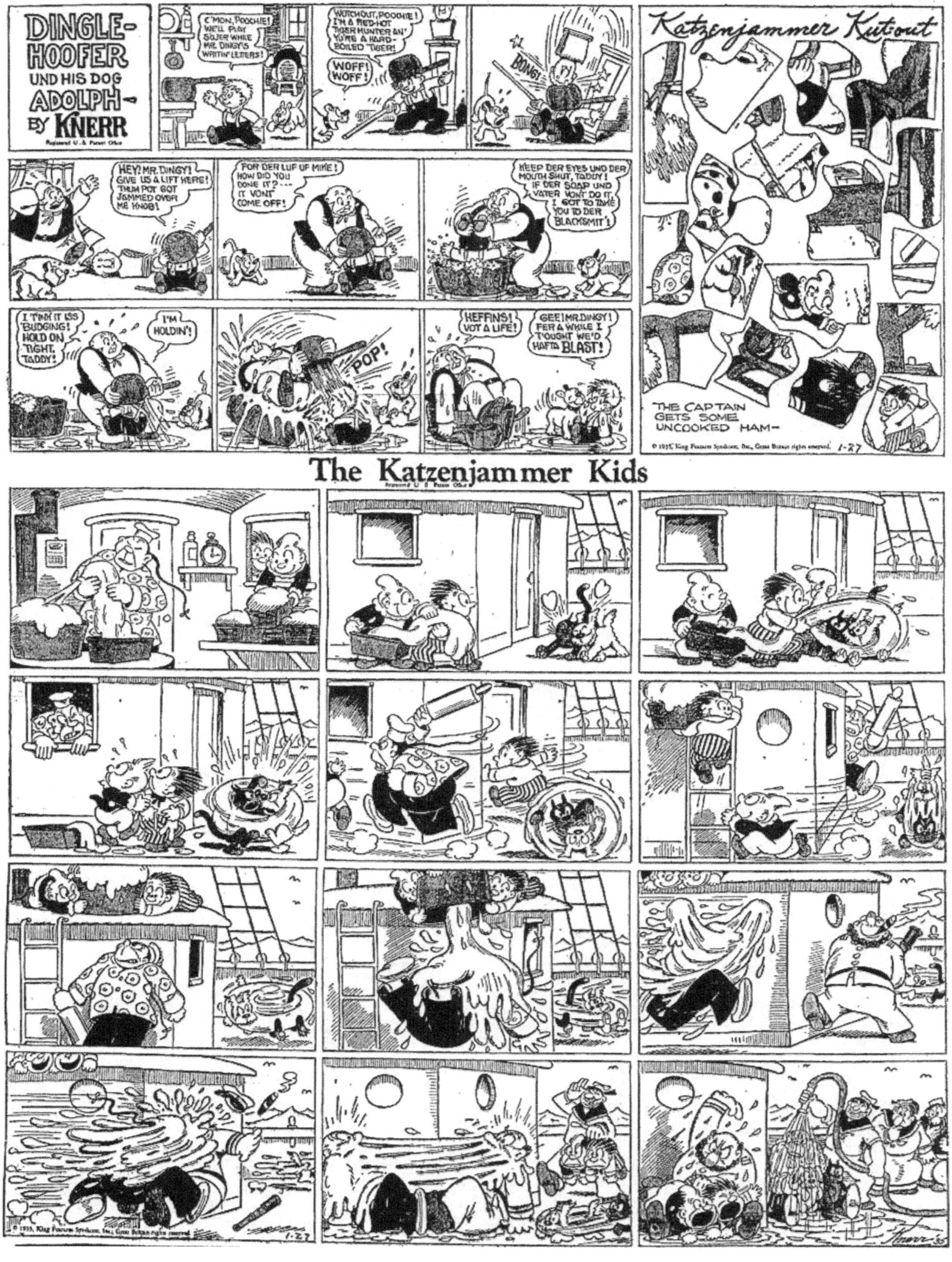
DINGLE-HOOFER UND HIS DOG ADOLPH - BY KNERR
Registered U. S. Patent Office
C'MON, POOCHIE! WE'LL PLAY SOJER WHILE MR. DINGY'S WRITIN' LETTERS!
WATCHOUT, POOCHIE! I'M A RED-HOT TIGER HUNTER AN' YU'RE A HARD-BOILED TIGER!
WOFF! WOFF!
BONG!
HEY! MR. DINGY! GIVE US A LIFT HERE! THUH POT GOT JAMMED OVER ME KNOB!
FOR DER LUF UF MIKE! HOW DID YOU DONE IT? --- IT VONT COME OFF!
KEEP DER EYES UND DER MOUTH SHUT, TADDY! IF DER SOAP UND VATER VONT DO IT, I GOT TO TAKE YOU TO DER BLACKSMIT'!
I TINK IT ISS BUDGING! HOLD ON TIGHT, TADDY!
I'M HOLDIN'!
POP!
HEFFINS! VOT A LIFE!
GEE! MR. DINGY! FER A WHILE I T'OUGHT WE'D HAFTA BLAST!
Katzenjammer Kut-out
THE CAPTAIN GETS SOME UNCOOKED HAM—
1-27
The Katzenjammer Kids
Registered U. S. Patent Office
1-27
Knerr '35

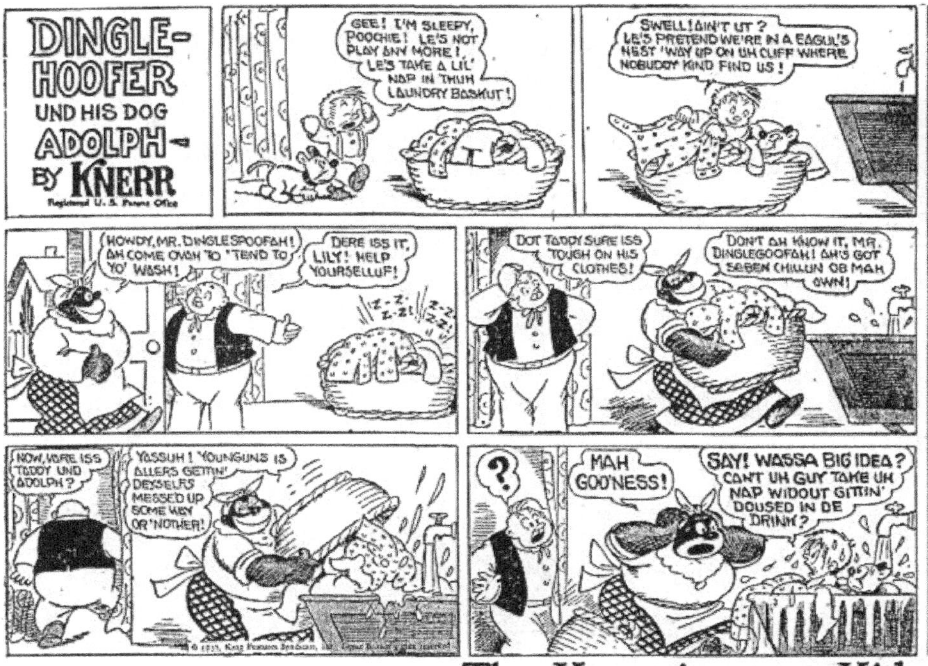
DINGLE-HOOFER UND HIS DOG ADOLPH BY KNERR
Registered U.S. Patent Office
GEE! I'M SLEEPY, POOCHIE! LE'S NOT PLAY ANY MORE! LE'S TAKE A LIL' NAP IN THUH LAUNDRY BASKUT!
SWELL! AIN'T UT? LE'S PRETEND WE'RE IN A EAGUL'S NEST 'WAY UP ON UH CLIFF WHERE NOBUDDY KIND FIND US!
HOWDY, MR. DINGLESPOOFAH! AH COME OVAH TO 'TEND TO YO' WASH!
DERE ISS IT, LILY! HELP YOURSELLUF!
DOT TEDDY SURE ISS TOUGH ON HIS CLOTHES!
DON'T AH KNOW IT, MR. DINGLEGOOFAH! AH'S GOT SEBEN CHILLUN OB MAH OWN!
NOW, VERE ISS TEDDY UND ADOLPH?
YASSUH! YOUNGUNS IS ALLERS GITTIN' DEYSELFS MESSED UP SOME WAY OR 'NOTHER!
?
MAH GOO'NESS!
SAY! WASSA BIG IDEA? CAN'T UH GUY TAKE UH NAP WIDOUT GITTIN' DOUSED IN DE DRINK?

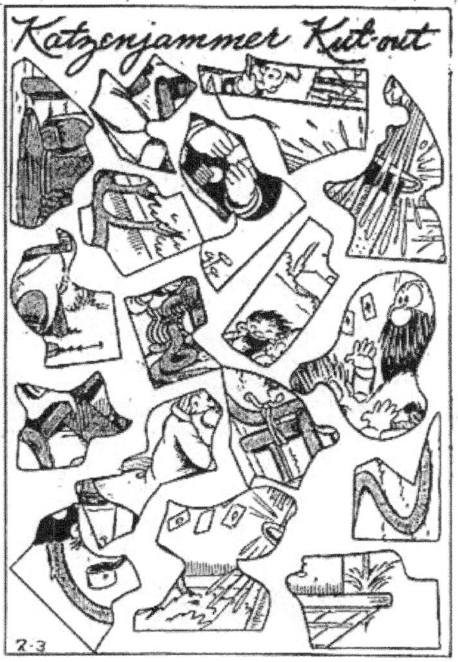
Katzenjammer Kut-out
2-3

The Katzenjammer Kids

Registered U.S. Patent Office

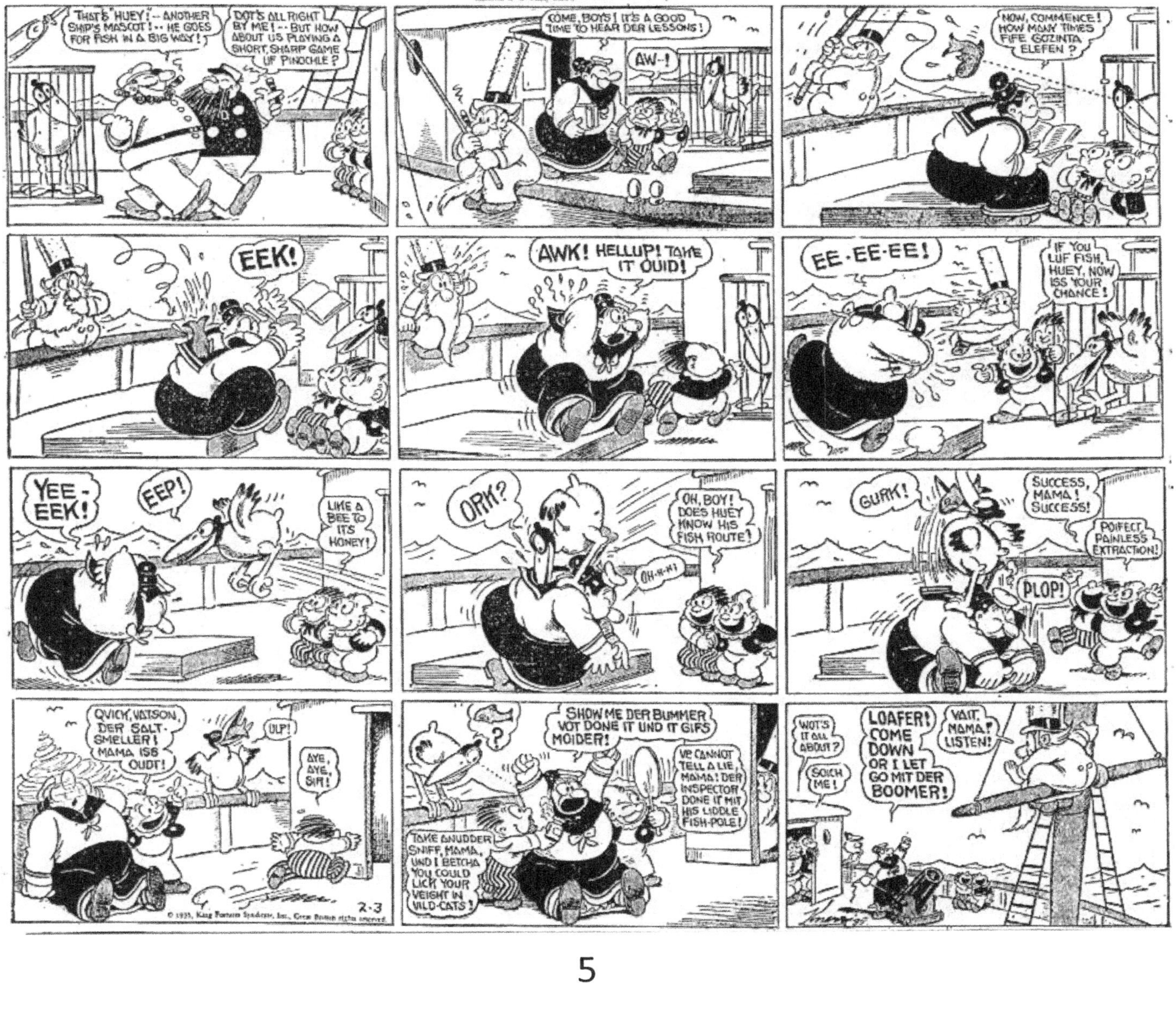
THAT'S HUEY! -- ANOTHER SHIP'S MASCOT! -- HE GOES FOR FISH IN A BIG WAY!
DOT'S ALL RIGHT BY ME! -- BUT HOW ABOUT US PLAYING A SHORT, SHARP GAME UF PINOCHLE?
COME, BOYS! IT'S A GOOD TIME TO HEAR DER LESSONS!
AW-!
NOW, COMMENCE! HOW MANY TIMES FIFE GOZINTA ELEFEN?
EEK!
AWK! HELLUP! TAKE IT OUID!
EE-EE-EE!
IF YOU LUF FISH, HUEY, NOW ISS YOUR CHANCE!
YEE-EEK!
EEP!
LIKE A BEE TO ITS HONEY!
ORK?
OH, BOY! DOES HUEY KNOW HIS FISH ROUTE!
OH-H-H!
GURK!
SUCCESS, MAMA! SUCCESS!
POIFECT, PAINLESS EXTRACTION!
PLOP!
QVICK, VATSON, DER SALT-SMELLER! MAMA ISS OUDT!
ULP!
AYE, AYE, SIR!
2-3
?
SHOW ME DER BUMMER VOT DONE IT UND IT GIFS MOIDER!
VE CANNOT TELL A LIE, MAMA! DER INSPECTOR DONE IT MIT HIS LIDDLE FISH-POLE!
TAKE ANUDDER SNIFF, MAMA, UND I BETCHA YOU COULD LICK YOUR VEIGHT IN VILD-CATS!
WOT'S IT ALL ABOUT?
SOICH ME!
LOAFER! COME DOWN OR I LET GO MIT DER BOOMER!
VAIT, MAMA! LISTEN!

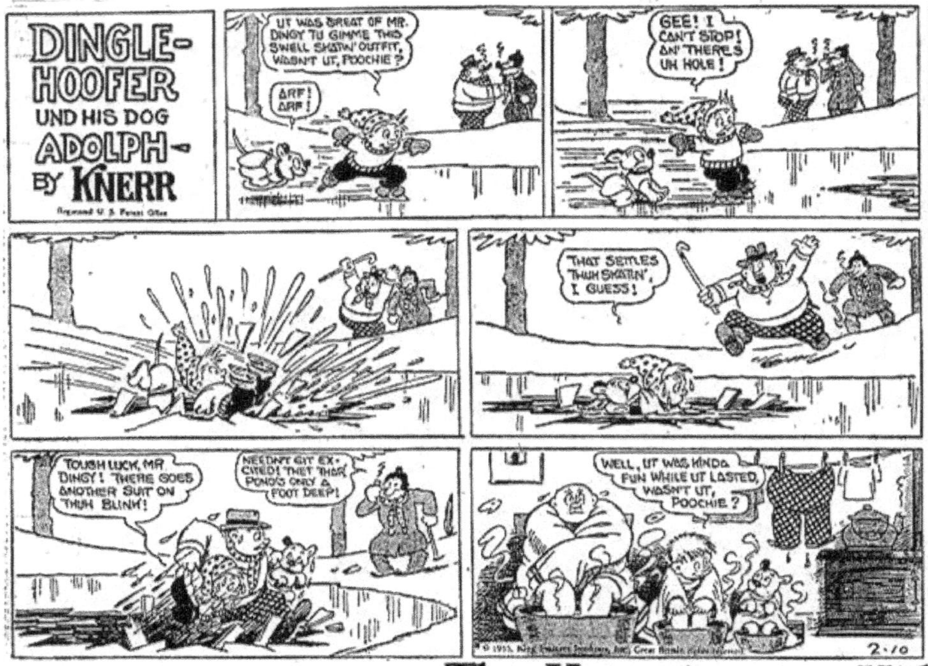
DINGLE-HOOFER UND HIS DOG ADOLPH BY KNERR
Registered U. S. Patent Office
UT WAS GREAT OF MR. DINGY TU GIMME THIS SWELL SKATIN' OUTFIT, WASN'T UT, POOCHIE?
ARF! ARF!
GEE! I CAN'T STOP! AN' THERE'S UH HOLE!
THAT SETTLES THUH SKATIN', I GUESS!
TOUGH LUCK, MR. DINGY! THERE GOES ANOTHER SUIT ON THUH BLINK!
NEEDN'T GIT EXCITED! THET THAR POND'S ONLY A FOOT DEEP!
WELL, UT WAS KINDA FUN WHILE UT LASTED, WASN'T UT, POOCHIE?
2-10

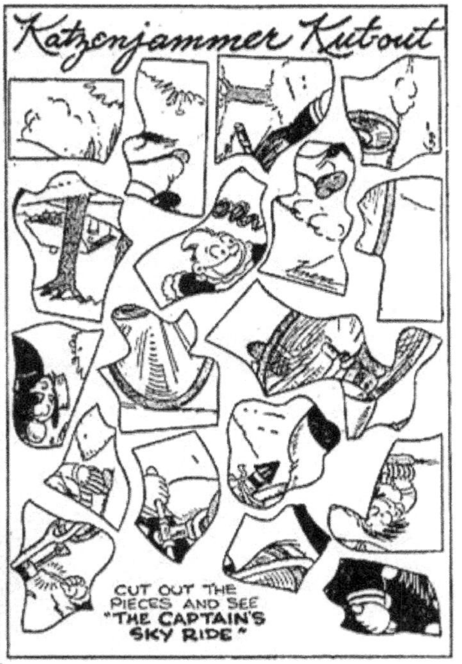
Katzenjammer Kutout
CUT OUT THE PIECES AND SEE "THE CAPTAIN'S SKY RIDE"

The Katzenjammer Kids

Registered U. S. Patent Office

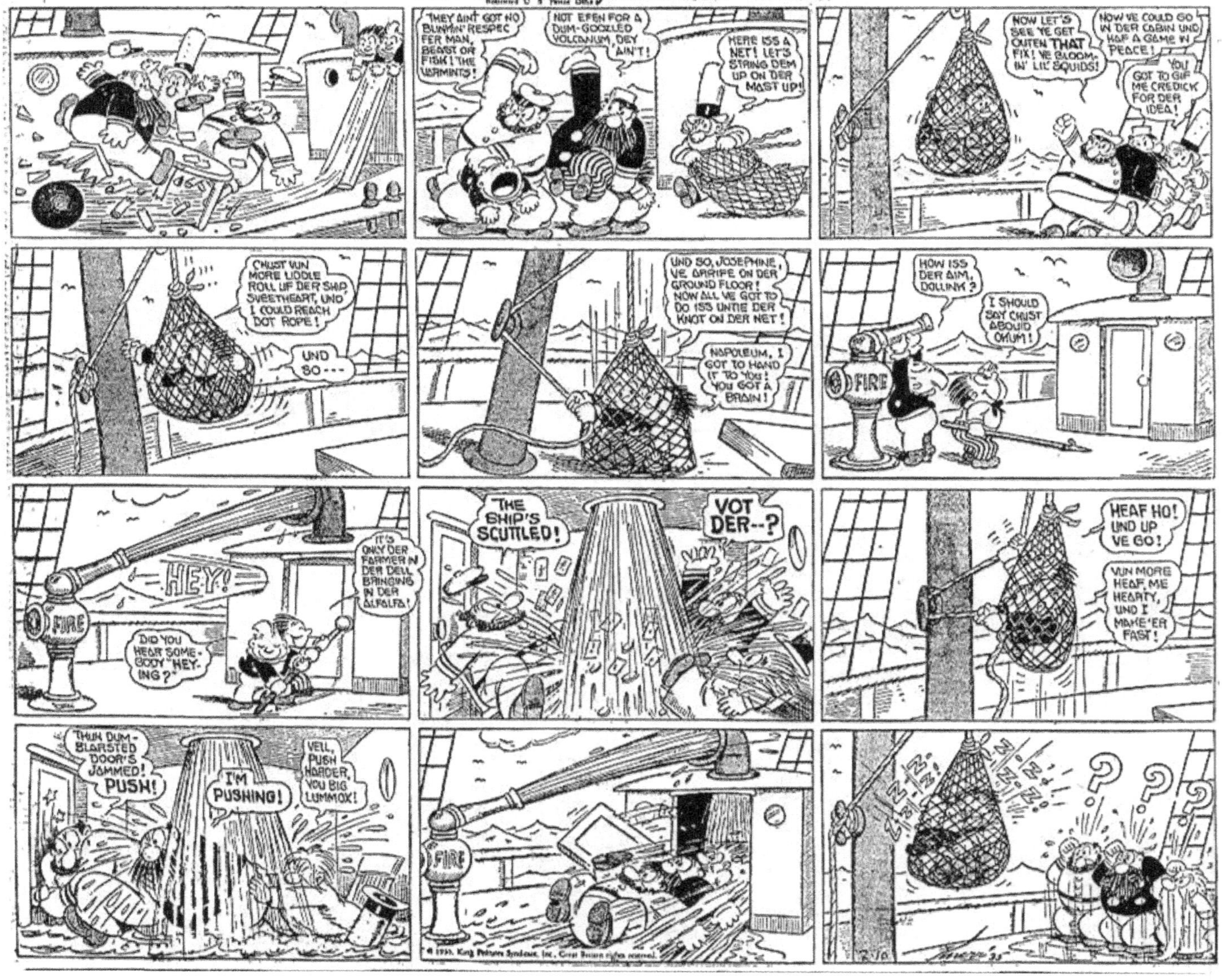
THEY AIN'T GOT NO BLINKIN' RESPEC FER MAN, BEAST OR FISH! THE VARMINTS!
NOT EFEN FOR A DUM-GOOZLED VOLCANUM, DEY AIN'T!
HERE ISS A NET! LET'S STRING DEM UP ON DER MAST UP!
NOW LET'S SEE YE GET OUTEN THAT FIX! YE BLOOMIN' LIL' SQUIDS!
NOW VE COULD GO IN DER CABIN UND HAF A GAME IN PEACE!
YOU GOT TO GIF ME CREDICK FOR DER IDEA!
CHUST VUN MORE LIDDLE ROLL UF DER SHIP, SVEETHEART, UND I COULD REACH DOT ROPE!
UND SO---
UND SO, JOSEPHINE, VE ARRIFE ON DER GROUND FLOOR! NOW ALL VE GOT TO DO ISS UNTIE DER KNOT ON DER NET!
NAPOLEUM, I GOT TO HAND IT TO YOU! YOU GOT A BRAIN!
HOW ISS DER AIM, DOLLINK?
I SHOULD SAY CHUST ABOUD OHUM!
FIRE
HEY!
DID YOU HEAR SOMEBODY "HEY-ING?"
IT'S ONLY DER FARMER IN DER DELL BRINGING IN DER ALFALFA!
THE SHIP'S SCUTTLED!
VOT DER--?
HEAF HO! UND UP VE GO!
VUN MORE HEAF, ME HEARTY, UND I MAKE 'ER FAST!
THUH DUM-BLARSTED DOOR'S JAMMED! PUSH!
I'M PUSHING!
VELL, PUSH HARDER, YOU BIG LUMMOX!
2-10

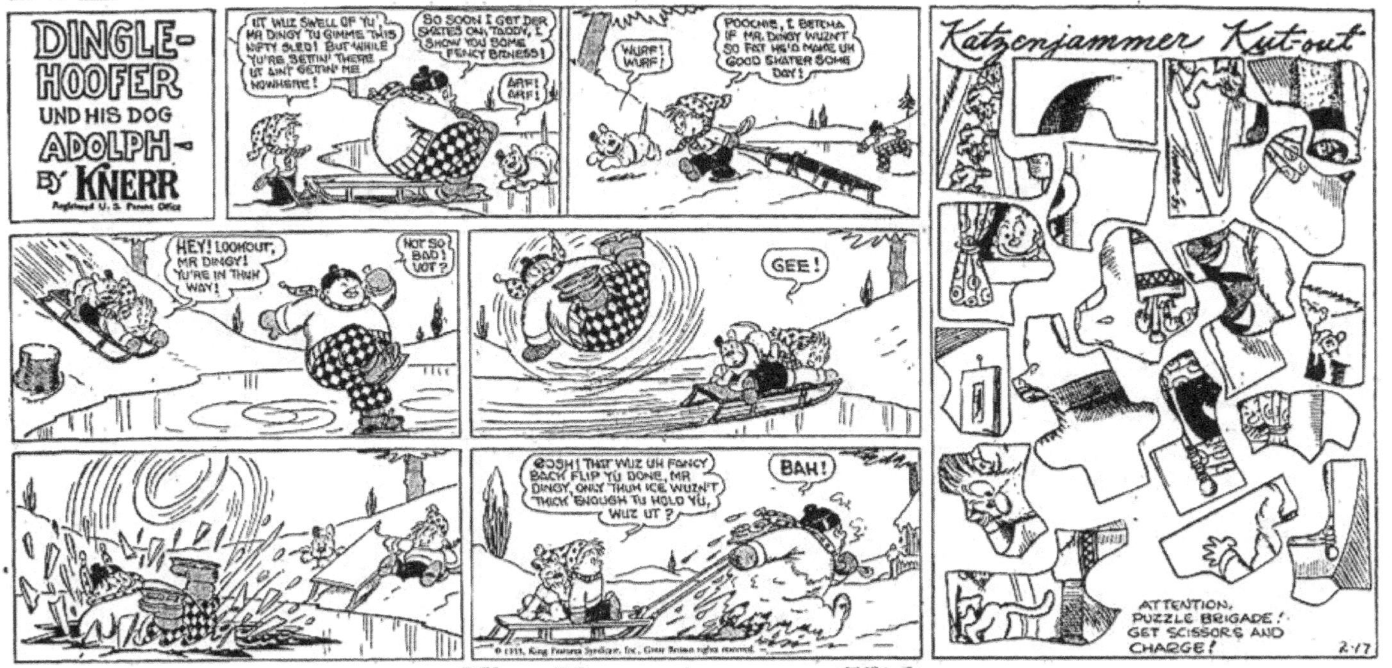
DINGLE-HOOFER
UND HIS DOG
ADOLPH
BY KNERR
UT WUZ SWELL OF YU' MR DINGY TU GIMME THIS NIFTY SLED! BUT WHILE YU'RE SETTIN' THERE UT AIN'T GETTIN' ME NOWHERE!
SO SOON I GET DER SKATES ON, TADDY, I SHOW YOU SOME FENCY BIZNESS!
ARF! ARF!
WURF! WURF!
POOCHIE, I BETCHA IF MR. DINGY WUZN'T SO FAT HE'D MAKE UH GOOD SKATER SOME DAY!
HEY! LOOKOUT, MR DINGY! YU'RE IN THUH WAY!
NOT SO BAD! VOT?
GEE!
GOSH! THAT WUZ UH FANCY BACK FLIP YU DONE, MR DINGY, ONLY THUH ICE WUZN'T THICK ENOUGH TU HOLD YU, WUZ UT?
BAH!
Katzenjammer Kut-out
ATTENTION, PUZZLE BRIGADE! GET SCISSORS AND CHARGE!
2-17

The Katzenjammer Kids

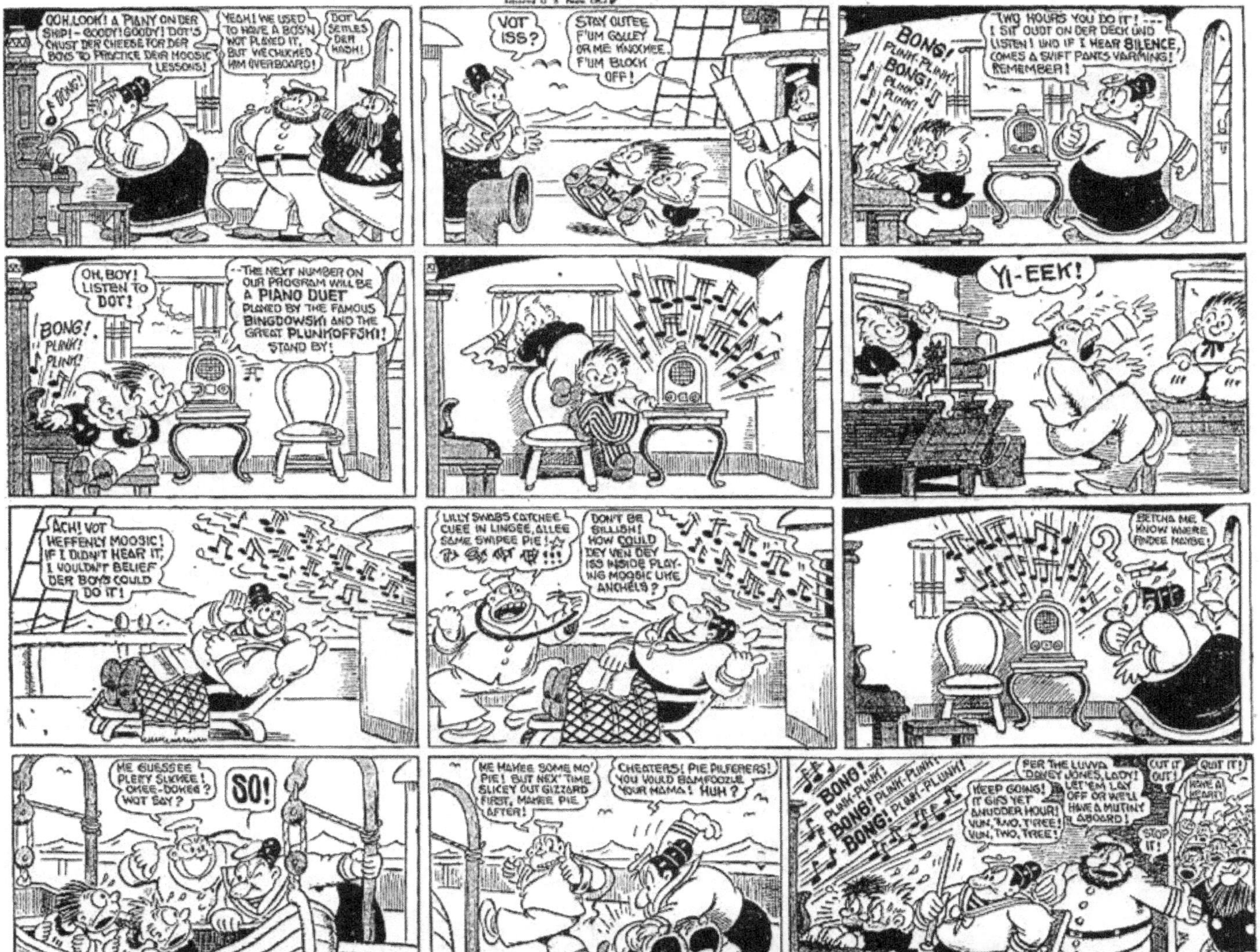
OOH, LOOK! A PIANY ON DER SHIP! - GOODY! GOODY! DOT'S CHUST DER CHEESE FOR DER BOYS TO PRACTICE DEIR MOOSIC LESSONS!
BONG!
YEAH! WE USED TO HAVE A BOS'N WOT PLAYED IT, BUT WE CHUCKED HIM OVERBOARD!
DOT SETTLES DER HASH!
VOT ISS?
STAY OUTEE F'UM GALLEY OR ME KNOCKEE F'UM BLOCK OFF!
TWO HOURS YOU DO IT! --- I SIT OUDT ON DER DECK UND LISTEN! UND IF I HEAR SILENCE, COMES A SWIFT PANTS VARMING! REMEMBER!
BONG! PLINK-PLINK! BONG! PLINK-PLINK!
OH, BOY! LISTEN TO DOT!
BONG! PLINK! PLINK!
--THE NEXT NUMBER ON OUR PROGRAM WILL BE A PIANO DUET PLAYED BY THE FAMOUS BINGDOWSKI AND THE GREAT PLUNKOFFSKI! STAND BY!
YI-EEK!
ACH! VOT HEFFENLY MOOSIC! IF I DIDN'T HEAR IT, I VOULDN'T BELIEF DER BOYS COULD DO IT!
LILLY SWABS CATCHEE CUEE IN LINGEE, ALLEE SAME SWIPEE PIE!
DON'T BE SILLISH! HOW COULD DEY VEN DEY ISS INSIDE PLAYING MOOSIC LIKE ANCHELS?
BETCHA ME KNOW WHERE FINDEE MAYBE!
ME GUESSEE PLENTY SUCKEE! OKEE-DOKEE? WOT SAY?
SO!
ME MAKEE SOME MO' PIE! BUT NEX' TIME SLICEY OUT GIZZARD FIRST, MAKEE PIE AFTER!
CHEATERS! PIE PILFERERS! YOU VOULD BAMFOOZLE YOUR MAMA! HUH?
BONG! PLINK-PLINK! BONG! PLINK-PLINK! BONG! PLINK-PLUNK!
KEEP GOING! IT GIFS YET ANUDDER HOUR! VUN, TWO, TREE! VUN, TWO, TREE!
FER THE LUVVA DAVEY JONES, LADY! LET 'EM LAY OFF OR WE'LL HAVE A MUTINY ABOARD!
CUT IT OUT!
QUIT IT!
HAVE A HEART!
STOP IT!
2-17

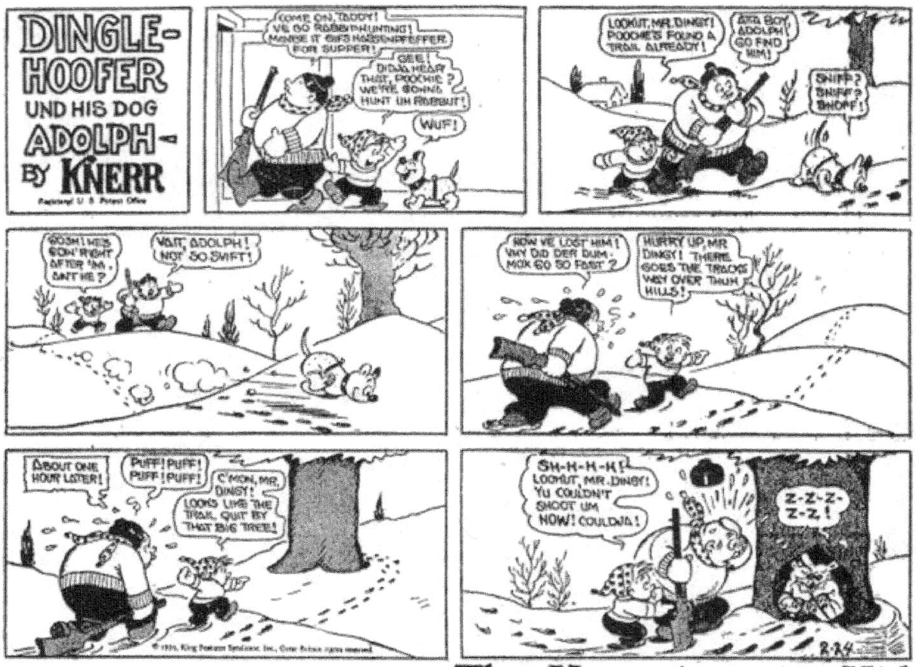
DINGLE-HOOFER UND HIS DOG ADOLPH - BY KNERR
COME ON, TADDY! VE GO RABBITHUNTING! MEBBE IT GIFS HASSENPFEFFER FOR SUPPER!
GEE! DIDJA HEAR THAT, POOCHIE? WE'RE GONNA HUNT UH RABBIT!
WUF!
LOOKUT, MR. DINGY! POOCHIE'S FOUND A TRAIL ALREADY!
ATTA BOY, ADOLPH! GO FIND HIM!
SNIFF? SNIFF? SNOFF!
GOSH! HE'S GOIN' RIGHT AFTER 'IM, AIN'T HE?
VAIT, ADOLPH! NOT SO SWIFT!
NOW VE LOST HIM! VHY DID DER DUMMOX GO SO FAST?
HURRY UP, MR DINGY! THERE GOES THE TRACKS WAY OVER THUH HILLS!
ABOUT ONE HOUR LATER!
PUFF! PUFF! PUFF! PUFF!
C'MON, MR. DINGY! LOOKS LIKE THE TRAIL QUIT BY THAT BIG TREE!
SH-H-H-K! LOOKUT, MR. DINGY! YU COULDN'T SHOOT UM NOW! COULDJA!
Z-Z-Z-Z-Z!
2-24

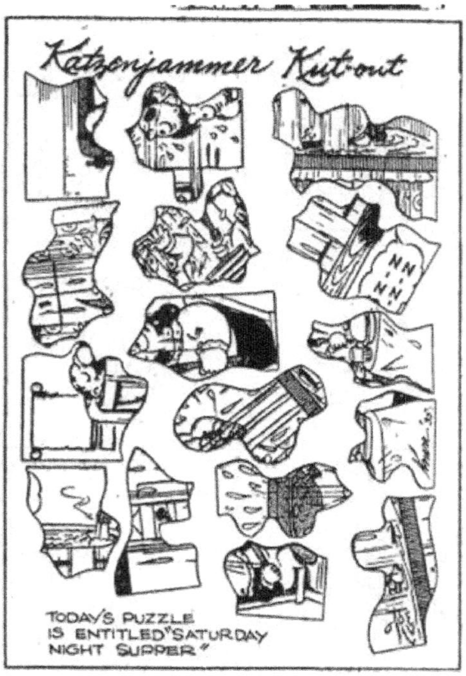
Katzenjammer Kut-out
NN-NN!
TODAY'S PUZZLE IS ENTITLED "SATURDAY NIGHT SUPPER"

The Katzenjammer Kids

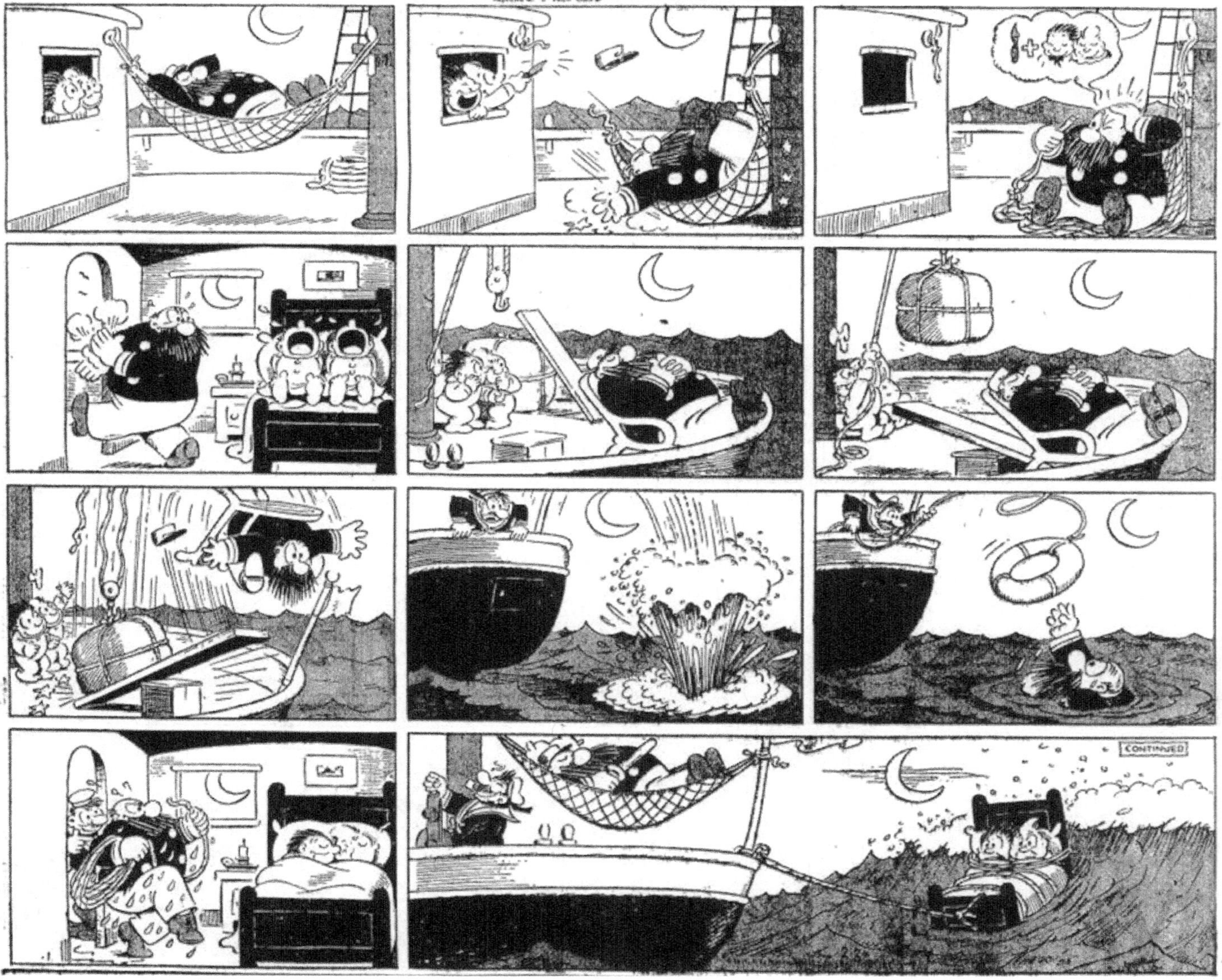
CONTINUED

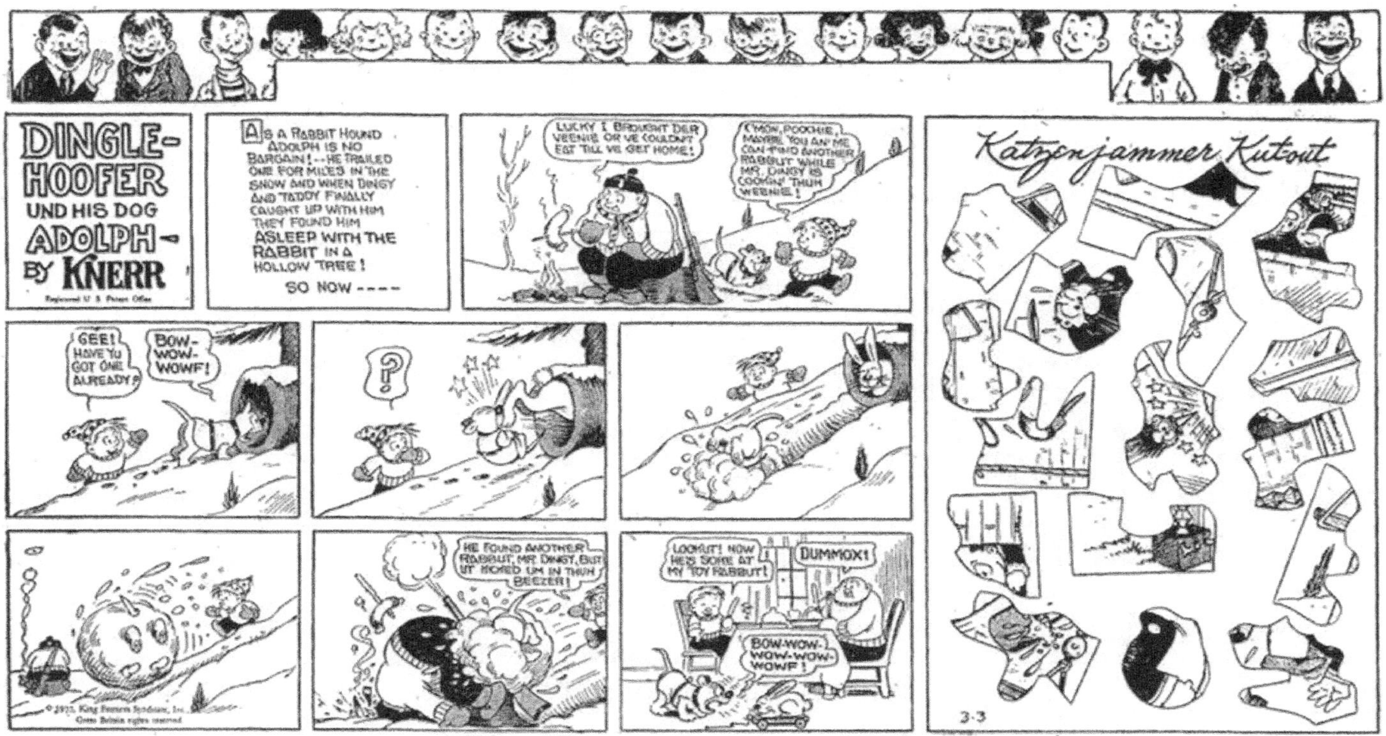
DINGLE-HOOFER UND HIS DOG ADOLPH - BY KNERR
AS A RABBIT HOUND ADOLPH IS NO BARGAIN! -- HE TRAILED ONE FOR MILES IN THE SNOW AND WHEN DINGY AND TADDY FINALLY CAUGHT UP WITH HIM THEY FOUND HIM ASLEEP WITH THE RABBIT IN A HOLLOW TREE! SO NOW ----
LUCKY I BROUGHT DER VEENIE OR VE COULDN'T EAT TILL VE GET HOME!
C'MON, POOCHIE, MAYBE YOU AN' ME CAN FIND ANOTHER RABBIT WHILE MR. DINGY IS COOKIN' THUH WEENIE!
GEE! HAVE YU GOT ONE ALREADY?
BOW-WOW-WOWF!
?
HE FOUND ANOTHER RABBIT, MR. DINGY, BUT UT KICKED UM IN THUH BEEZER!
LOOKUT! NOW HE'S SORE AT MY TOY RABBIT!
DUMMOX!
BOW-WOW-WOW-WOW-WOWF!
Katzenjammer Kutout
3-3

The Katzenjammer Kids

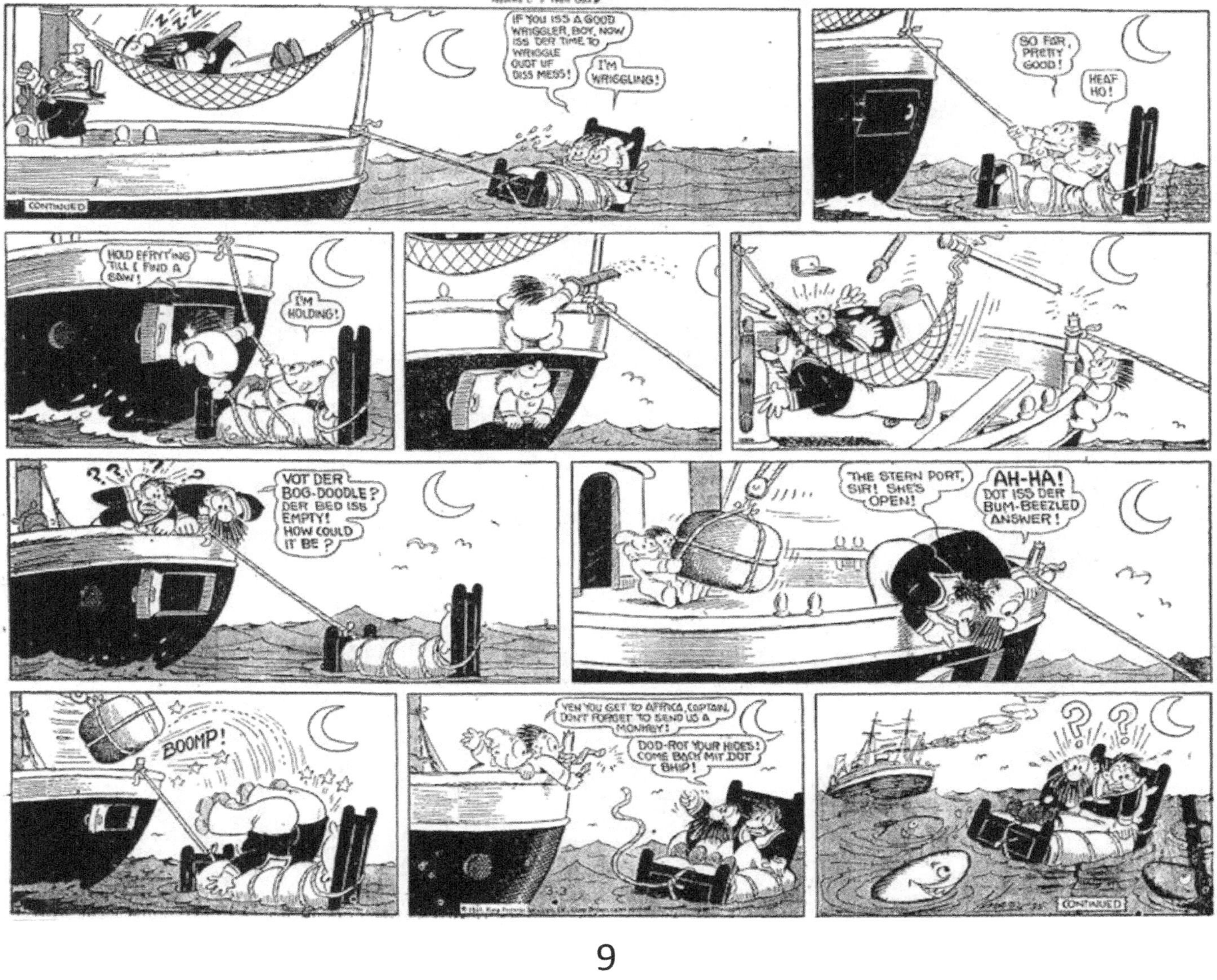
IF YOU ISS A GOOD WRIGGLER, BOY, NOW ISS DER TIME TO WRIGGLE OUDT UF DISS MESS!
I'M WRIGGLING!
CONTINUED
SO FAR, PRETTY GOOD!
HEAF HO!
HOLD EFRYT'ING TILL I FIND A SAW!
I'M HOLDING!
VOT DER BOG-DOODLE? DER BED ISS EMPTY! HOW COULD IT BE?
THE STERN PORT, SIR! SHE'S OPEN!
AH-HA! DOT ISS DER BUM-BEEZLED ANSWER!
BOOMP!
VEN YOU GET TO AFRICA, CAPTAIN, DON'T FORGET TO SEND US A MONKEY!
DOD-ROT YOUR HIDES! COME BACK MIT DOT SHIP!
CONTINUED

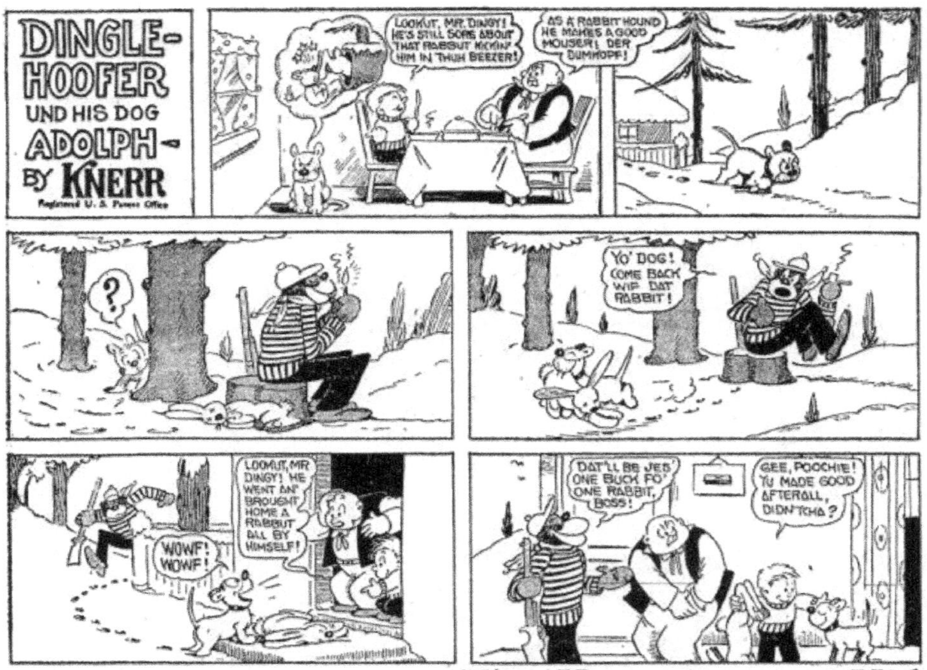
DINGLE-HOOFER UND HIS DOG ADOLPH BY KNERR
Registered U. S. Patent Office
LOOKUT, MR. DINGY! HE'S STILL SORE ABOUT THAT RABBIT KICKIN' HIM IN THUH BEEZER!
AS A RABBIT HOUND HE MAKES A GOOD MOUSER! DER DUMKOPF!
?
YO' DOG! COME BACK WIF DAT RABBIT!
LOOKUT, MR DINGY! HE WENT AN' BROUGHT HOME A RABBIT ALL BY HIMSELF!
WOWF! WOWF!
DAT'LL BE JES' ONE BUCK FO' ONE RABBIT, BOSS!
GEE, POOCHIE! YU MADE GOOD AFTERALL, DIDN'TCHA?

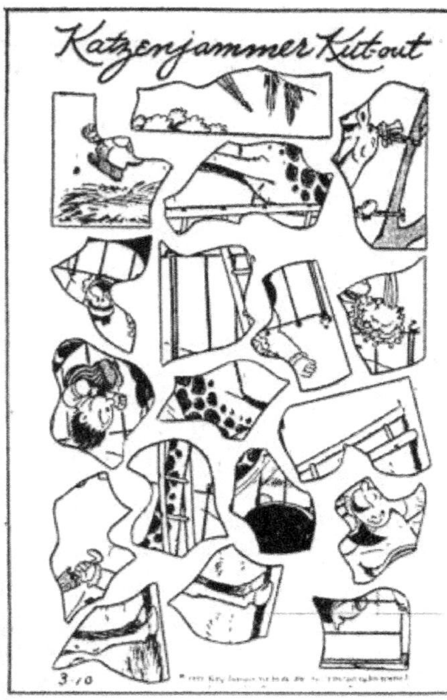
Katzenjammer Kut-out
3-10

The Katzenjammer Kids

Registered U. S. Patent Office

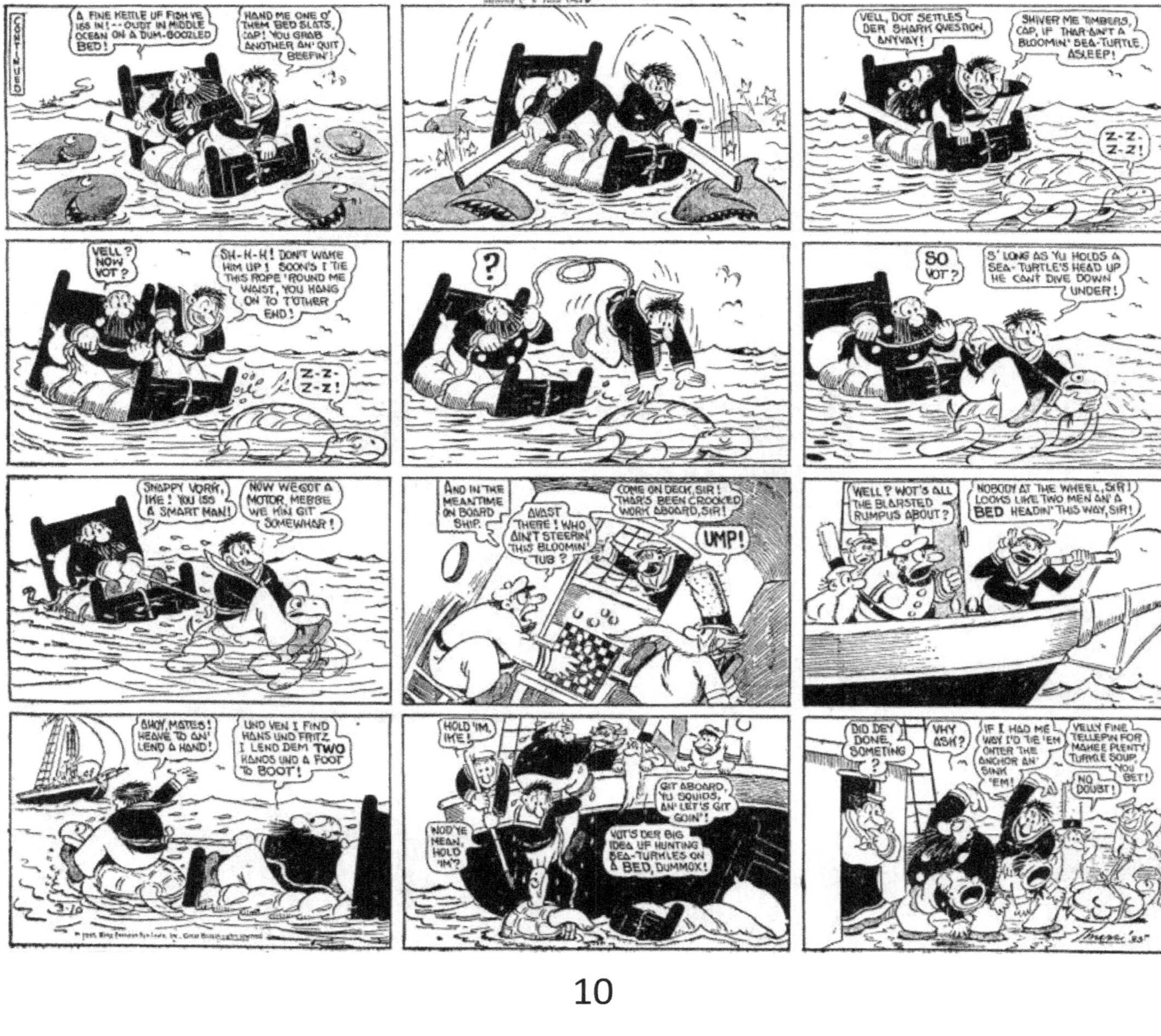
CONTINUED
A FINE KETTLE UF FISH YE ISS IN! -- OUDT IN MIDDLE OCEAN ON A DUM-GOOZLED BED!
HAND ME ONE O' THEM BED SLATS, CAP! YOU GRAB ANOTHER AN' QUIT BEEFIN'!
VELL, DOT SETTLES DER SHARK QVESTION, ANYVAY!
SHIVER ME TIMBERS, CAP, IF THAR AIN'T A BLOOMIN' SEA-TURTLE, ASLEEP!
Z-Z. Z-Z!
VELL? NOW VOT?
SH-H-H! DON'T WAKE HIM UP! SOON'S I TIE THIS ROPE 'ROUND ME WAIST, YOU HANG ON TO T'OTHER END!
Z-Z. Z-Z!
?
SO VOT?
S' LONG AS YU HOLDS A SEA-TURTLE'S HEAD UP HE CAN'T DIVE DOWN UNDER!
SNAPPY VORK, IKE! YOU ISS A SMART MAN!
NOW WE GOT A MOTOR, MEBBE WE KIN GIT SOMEWHAR!
AND IN THE MEANTIME ON BOARD SHIP.
COME ON DECK, SIR! THAR'S BEEN CROOKED WORK ABOARD, SIR!
AVAST THERE! WHO AIN'T STEERIN' THIS BLOOMIN' TUB?
UMP!
WELL? WOT'S ALL THE BLARSTED RUMPUS ABOUT?
NOBODY AT THE WHEEL, SIR! LOOKS LIKE TWO MEN AN' A BED HEADIN' THIS WAY, SIR!
AHOY, MATES! HEAVE TO AN' LEND A HAND!
UND VEN I FIND HANS UND FRITZ I LEND DEM TWO HANDS UND A FOOT TO BOOT!
3-10
HOLD 'IM, IKE!
WOT YE MEAN, HOLD 'IM?
GIT ABOARD, YU SQUIDS, AN' LET'S GIT GOIN'!
WOT'S DER BIG IDEA UF HUNTING SEA-TURKLES ON A BED, DUMMOX!
DID DEY DONE SOMETING?
WHY ASK?
IF I HAD ME WAY I'D TIE 'EM ONTER THE ANCHOR AN' SINK 'EM!
VELLY FINE TELLEPIN FOR MAHEE PLENTY TURKLE SOUP, YOU BET!
NO DOUBT!
Knerr '35

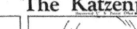

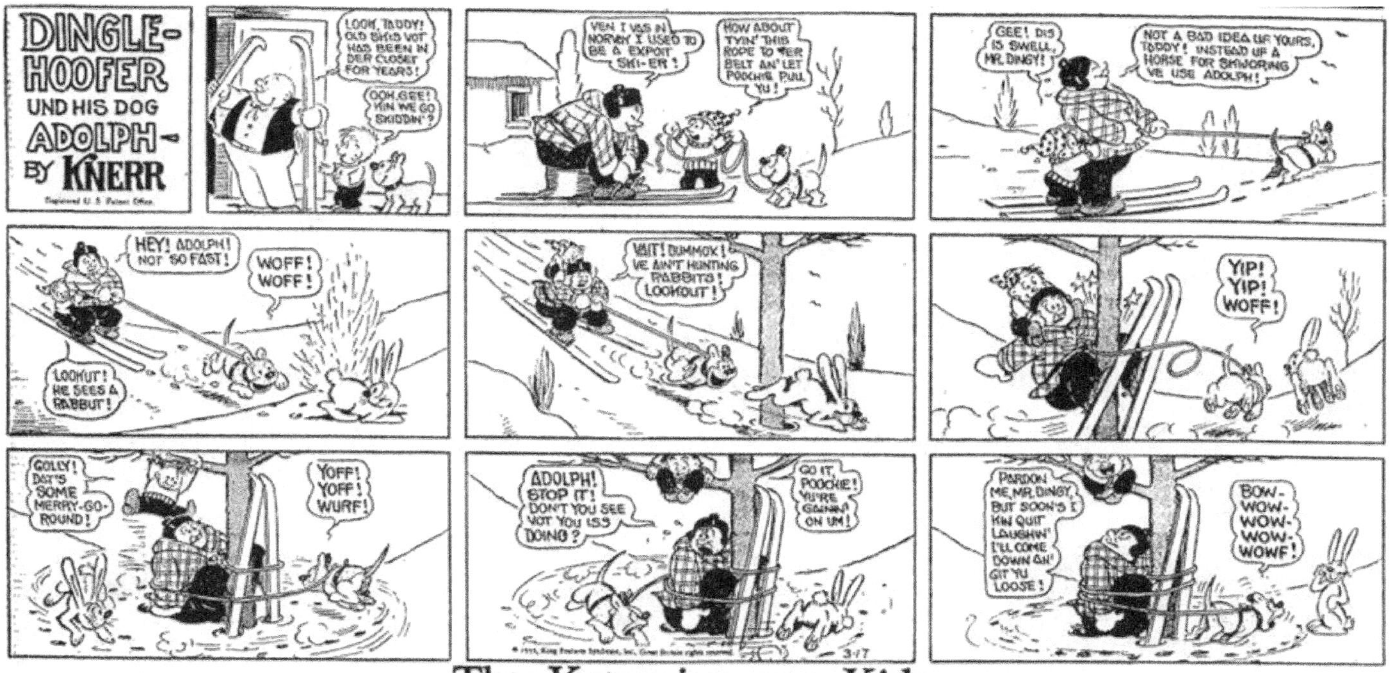

DINGLE-HOOFER UND HIS DOG ADOLPH BY KNERR
LOOK, TADDY! OLD SKIS VOT HAS BEEN IN DER CLOSET FOR YEARS!
OOH, GEE! KIN WE GO SKIDDIN'?
VEN I VAS IN NORVAY I USED TO BE A EXPOIT SKI-ER!
HOW ABOUT TYIN' THIS ROPE TO YER BELT AN' LET POOCHIE PULL YU!
GEE! DIS IS SWELL, MR. DINGY!
NOT A BAD IDEA UF YOURS, TADDY! INSTEAD UF A HORSE FOR SKIJORING VE USE ADOLPH!
HEY! ADOLPH! NOT SO FAST!
WOFF! WOFF!
LOOKUT! HE SEES A RABBUT!
VAIT! DUMMOX! VE AIN'T HUNTING RABBITS! LOOKOUT!
YIP! YIP! WOFF!
GOLLY! DAT'S SOME MERRY-GO-ROUND!
YOFF! YOFF! WURF!
ADOLPH! STOP IT! DON'T YOU SEE VOT YOU ISS DOING?
GO IT, POOCHIE! YU'RE GAININ' ON UM!
PARDON ME, MR. DINGY, BUT SOON'S I KIN QUIT LAUGHIN' I'LL COME DOWN AN' GIT YU LOOSE!
BOW-WOW-WOW-WOW-WOWF!
3-17

The Katzenjammer Kids

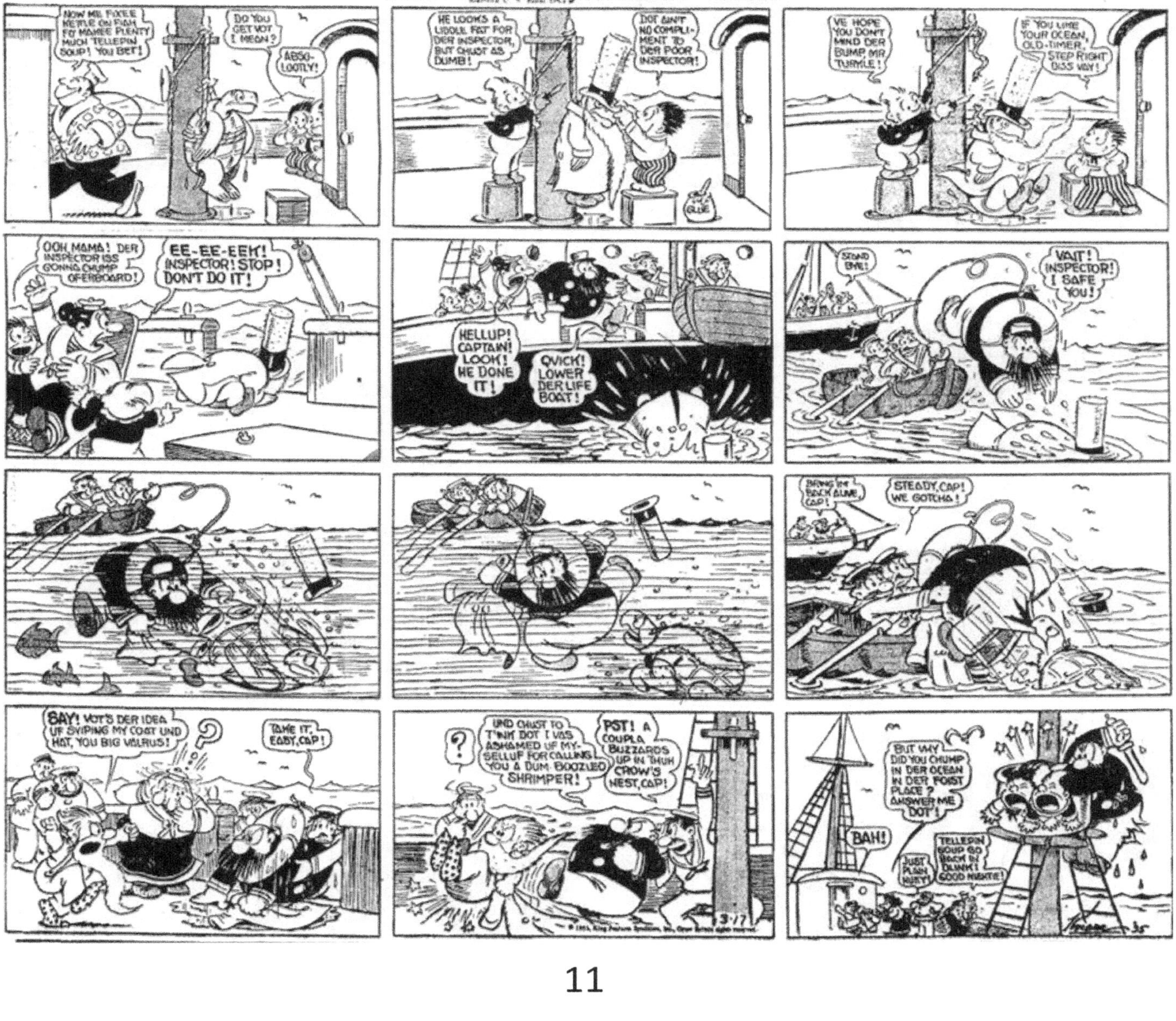

NOW ME FIXEE KETTLE ON FIAH FO' MAKEE PLENTY MUCH TELLEPIN SOUP! YOU BET!
DO YOU GET VOT I MEAN?
ABSO-LOOTLY!
HE LOOKS A LIDDLE FAT FOR DER INSPECTOR, BUT CHUST AS DUMB!
DOT AIN'T NO COMPLI-MENT TO DER POOR INSPECTOR!
GLUE
VE HOPE YOU DON'T MIND DER BUMP, MR. TURTLE!
IF YOU LIKE YOUR OCEAN, OLD-TIMER, STEP RIGHT DISS VAY!
OOH MAMA! DER INSPECTOR ISS GONNA CHUMP OFERBOARD!
EE-EE-EEK! INSPECTOR! STOP! DON'T DO IT!
HELLUP! CAPTAIN! LOOK! HE DONE IT!
QVICK! LOWER DER LIFE BOAT!
STAND BYE!
VAIT! INSPECTOR! I SAFE YOU!
BRING 'IM BACK ALIVE, CAP!
STEADY, CAP! WE GOTCHA!
SAY! VOT'S DER IDEA UF SVIPING MY COAT UND HAT, YOU BIG VALRUS!
TAKE IT EASY, CAP!
UND CHUST TO T'INK DOT I VAS ASHAMED UF MY-SELLUF FOR CALLING YOU A DUM-BOOZLED SHRIMPER!
PST! A COUPLA BUZZARDS UP IN THUH CROW'S NEST, CAP!
3-17
BUT VHY DID YOU CHUMP IN DER OCEAN IN DER FOIST PLACE? ANSWER ME DOT!
BAH!
JUST PLAIN NUTTY!
TELLEPIN SOUP GO BACK IN DLINK! GOOD NIGHTIE!

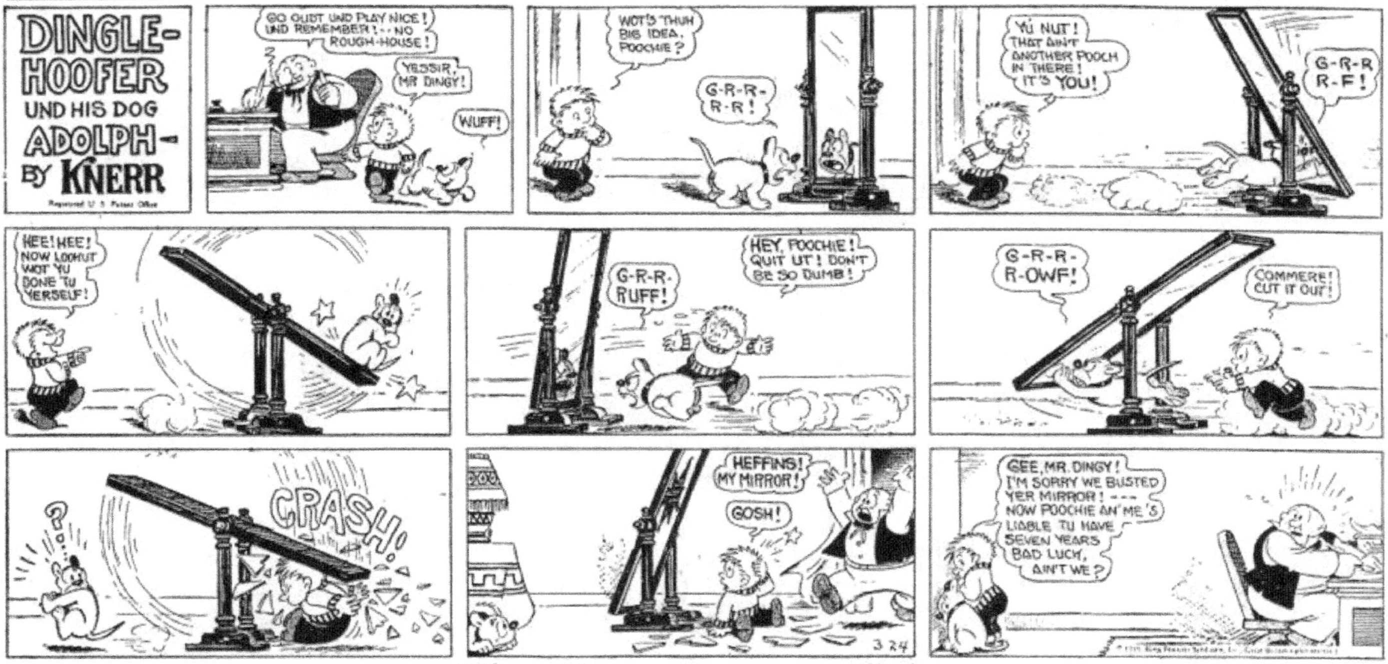
DINGLE-HOOFER UND HIS DOG ADOLPH- BY KNERR
Registered U. S. Patent Office
GO OUDT UND PLAY NICE! UND REMEMBER!-- NO ROUGH-HOUSE!
YESSIR, MR DINGY!
WUFF!
WOT'S THUH BIG IDEA, POOCHIE?
G-R-R-R-R!
YU NUT! THAT AIN'T ANOTHER POOCH IN THERE! IT'S YOU!
G-R-R R-F!
HEE! HEE! NOW LOOKUT WOT YU DONE TU YERSELF!
G-R-R-RUFF!
HEY, POOCHIE! QUIT UT! DON'T BE SO DUMB!
G-R-R-R-OWF!
COMMERE! CUT IT OUT!
CRASH!
HEFFINS! MY MIRROR!
GOSH!
GEE, MR. DINGY! I'M SORRY WE BUSTED YER MIRROR! --- NOW POOCHIE AN' ME'S LIABLE TU HAVE SEVEN YEARS BAD LUCK, AIN'T WE?
3-24

The Katzenjammer Kids

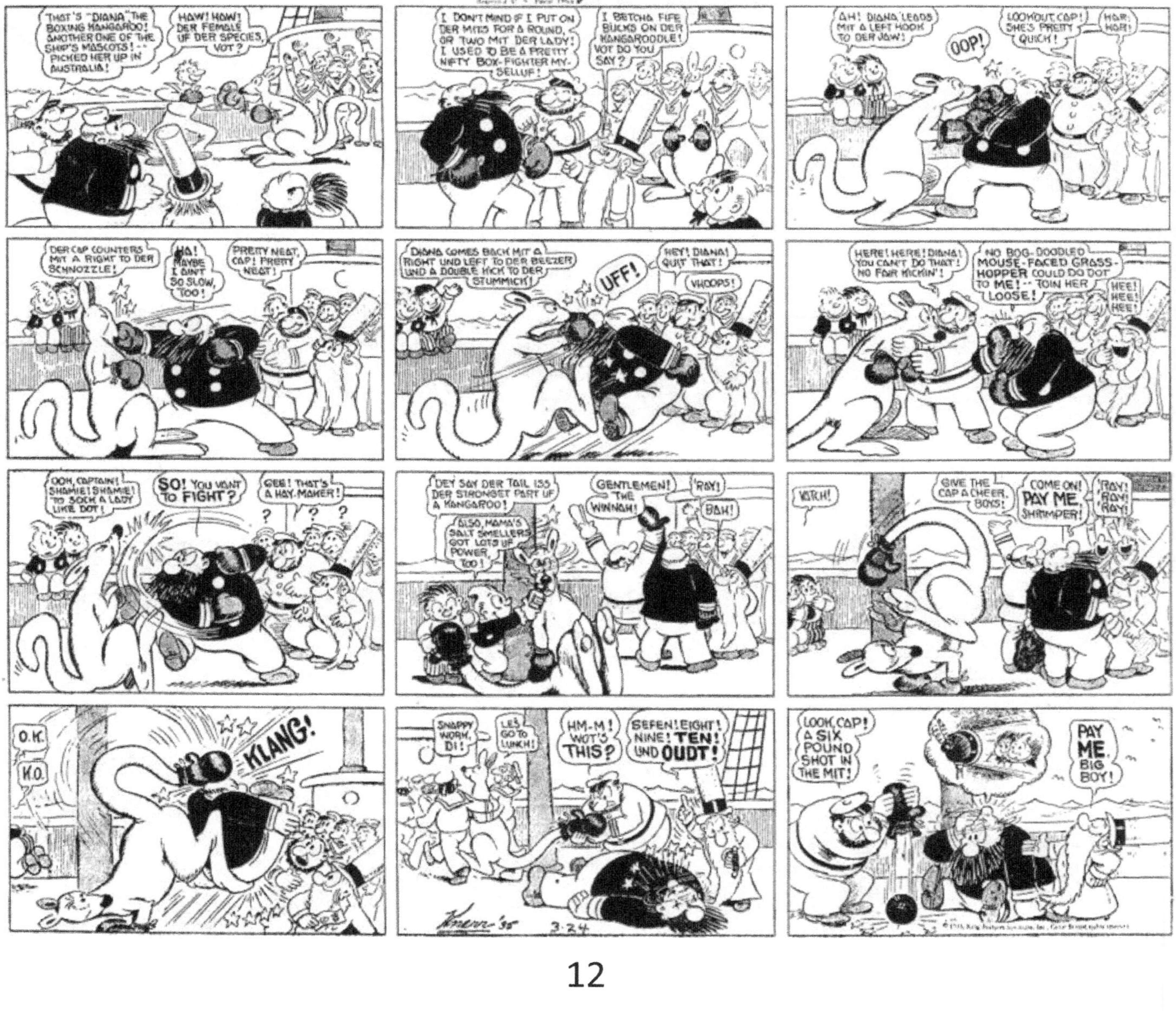
THAT'S "DIANA" THE BOXING KANGAROO! ANOTHER ONE OF THE SHIP'S MASCOTS! -- PICKED HER UP IN AUSTRALIA!
HAW! HAW! DER FEMALE UF DER SPECIES, VOT?
I DON'T MIND IF I PUT ON DER MITS FOR A ROUND, OR TWO MIT DER LADY! I USED TO BE A PRETTY NIFTY BOX-FIGHTER MY-SELLUF!
I BETCHA FIFE BUCKS ON DER KANGAROODLE! VOT DO YOU SAY?
AH! DIANA LEADS MIT A LEFT HOOK TO DER JAW!
OOP!
LOOKOUT, CAP! SHE'S PRETTY QUICK!
HAR! HAR!
DER CAP COUNTERS MIT A RIGHT TO DER SCHNOZZLE!
HA! MAYBE I AIN'T SO SLOW, TOO!
PRETTY NEAT, CAP! PRETTY NEAT!
DIANA COMES BACK MIT A RIGHT UND LEFT TO DER BEEZER UND A DOUBLE KICK TO DER STUMMICK!
UFF!
HEY! DIANA! QUIT THAT!
WHOOPS!
HERE! HERE! DIANA! YOU CAN'T DO THAT! NO FAIR KICKIN'!
NO BOG-DOODLED MOUSE-FACED GRASS-HOPPER COULD DO DOT TO ME! -- TOIN HER LOOSE!
HEE! HEE! HEE!
OOH, CAPTAIN! SHAME! SHAME! TO SOCK A LADY LIKE DOT!
SO! YOU VANT TO FIGHT?
GEE! THAT'S A HAY-MAKER!
? ? ?
DEY SAY DER TAIL ISS DER STRONGEST PART UF A KANGAROO!
ALSO, MAMA'S SALT SMELLERS GOT LOTS UF POWER, TOO!
GENTLEMEN! THE WINNAH!
'RAY!
BAH!
WATCH!
GIVE THE CAP A CHEER, BOYS!
COME ON! PAY ME, SHRIMPER!
'RAY! 'RAY! 'RAY!
O.K.
K.O.
KLANG!
SNAPPY WORK, DI!
LES GO TO LUNCH!
HM-M! WOT'S THIS?
SEFEN! EIGHT! NINE! TEN! UND OUDT!
LOOK, CAP! A SIX POUND SHOT IN THE MIT!
PAY ME, BIG BOY!
Knerr '35
3-24

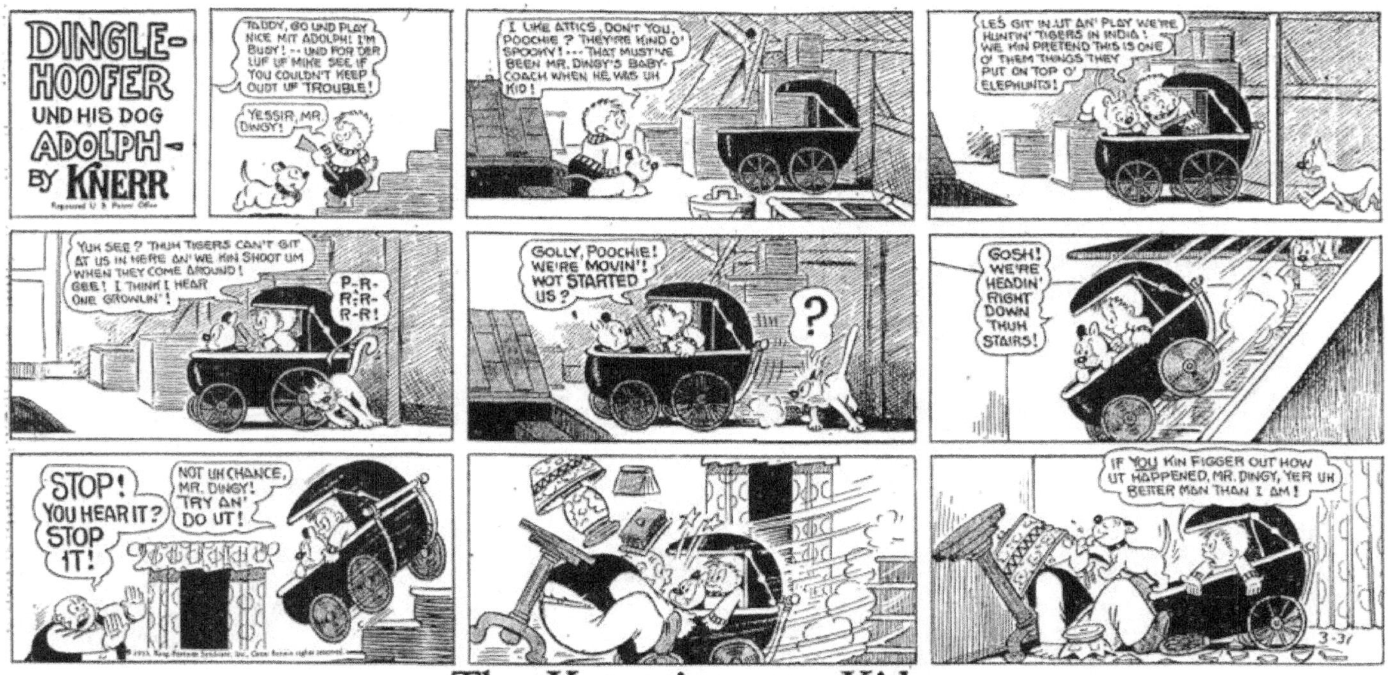
DINGLE-HOOFER UND HIS DOG ADOLPH - BY KNERR
TADDY, GO UND PLAY NICE MIT ADOLPH! I'M BUSY! -- UND FOR DER LUF UF MIKE SEE IF YOU COULDN'T KEEP OUDT UF TROUBLE!
YESSIR, MR. DINGY!
I LIKE ATTICS, DON'T YOU, POOCHIE? THEY'RE KIND O' SPOOKY! --- THAT MUST'VE BEEN MR. DINGY'S BABY-COACH WHEN HE WAS UH KID!
LE'S GIT IN UT AN' PLAY WE'RE HUNTIN' TIGERS IN INDIA! WE KIN PRETEND THIS IS ONE O' THEM THINGS THEY PUT ON TOP O' ELEPHUNTS!
YUH SEE? THUH TIGERS CAN'T GIT AT US IN HERE AN' WE KIN SHOOT UM WHEN THEY COME AROUND! GEE! I THINK I HEAR ONE GROWLIN'!
P-R-R-R-R-R!
GOLLY, POOCHIE! WE'RE MOVIN'! WOT STARTED US?
?
GOSH! WE'RE HEADIN' RIGHT DOWN THUH STAIRS!
STOP! YOU HEAR IT? STOP IT!
NOT UH CHANCE, MR. DINGY! TRY AN' DO UT!
IF YOU KIN FIGGER OUT HOW UT HAPPENED, MR. DINGY, YER UH BETTER MAN THAN I AM!
3-31

The Katzenjammer Kids

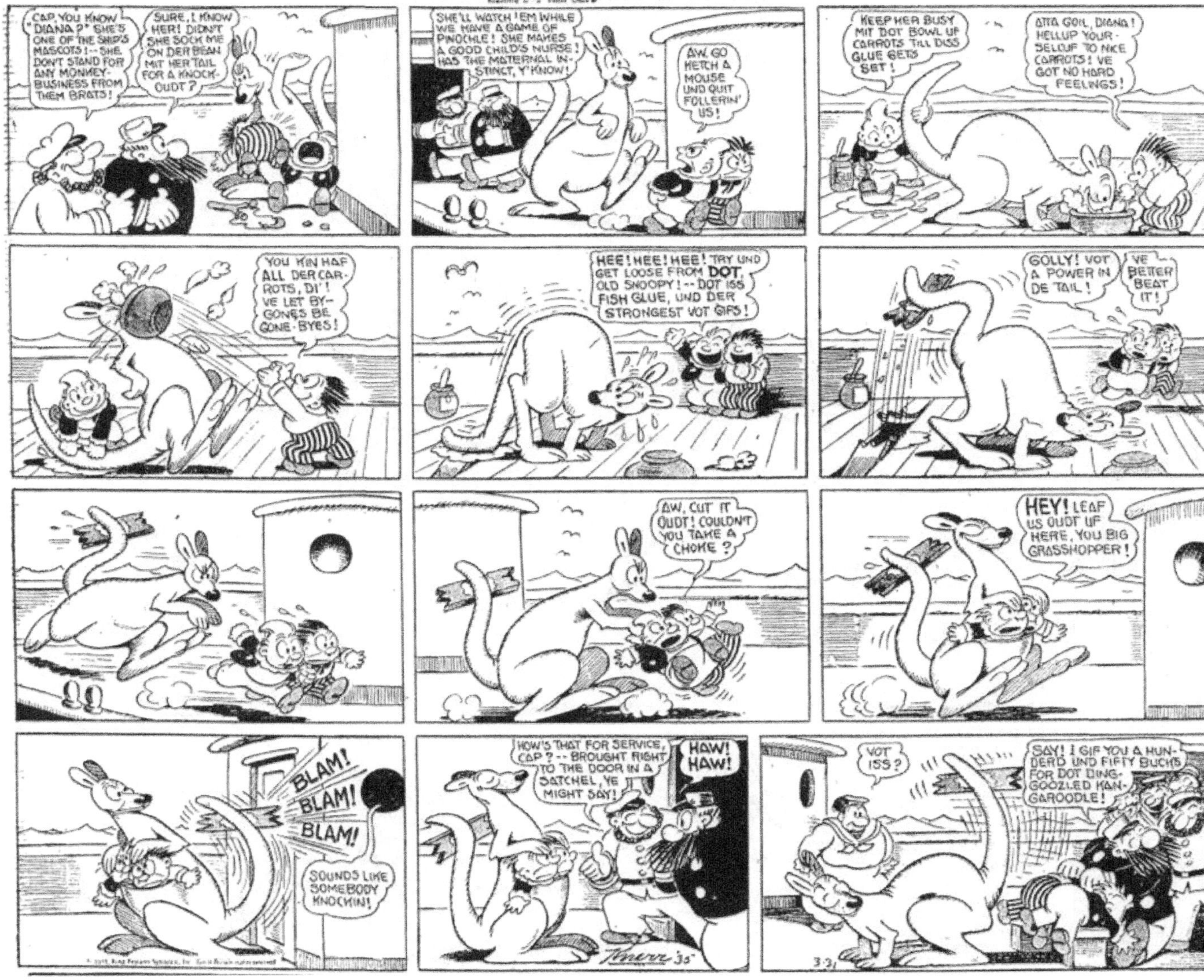
CAP, YOU KNOW "DIANA?" SHE'S ONE OF THE SHIP'S MASCOTS! -- SHE DON'T STAND FOR ANY MONKEY-BUSINESS FROM THEM BRATS!
SURE, I KNOW HER! DIDN'T SHE SOCK ME ON DER BEAN MIT HER TAIL FOR A KNOCK-OUDT?
SHE'LL WATCH 'EM WHILE WE HAVE A GAME OF PINOCHLE! SHE MAKES A GOOD CHILD'S NURSE! HAS THE MATERNAL IN-STINCT, Y'KNOW!
AW, GO KETCH A MOUSE UND QUIT FOLLERIN' US!
KEEP HER BUSY MIT DOT BOWL UF CARROTS TILL DISS GLUE GETS SET!
ATTA GOIL, DIANA! HELLUP YOUR-SELLUF TO NICE CARROTS! VE GOT NO HARD FEELINGS!
YOU KIN HAF ALL DER CAR-ROTS, DI'! VE LET BY-GONES BE GONE-BYES!
HEE! HEE! HEE! TRY UND GET LOOSE FROM DOT, OLD SNOOPY! -- DOT ISS FISH GLUE, UND DER STRONGEST VOT GIFS!
GOLLY! VOT A POWER IN DE TAIL!
VE BETTER BEAT IT!
AW, CUT IT OUDT! COULDN'T YOU TAKE A CHOKE?
HEY! LEAF US OUDT UF HERE, YOU BIG GRASSHOPPER!
BLAM! BLAM! BLAM!
SOUNDS LIKE SOMEBODY KNOCKIN'!
HOW'S THAT FOR SERVICE, CAP? -- BROUGHT RIGHT TO THE DOOR IN A SATCHEL, YE MIGHT SAY!
HAW! HAW!
VOT ISS?
SAY! I GIF YOU A HUN-DERD UND FIFTY BUCKS FOR DOT DING-GOOZLED KAN-GAROODLE!
Knerr '35
3-31

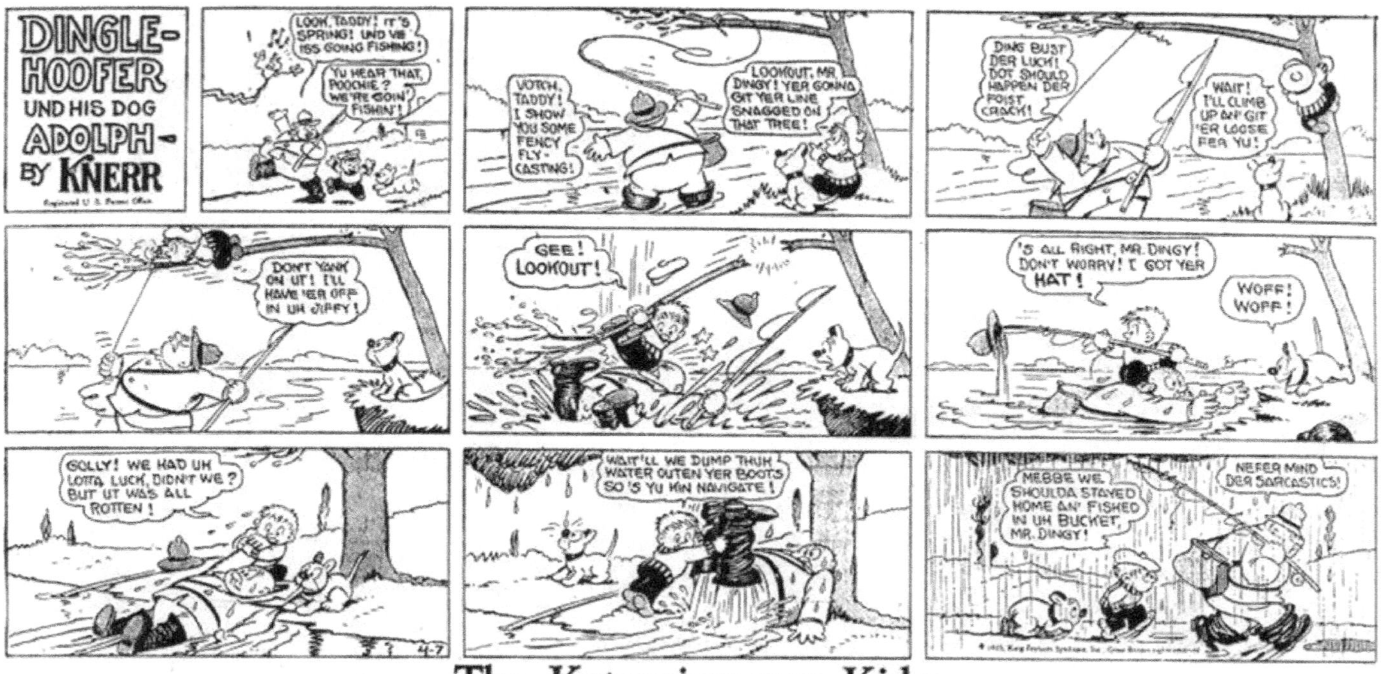
DINGLE-HOOFER UND HIS DOG ADOLPH - BY KNERR
LOOK, TADDY! IT'S SPRING! UND VE ISS GOING FISHING!
YU HEAR THAT, POOCHIE? WE'RE GOIN' FISHIN'!
VOTCH, TADDY! I SHOW YOU SOME FENCY FLY-CASTING!
LOOKOUT, MR. DINGY! YER GONNA GIT YER LINE SNAGGED ON THAT TREE!
DING BUST DER LUCK! DOT SHOULD HAPPEN DER FOIST CRACK!
WAIT! I'LL CLIMB UP AN' GIT 'ER LOOSE FER YU!
DON'T YANK ON UT! I'LL HAVE 'ER OFF IN UH JIFFY!
GEE! LOOKOUT!
'S ALL RIGHT, MR. DINGY! DON'T WORRY! I GOT YER HAT!
WOFF! WOFF!
GOLLY! WE HAD UH LOTTA LUCK, DIDN'T WE? BUT UT WAS ALL ROTTEN!
4-7
WAIT'LL WE DUMP THUH WATER OUTEN YER BOOTS SO'S YU KIN NAVIGATE!
MEBBE WE SHOULDA STAYED HOME AN' FISHED IN UH BUCKET, MR. DINGY!
NEFER MIND DER SARCASTICS!

The Katzenjammer Kids

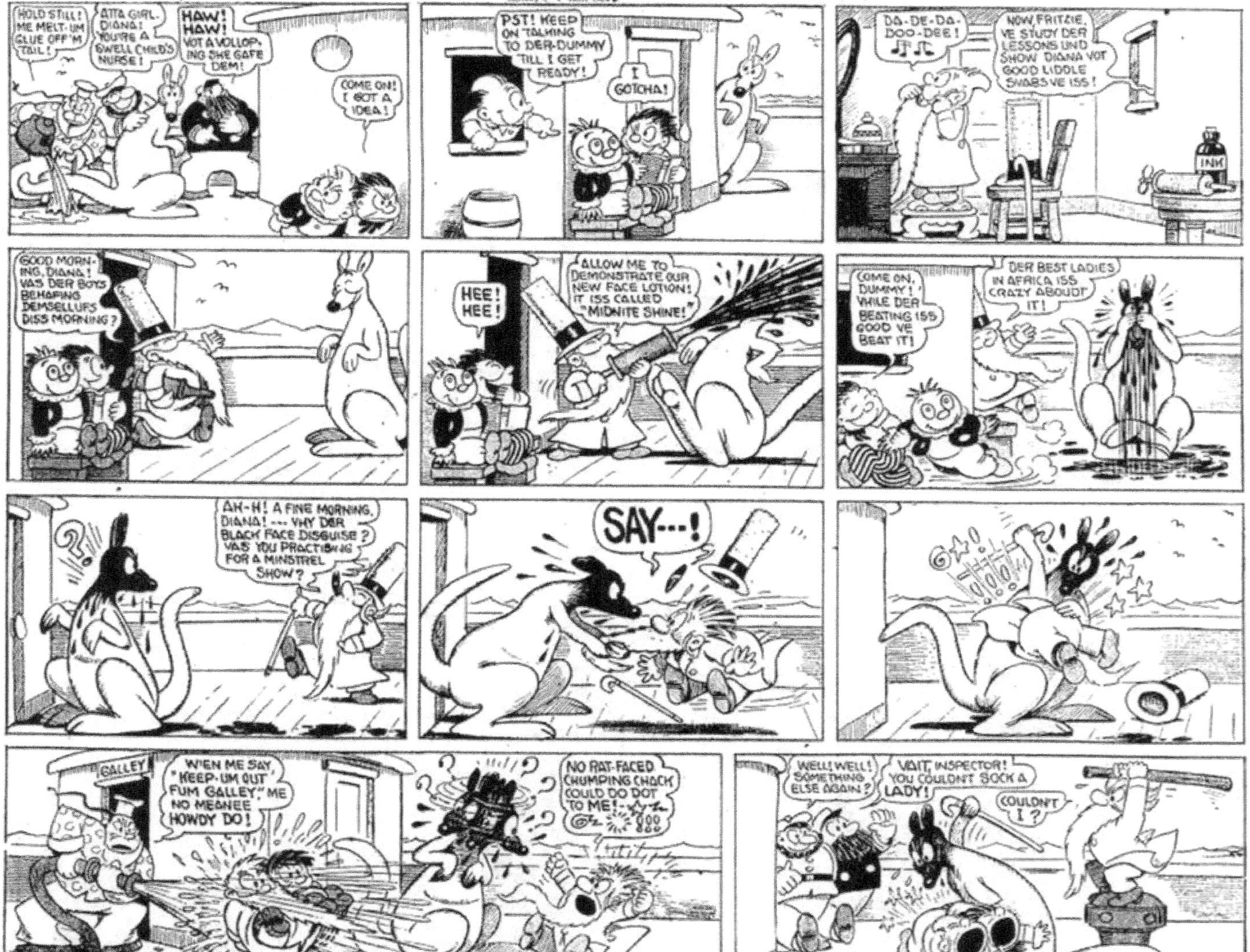
HOLD STILL! ME MELT-UM GLUE OFF 'M TAIL!
ATTA GIRL, DIANA! YOU'RE A SWELL CHILD'S NURSE!
HAW! HAW! VOT A VOLLOPING SHE GAFE DEM!
COME ON! I GOT A IDEA!
PST! KEEP ON TALKING TO DER-DUMMY 'TILL I GET READY!
I GOTCHA!
DA-DE-DA-DOO-DEE!
NOW, FRITZIE, VE STUDY DER LESSONS UND SHOW DIANA VOT GOOD LIDDLE SVABS VE ISS!
INK
GOOD MORNING, DIANA! VAS DER BOYS BEHAFING DEMSELLUFS DISS MORNING?
HEE! HEE!
ALLOW ME TO DEMONSTRATE OUR NEW FACE LOTION! IT ISS CALLED "MIDNITE SHINE!"
COME ON, DUMMY! VHILE DER BEATING ISS GOOD VE BEAT IT!
DER BEST LADIES IN AFRICA ISS CRAZY ABOUDT IT!
AH-H! A FINE MORNING, DIANA! --- VHY DER BLACK FACE DISGUISE? VAS YOU PRACTISING FOR A MINSTREL SHOW?
SAY---!
GALLEY
W'EN ME SAY, "KEEP-UM OUT FUM GALLEY," ME NO MEANEE HOWDY DO!
NO RAT-FACED CHUMPING CHACK COULD DO DOT TO ME!
WELL! WELL! SOMETHING ELSE AGAIN?
VAIT, INSPECTOR! YOU COULDN'T SOCK A LADY!
COULDN'T I?
Knerr 35
4-7

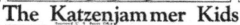

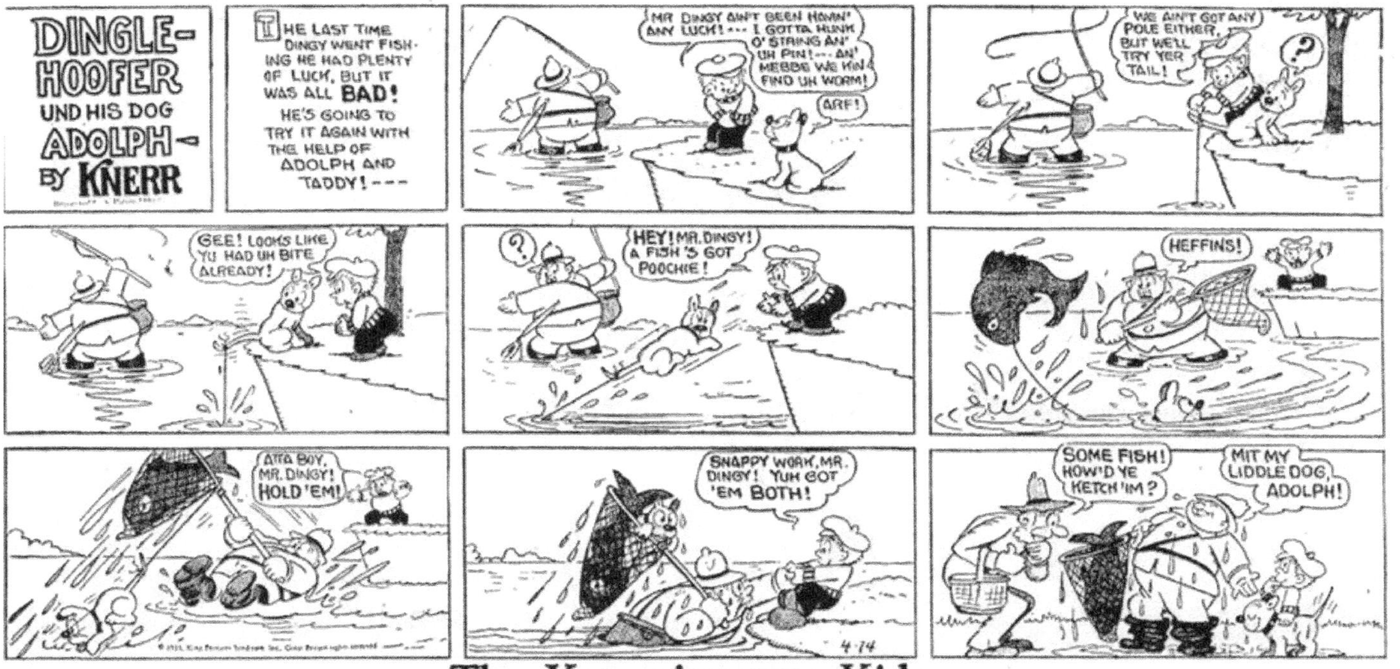
DINGLE-HOOFER UND HIS DOG ADOLPH - BY KNERR
THE LAST TIME DINGY WENT FISHING HE HAD PLENTY OF LUCK, BUT IT WAS ALL BAD! HE'S GOING TO TRY IT AGAIN WITH THE HELP OF ADOLPH AND TADDY! ---
MR DINGY AIN'T BEEN HAVIN' ANY LUCK! --- I GOTTA HUNK O' STRING AN' UH PIN! --- AN' MEBBE WE KIN FIND UH WORM!
ARF!
WE AIN'T GOT ANY POLE EITHER, BUT WE'LL TRY YER TAIL!
?
GEE! LOOKS LIKE YU HAD UH BITE ALREADY!
?
HEY! MR. DINGY! A FISH'S GOT POOCHIE!
HEFFINS!
ATTA BOY, MR. DINGY! HOLD 'EM!
SNAPPY WORK, MR. DINGY! YUH GOT 'EM BOTH!
4-14
SOME FISH! HOW'D YE KETCH 'IM?
MIT MY LIDDLE DOG, ADOLPH!

The Katzenjammer Kids

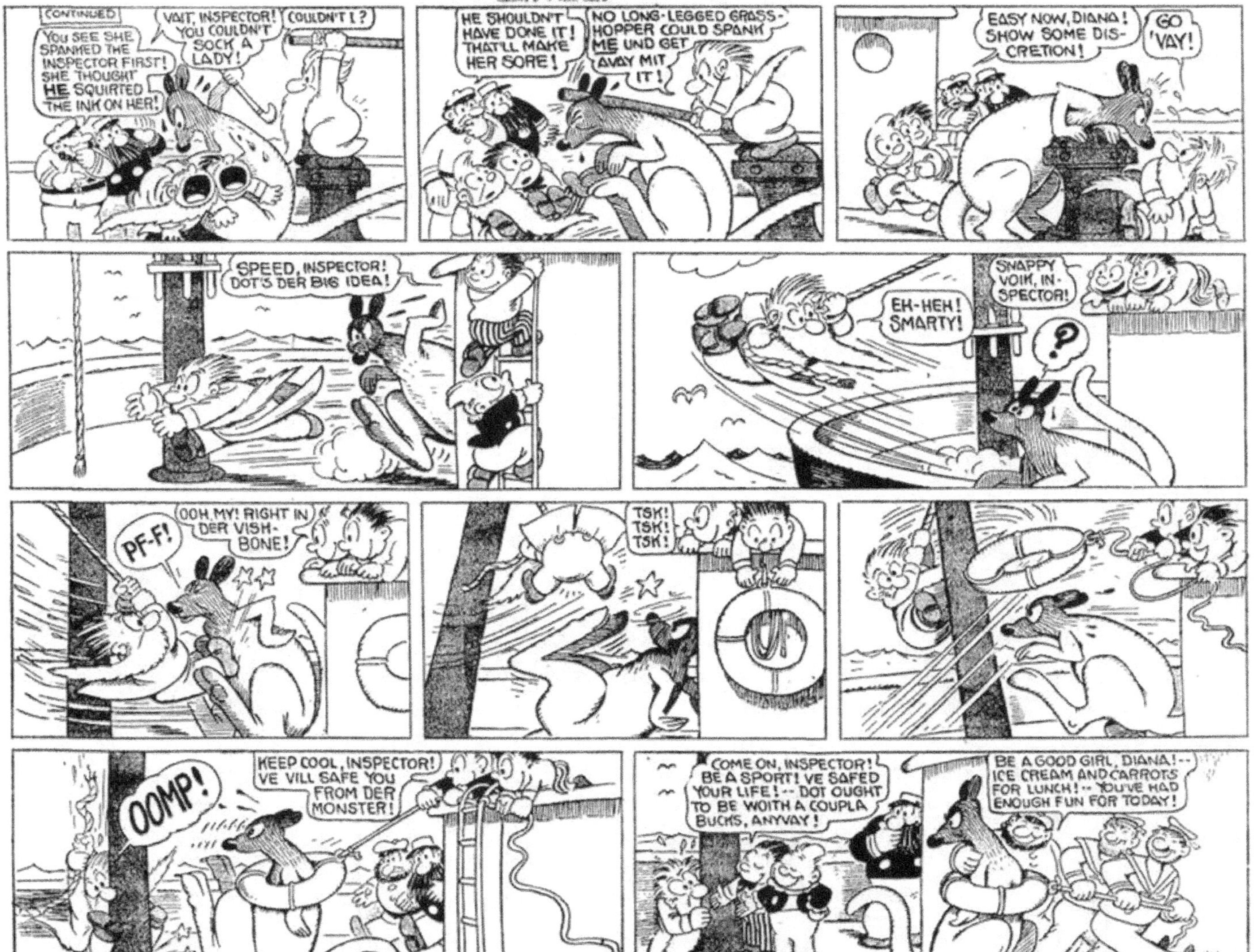
CONTINUED
YOU SEE SHE SPANKED THE INSPECTOR FIRST! SHE THOUGHT HE SQUIRTED THE INK ON HER!
VAIT, INSPECTOR! YOU COULDN'T SOCK A LADY!
COULDN'T I?
HE SHOULDN'T HAVE DONE IT! THAT'LL MAKE HER SORE!
NO LONG-LEGGED GRASSHOPPER COULD SPANK ME UND GET AVAY MIT IT!
EASY NOW, DIANA! SHOW SOME DISCRETION!
GO 'VAY!
SPEED, INSPECTOR! DOT'S DER BIG IDEA!
EH-HEH! SMARTY!
SNAPPY VOIK, INSPECTOR!
?
PF-F!
OOH, MY! RIGHT IN DER VISHBONE!
TSK! TSK! TSK!
OOMP!
KEEP COOL, INSPECTOR! VE VILL SAFE YOU FROM DER MONSTER!
COME ON, INSPECTOR! BE A SPORT! VE SAFED YOUR LIFE! -- DOT OUGHT TO BE WOITH A COUPLA BUCKS, ANYVAY!
BE A GOOD GIRL, DIANA! -- ICE CREAM AND CARROTS FOR LUNCH! -- YOU'VE HAD ENOUGH FUN FOR TODAY!
Knerr '35 4-14

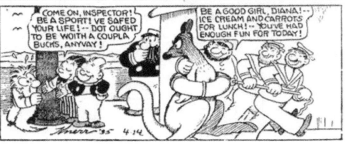

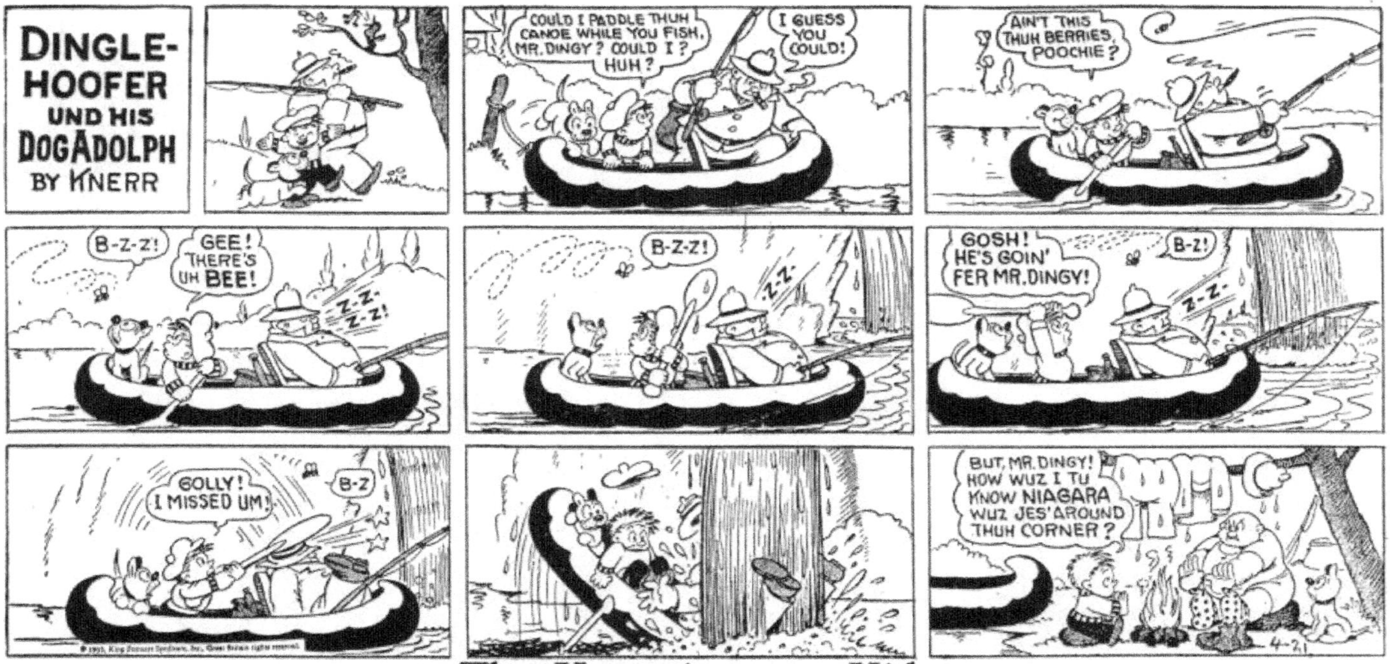
DINGLE-HOOFER UND HIS DOGADOLPH
BY KNERR
COULD I PADDLE THUH CANOE WHILE YOU FISH, MR. DINGY? COULD I? HUH?
I GUESS YOU COULD!
AIN'T THIS THUH BERRIES, POOCHIE?
B-Z-Z!
GEE! THERE'S UH BEE!
Z-Z-Z-Z!
B-Z-Z!
Z-Z-
GOSH! HE'S GOIN' FER MR. DINGY!
B-Z!
Z-Z-
GOLLY! I MISSED UM!
B-Z
BUT, MR. DINGY! HOW WUZ I TU KNOW NIAGARA WUZ JES' AROUND THUH CORNER?
4-21

The Katzenjammer Kids

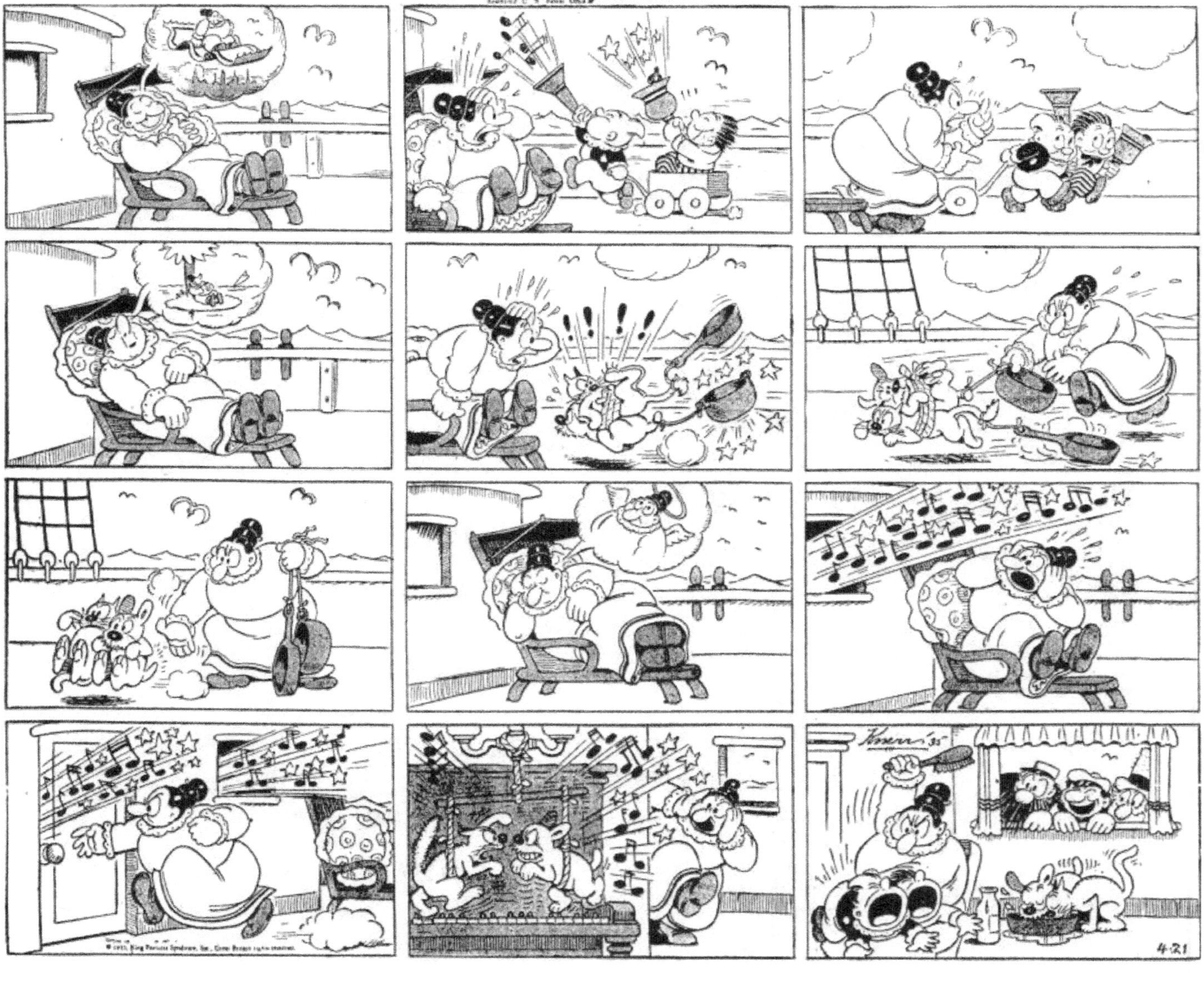
Knerr '35
4-21

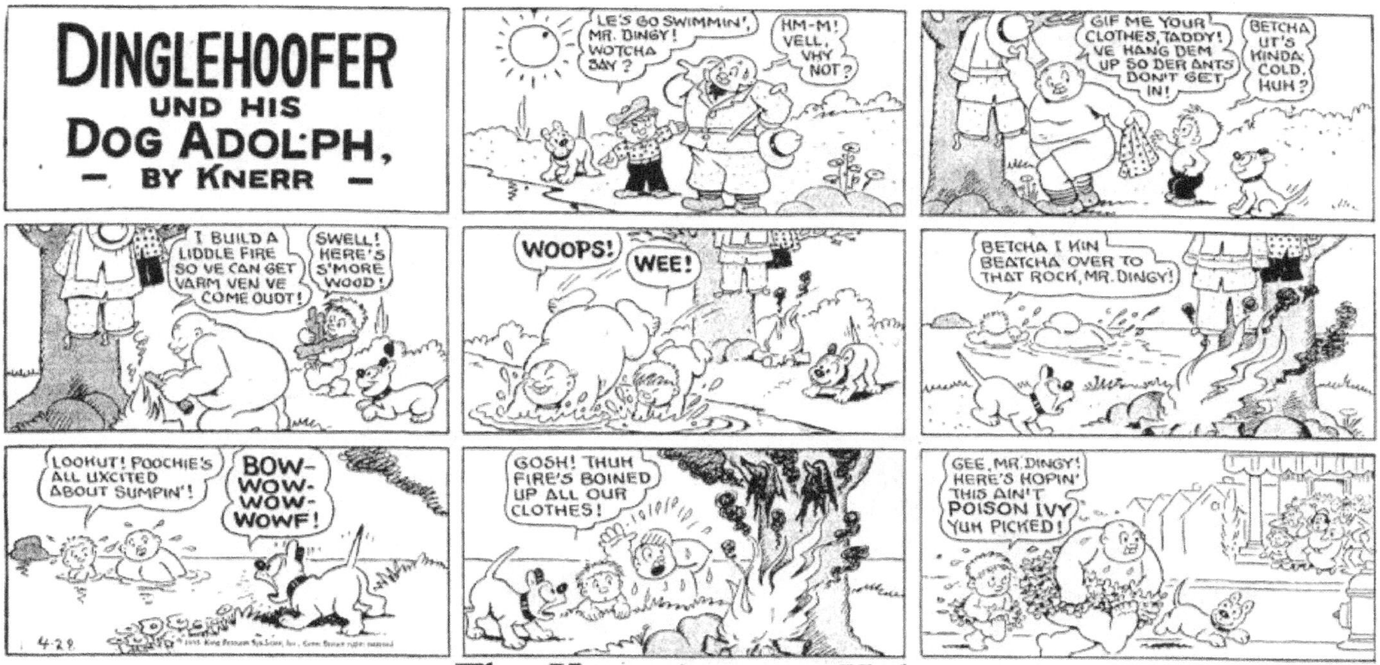
DINGLEHOOFER UND HIS DOG ADOLPH,
— BY KNERR —
LE'S GO SWIMMIN', MR. DINGY! WOTCHA SAY?
HM-M! VELL, VHY NOT?
GIF ME YOUR CLOTHES, TADDY! VE HANG DEM UP SO DER ANTS DON'T GET IN!
BETCHA UT'S KINDA COLD, HUH?
I BUILD A LIDDLE FIRE SO VE CAN GET VARM VEN VE COME OUDT!
SWELL! HERE'S S'MORE WOOD!
WOOPS!
WEE!
BETCHA I KIN BEATCHA OVER TO THAT ROCK, MR. DINGY!
LOOKUT! POOCHIE'S ALL UXCITED ABOUT SUMPIN'!
BOW-WOW-WOW-WOWF!
GOSH! THUH FIRE'S BOINED UP ALL OUR CLOTHES!
GEE, MR. DINGY! HERE'S HOPIN' THIS AIN'T POISON IVY YUH PICKED!
4-28

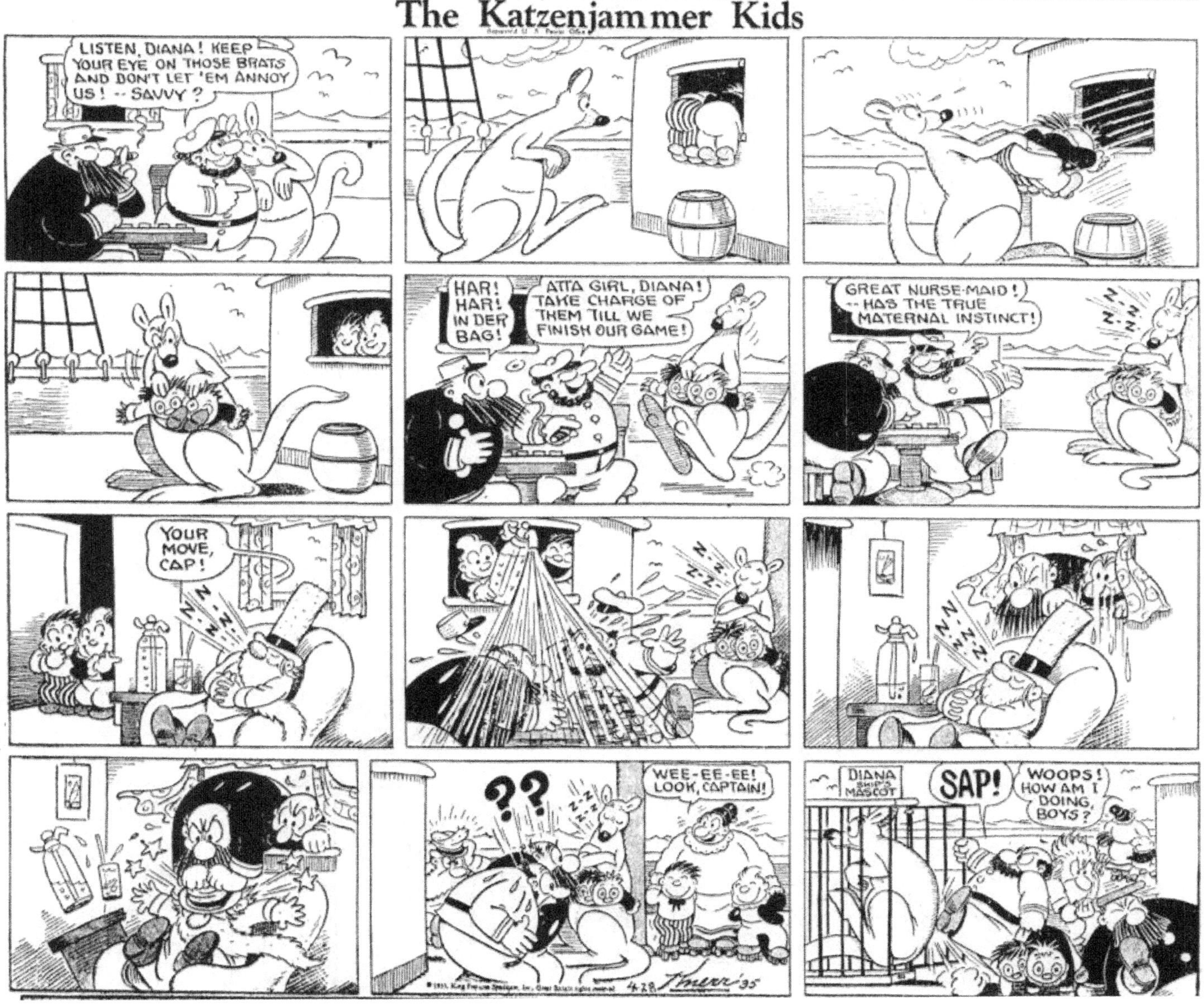
The Katzenjammer Kids
LISTEN, DIANA! KEEP YOUR EYE ON THOSE BRATS AND DON'T LET 'EM ANNOY US! -- SAVVY?
HAR! HAR! IN DER BAG!
ATTA GIRL, DIANA! TAKE CHARGE OF THEM TILL WE FINISH OUR GAME!
GREAT NURSE-MAID! -- HAS THE TRUE MATERNAL INSTINCT!
YOUR MOVE, CAP!
??
WEE-EE-EE! LOOK, CAPTAIN!
DIANA SHIP'S MASCOT
SAP!
WOOPS! HOW AM I DOING, BOYS?
4-28 Knerr '35

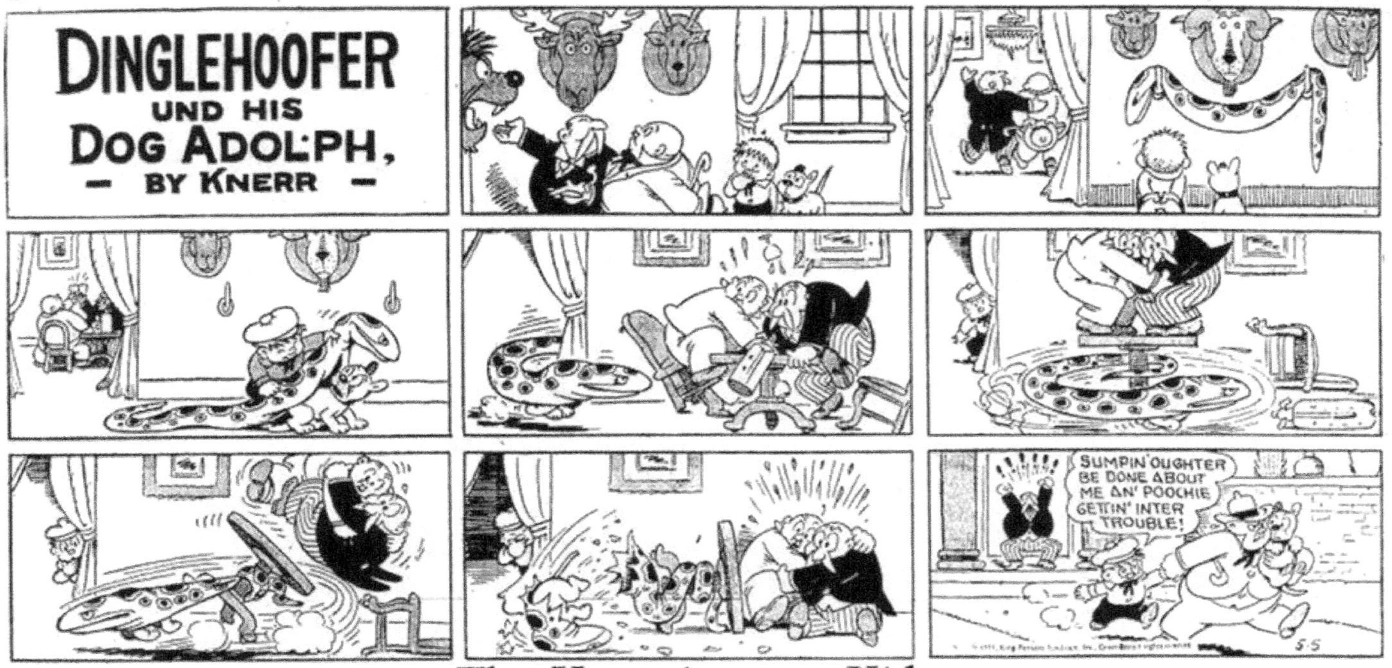
DINGLEHOOFER
UND HIS
DOG ADOL:PH,
— BY KNERR —
SUMPIN' OUGHTER BE DONE ABOUT ME AN' POOCHIE GETTIN' INTER TROUBLE!

The Katzenjammer Kids

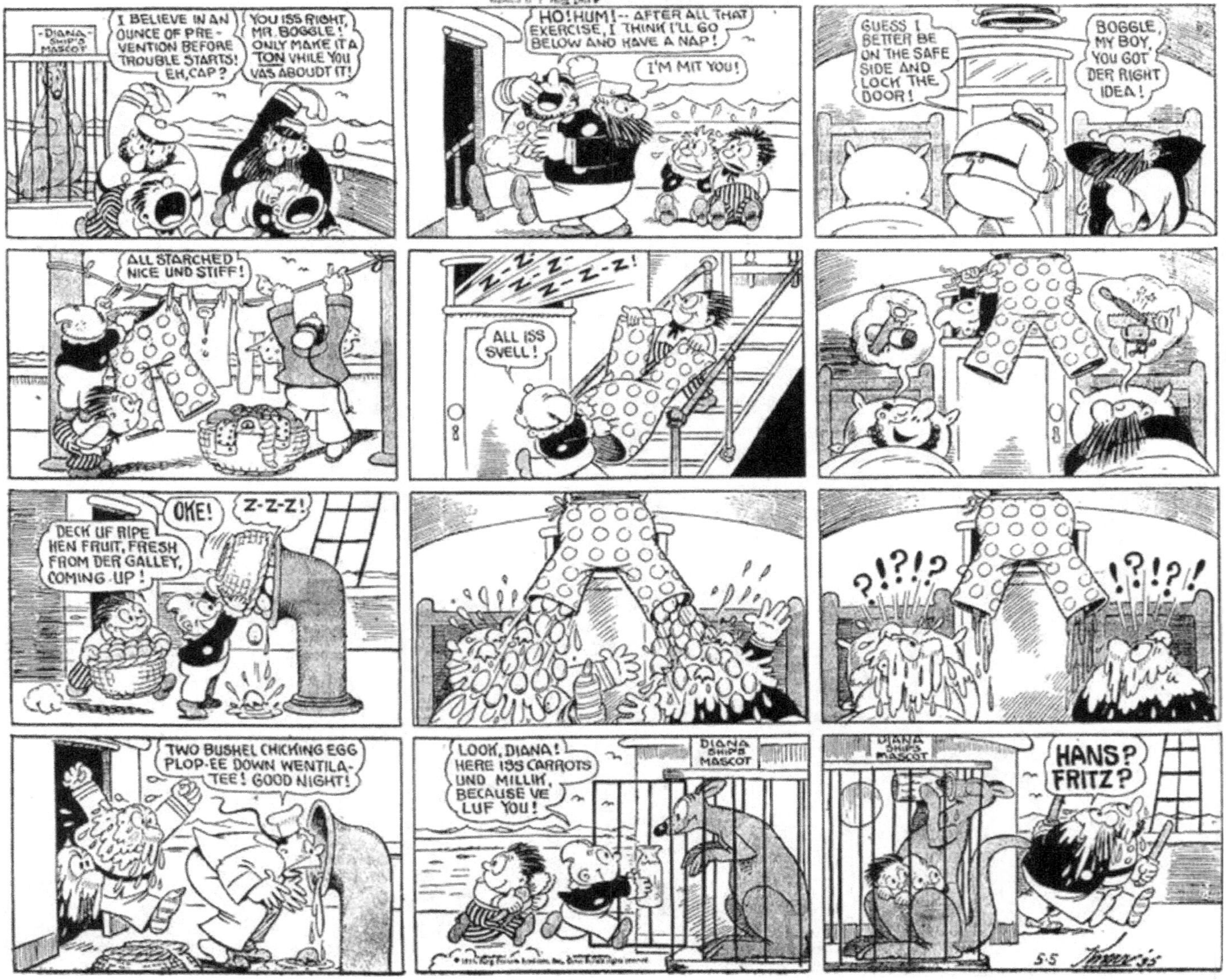
-DIANA- SHIP'S MASCOT
I BELIEVE IN AN OUNCE OF PRE-VENTION BEFORE TROUBLE STARTS! EH, CAP?
YOU ISS RIGHT, MR. BOGGLE! ONLY MAKE IT A TON VHILE YOU VAS ABOUDT IT!
HO! HUM! -- AFTER ALL THAT EXERCISE, I THINK I'LL GO BELOW AND HAVE A NAP!
I'M MIT YOU!
GUESS I BETTER BE ON THE SAFE SIDE AND LOCK THE DOOR!
BOGGLE, MY BOY, YOU GOT DER RIGHT IDEA!
ALL STARCHED NICE UND STIFF!
Z-Z-Z-Z-Z-Z-Z!
ALL ISS SVELL!
OKE!
Z-Z-Z!
DECK UF RIPE HEN FRUIT, FRESH FROM DER GALLEY, COMING UP!
?!?!?
!?!?!
TWO BUSHEL CHICKING EGG PLOP-EE DOWN WENTILA-TEE! GOOD NIGHT!
LOOK, DIANA! HERE ISS CARROTS UND MILLIK, BECAUSE VE LUF YOU!
DIANA SHIP'S MASCOT
HANS? FRITZ?

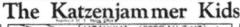

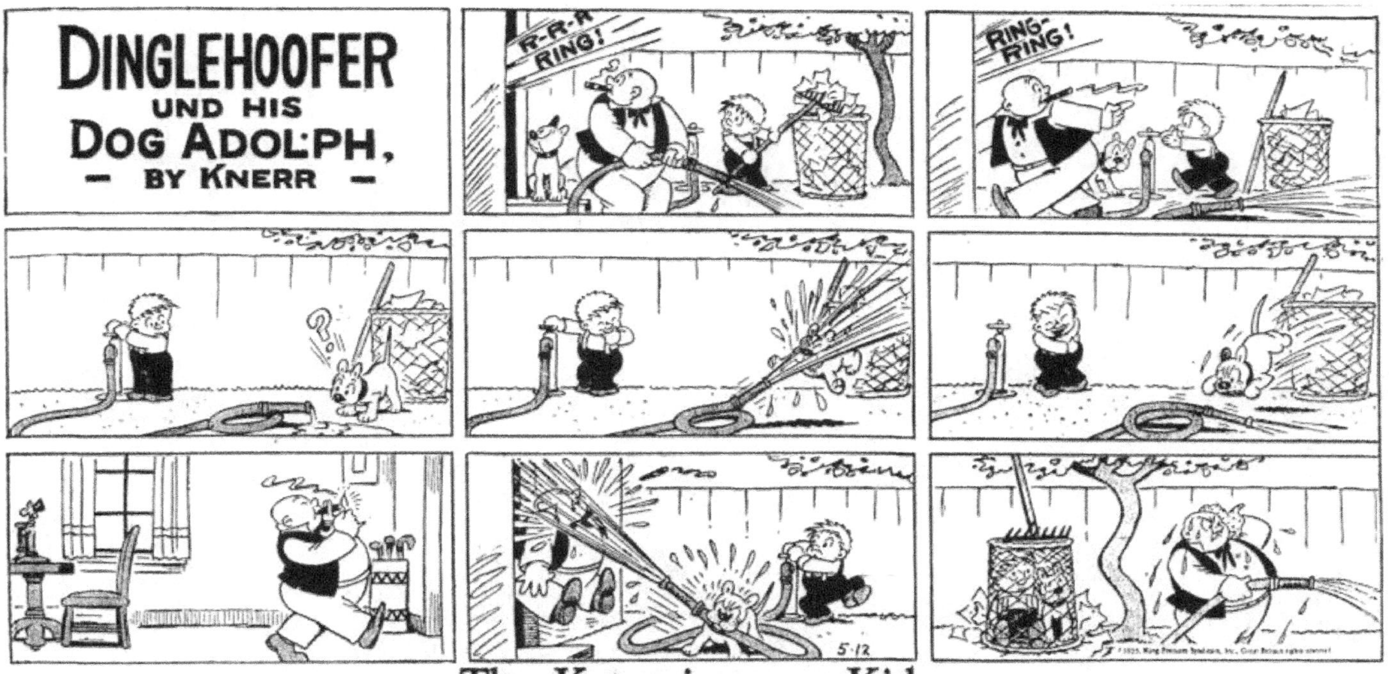
DINGLEHOOFER
UND HIS
DOG ADOL'PH,
— BY KNERR —
R-R-R RING!
RING-RING!
?
5-12

The Katzenjammer Kids

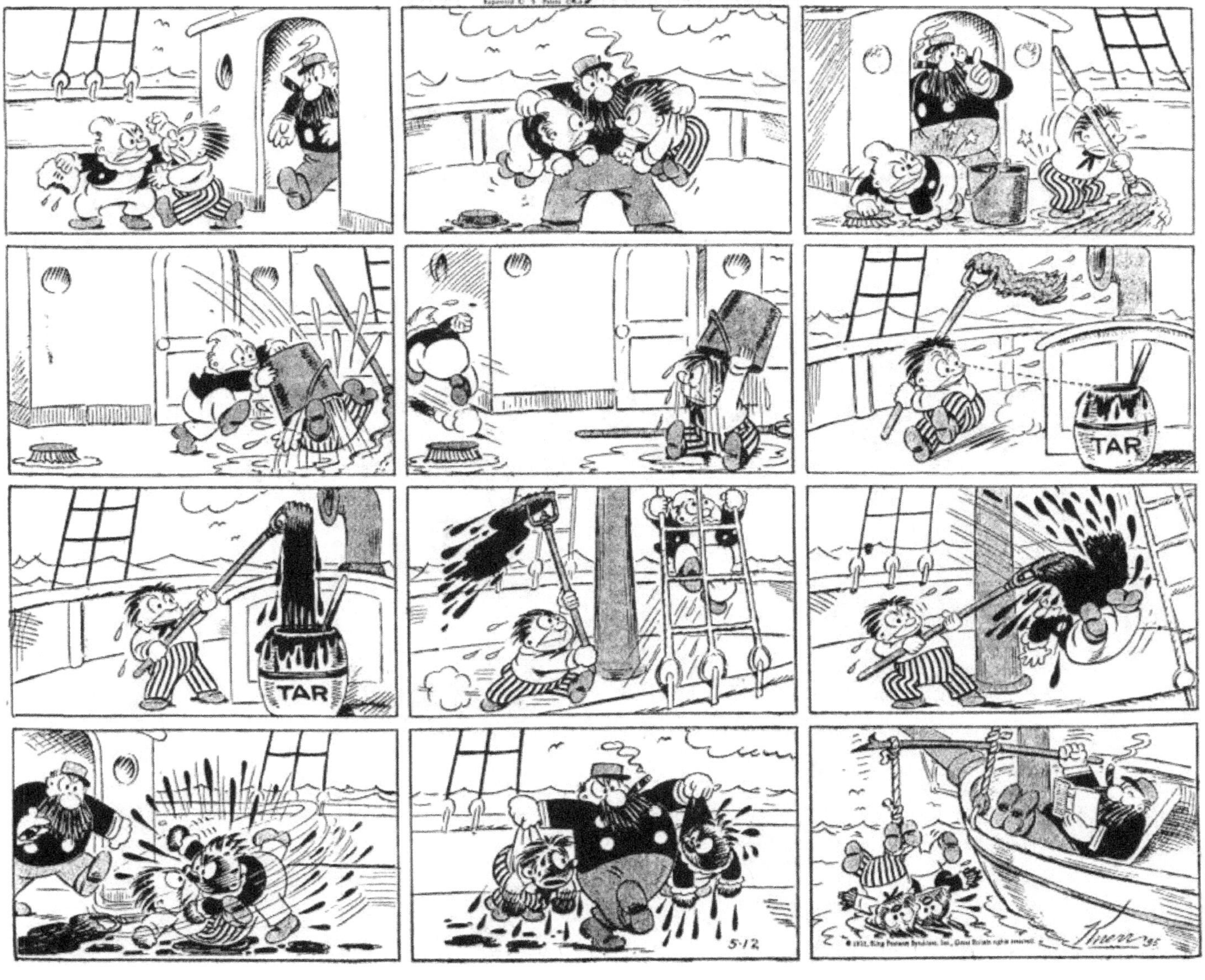
TAR
TAR
5-12
Knerr

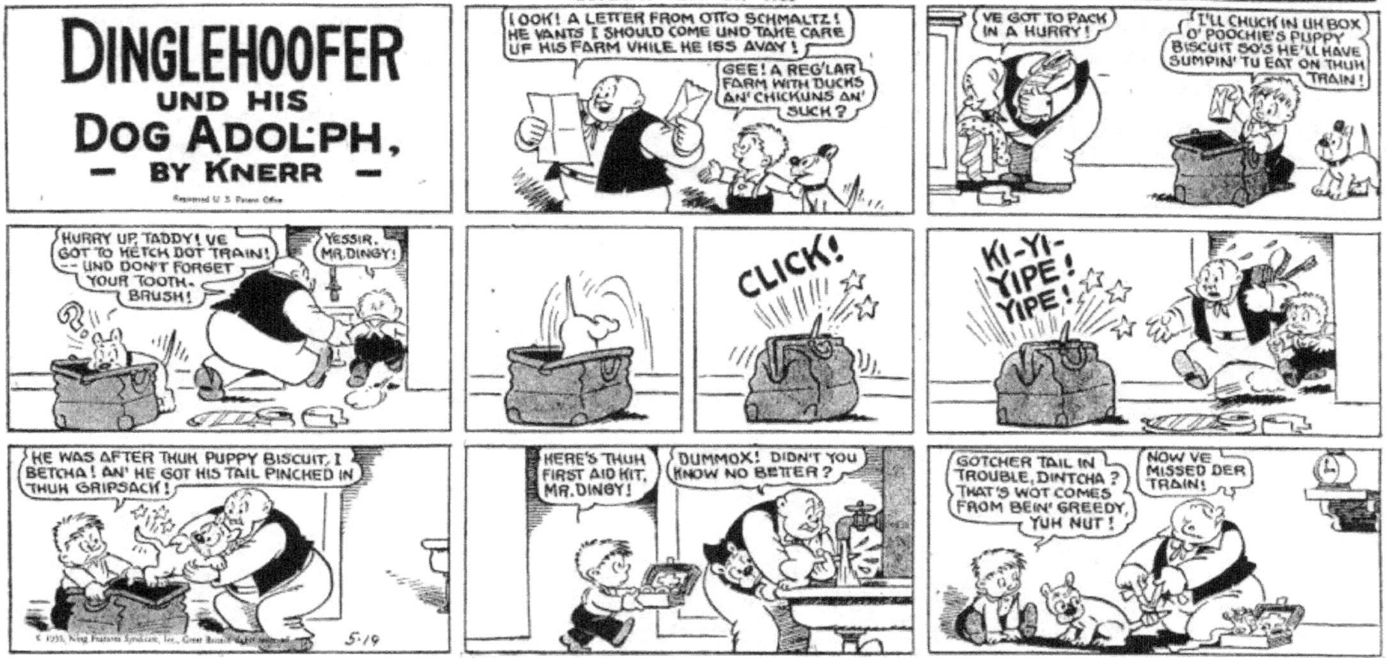
DINGLEHOOFER
UND HIS
DOG ADOLPH,
— BY KNERR —
LOOK! A LETTER FROM OTTO SCHMALTZ! HE VANTS I SHOULD COME UND TAKE CARE UF HIS FARM VHILE HE ISS AVAY!
GEE! A REG'LAR FARM WITH DUCKS AN' CHICKUNS AN' SUCH?
VE GOT TO PACK IN A HURRY!
I'LL CHUCK IN UH BOX O' POOCHIE'S PUPPY BISCUIT SO'S HE'LL HAVE SUMPIN' TU EAT ON THUH TRAIN!
HURRY UP, TADDY! VE GOT TO KETCH DOT TRAIN! -- UND DON'T FORGET YOUR TOOTH-BRUSH!
YESSIR, MR. DINGY!
CLICK!
KI-YI-YIPE! YIPE!
HE WAS AFTER THUH PUPPY BISCUIT, I BETCHA! AN' HE GOT HIS TAIL PINCHED IN THUH GRIPSACK!
HERE'S THUH FIRST AID KIT, MR. DINGY!
DUMMOX! DIDN'T YOU KNOW NO BETTER?
GOTCHER TAIL IN TROUBLE, DINTCHA? THAT'S WOT COMES FROM BEIN' GREEDY, YUH NUT!
NOW VE MISSED DER TRAIN!
5-19

The Katzenjammer Kids

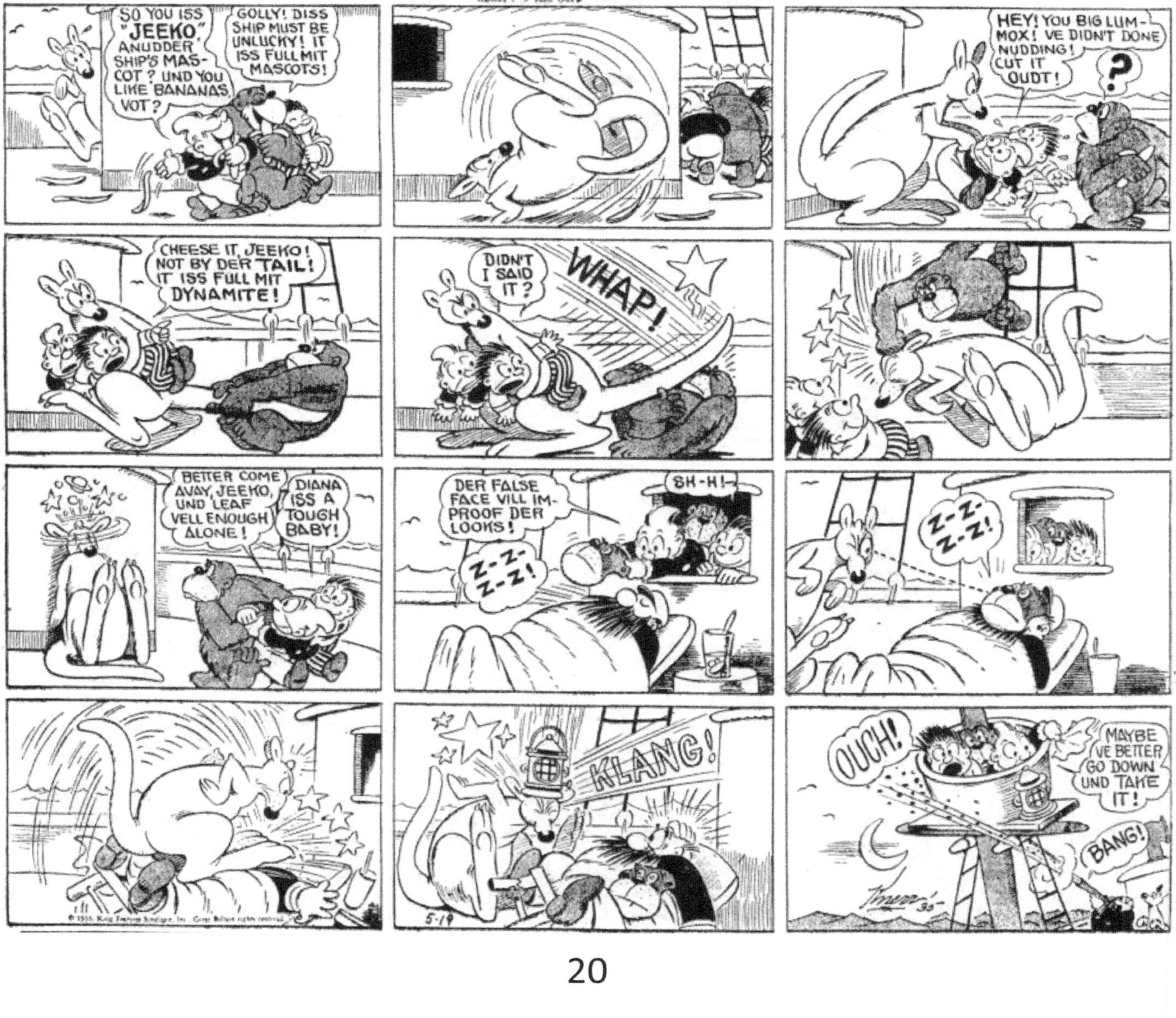
SO YOU ISS "JEEKO" ANUDDER SHIP'S MAS-COT? UND YOU LIKE BANANAS, VOT?
GOLLY! DISS SHIP MUST BE UNLUCKY! IT ISS FULL MIT MASCOTS!
HEY! YOU BIG LUM-MOX! VE DIDN'T DONE NUDDING! CUT IT OUDT!
?
CHEESE IT, JEEKO! NOT BY DER TAIL! IT ISS FULL MIT DYNAMITE!
DIDN'T I SAID IT?
WHAP!
BETTER COME AVAY, JEEKO, UND LEAF VELL ENOUGH ALONE!
DIANA ISS A TOUGH BABY!
DER FALSE FACE VILL IM-PROOF DER LOOKS!
SH-H!
Z-Z-Z-Z!
Z-Z-Z-Z!
KLANG!
5-19
OUCH!
MAYBE VE BETTER GO DOWN UND TAKE IT!
BANG!

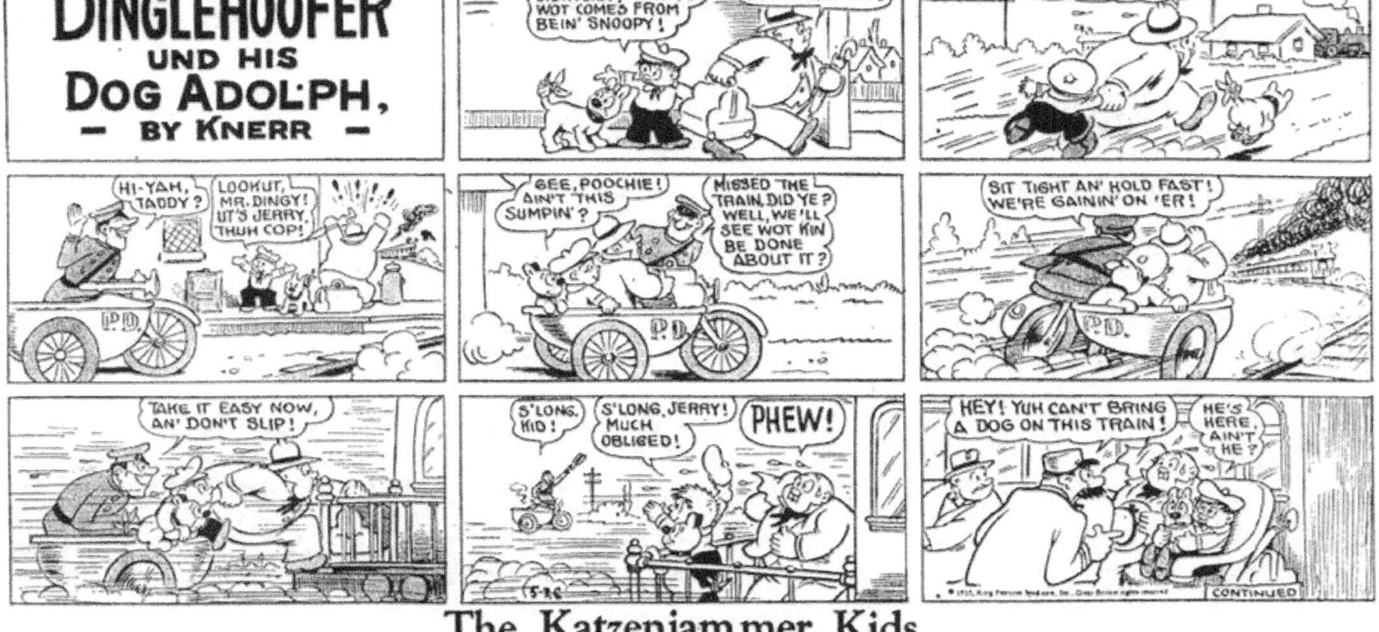
DINGLEHOOFER UND HIS DOG ADOLPH,
— BY KNERR —
GOTCHER TAIL PINCHED IN THUH GRIPSACK, DIDN'TCHA ?-- THAT'S WOT COMES FROM BEIN' SNOOPY!
COME ON! VE MISSED VUN TRAIN ALREADY!
HURRY UP! DOT'S DER LAST TRAIN!
HI-YAH, TADDY?
LOOKUT, MR. DINGY! UT'S JERRY, THUH COP!
SEE, POOCHIE! AIN'T THIS SUMPIN'?
MISSED THE TRAIN, DID YE? WELL, WE'LL SEE WOT KIN BE DONE ABOUT IT?
P.D.
SIT TIGHT AN' HOLD FAST! WE'RE GAININ' ON 'ER!
TAKE IT EASY NOW, AN' DON'T SLIP!
S'LONG, KID!
S'LONG, JERRY! MUCH OBLIGED!
PHEW!
HEY! YUH CAN'T BRING A DOG ON THIS TRAIN!
HE'S HERE, AIN'T HE?
5-26
CONTINUED

The Katzenjammer Kids

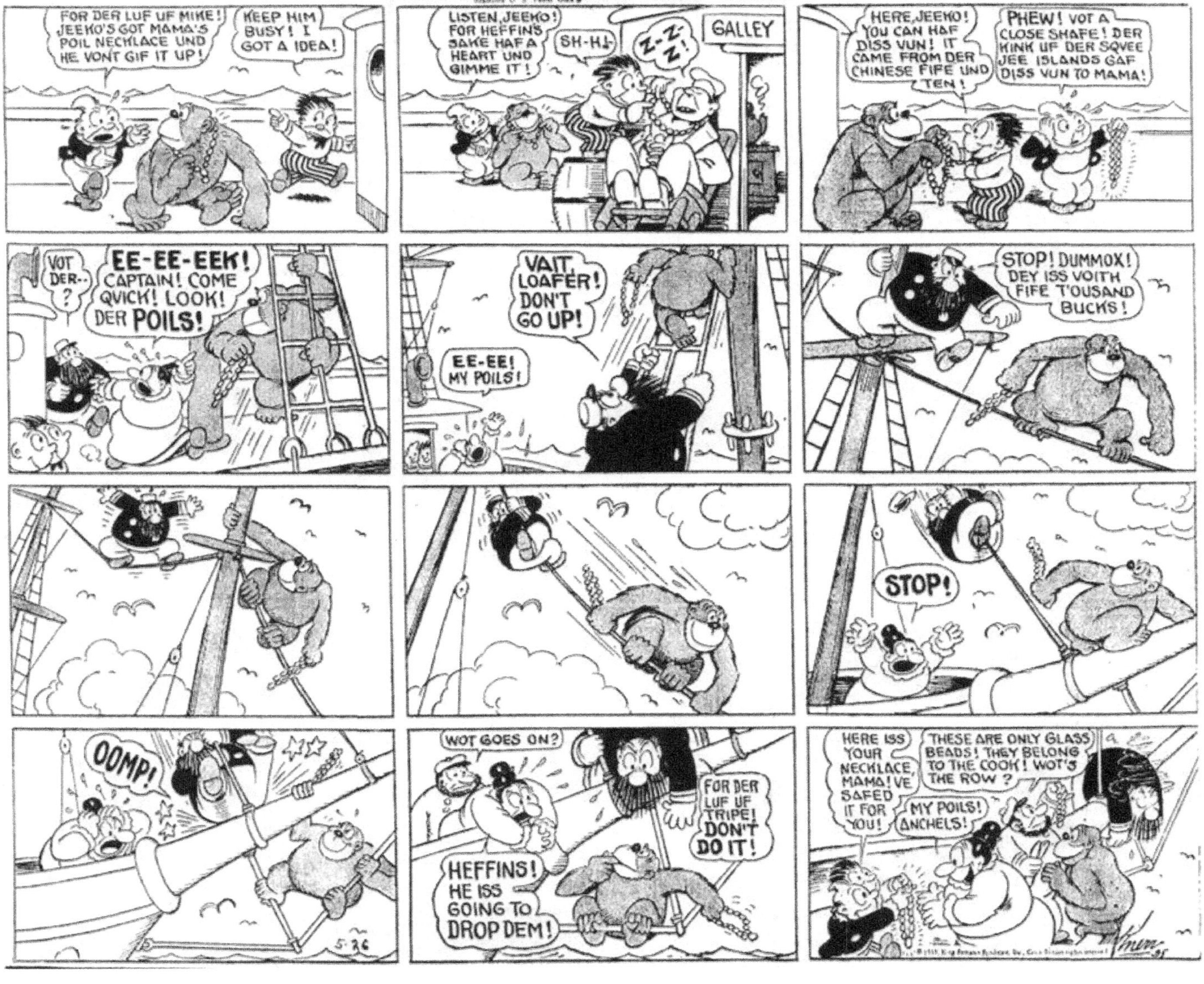
FOR DER LUF UF MIKE! JEEKO'S GOT MAMA'S POIL NECKLACE UND HE VONT GIF IT UP!
KEEP HIM BUSY! I GOT A IDEA!
LISTEN, JEEKO! FOR HEFFIN'S SAKE HAF A HEART UND GIMME IT!
SH-H!
Z-Z-Z!
GALLEY
HERE, JEEKO! YOU CAN HAF DISS VUN! IT CAME FROM DER CHINESE FIFE UND TEN!
PHEW! VOT A CLOSE SHAFE! DER KINK UF DER SQVEE JEE ISLANDS GAF DISS VUN TO MAMA!
VOT DER..?
EE-EE-EEK! CAPTAIN! COME QVICK! LOOK! DER POILS!
VAIT, LOAFER! DON'T GO UP!
EE-EE! MY POILS!
STOP! DUMMOX! DEY ISS VOITH FIFE T'OUSAND BUCKS!
STOP!
OOMP!
WOT GOES ON?
FOR DER LUF UF TRIPE! DON'T DO IT!
HEFFINS! HE ISS GOING TO DROP DEM!
5-26
HERE ISS YOUR NECKLACE, MAMA! VE SAFED IT FOR YOU!
THESE ARE ONLY GLASS BEADS! THEY BELONG TO THE COOK! WOT'S THE ROW?
MY POILS! ANCHELS!

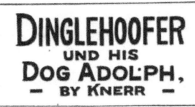

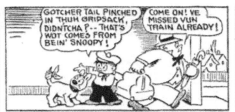

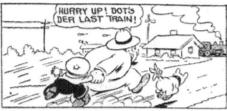

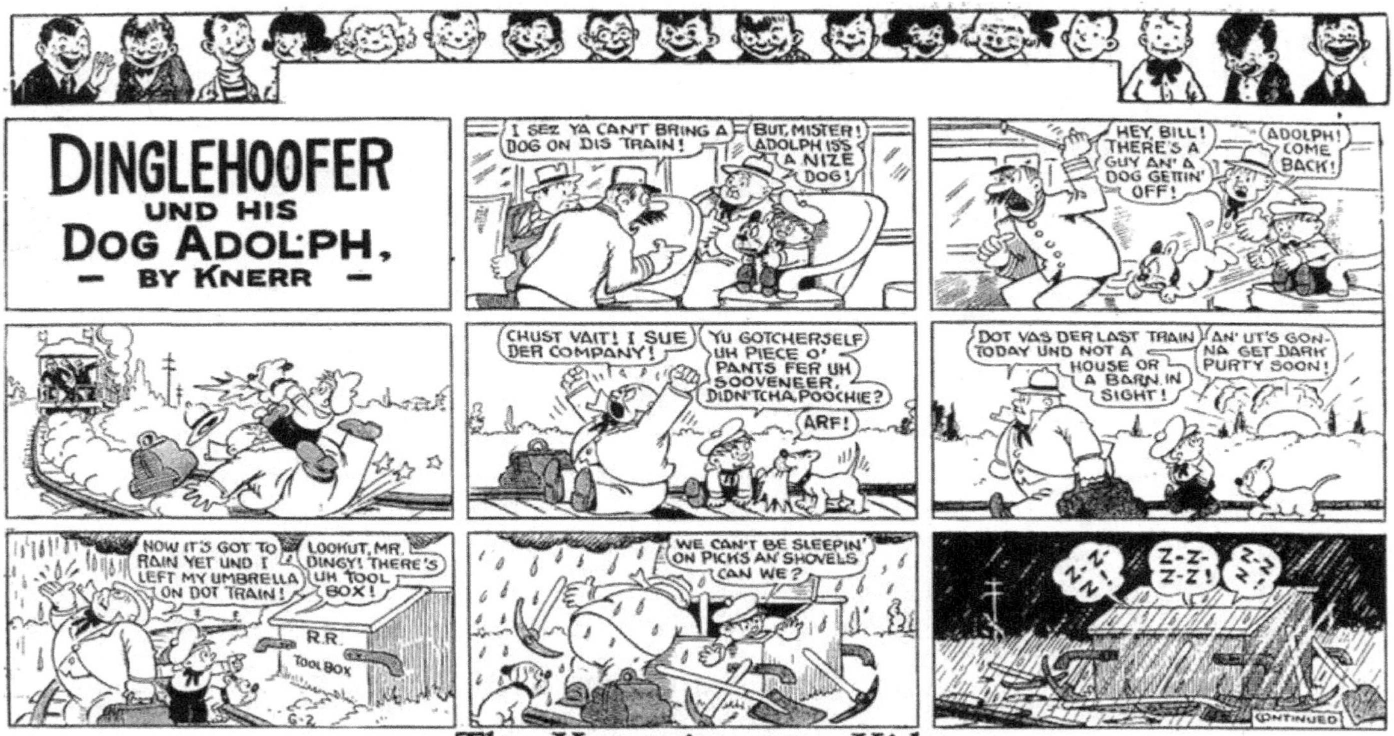
DINGLEHOOFER UND HIS DOG ADOLPH, — BY KNERR —
I SEZ YA CAN'T BRING A DOG ON DIS TRAIN!
BUT, MISTER! ADOLPH ISS A NIZE DOG!
HEY, BILL! THERE'S A GUY AN' A DOG GETTIN' OFF!
ADOLPH! COME BACK!
CHUST VAIT! I SUE DER COMPANY!
YU GOTCHERSELF UH PIECE O' PANTS FER UH SOOVENEER, DIDN'TCHA, POOCHIE?
ARF!
DOT VAS DER LAST TRAIN TODAY UND NOT A HOUSE OR A BARN IN SIGHT!
AN' UT'S GONNA GET DARK PURTY SOON!
NOW IT'S GOT TO RAIN YET UND I LEFT MY UMBRELLA ON DOT TRAIN!
LOOKUT, MR. DINGY! THERE'S UH TOOL BOX!
R.R. TOOL BOX
WE CAN'T BE SLEEPIN' ON PICKS AN' SHOVELS CAN WE?
Z-Z-Z!
Z-Z-Z-Z!
Z-Z-Z!
CONTINUED

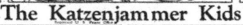

The Katzenjammer Kids

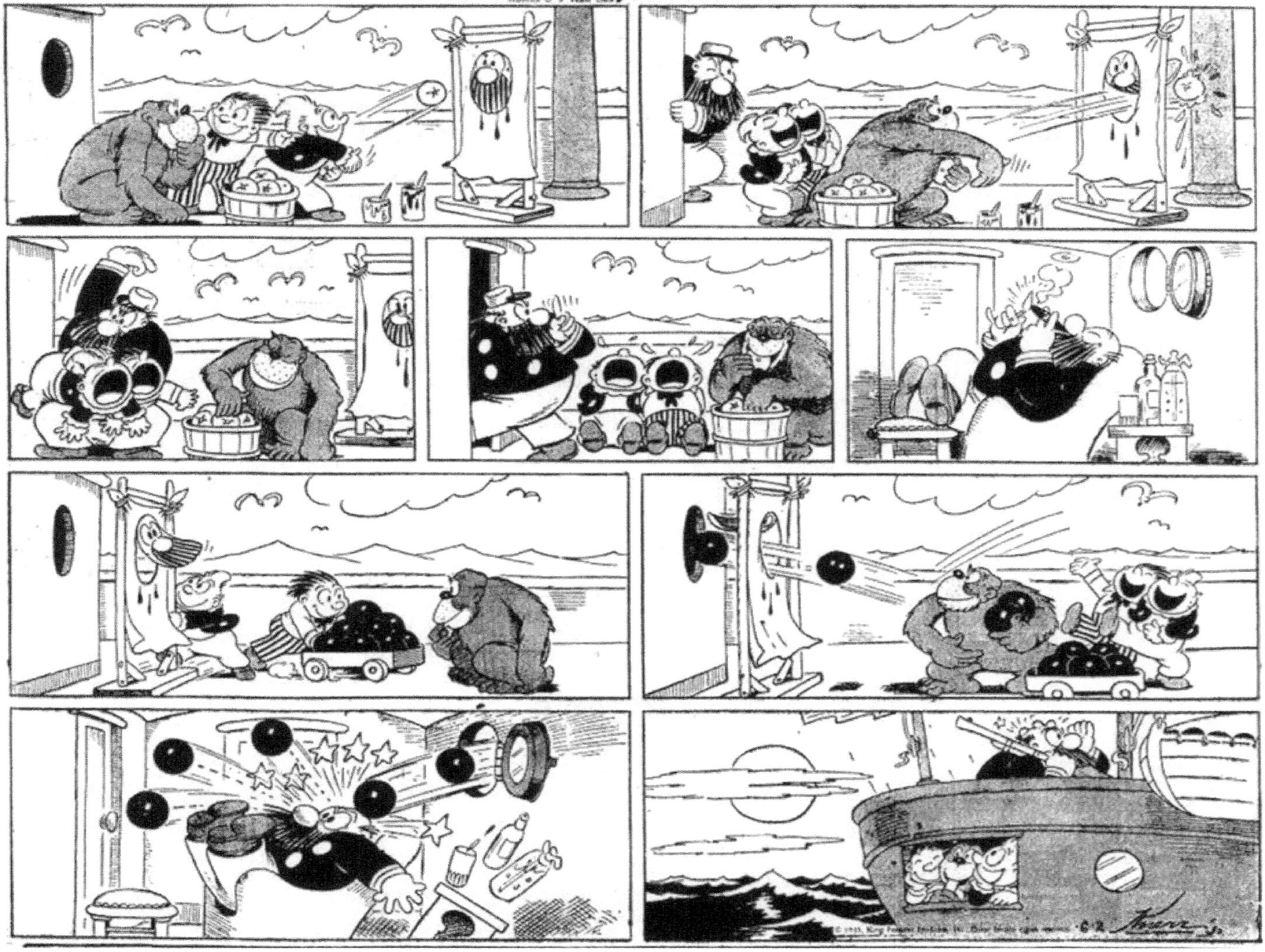

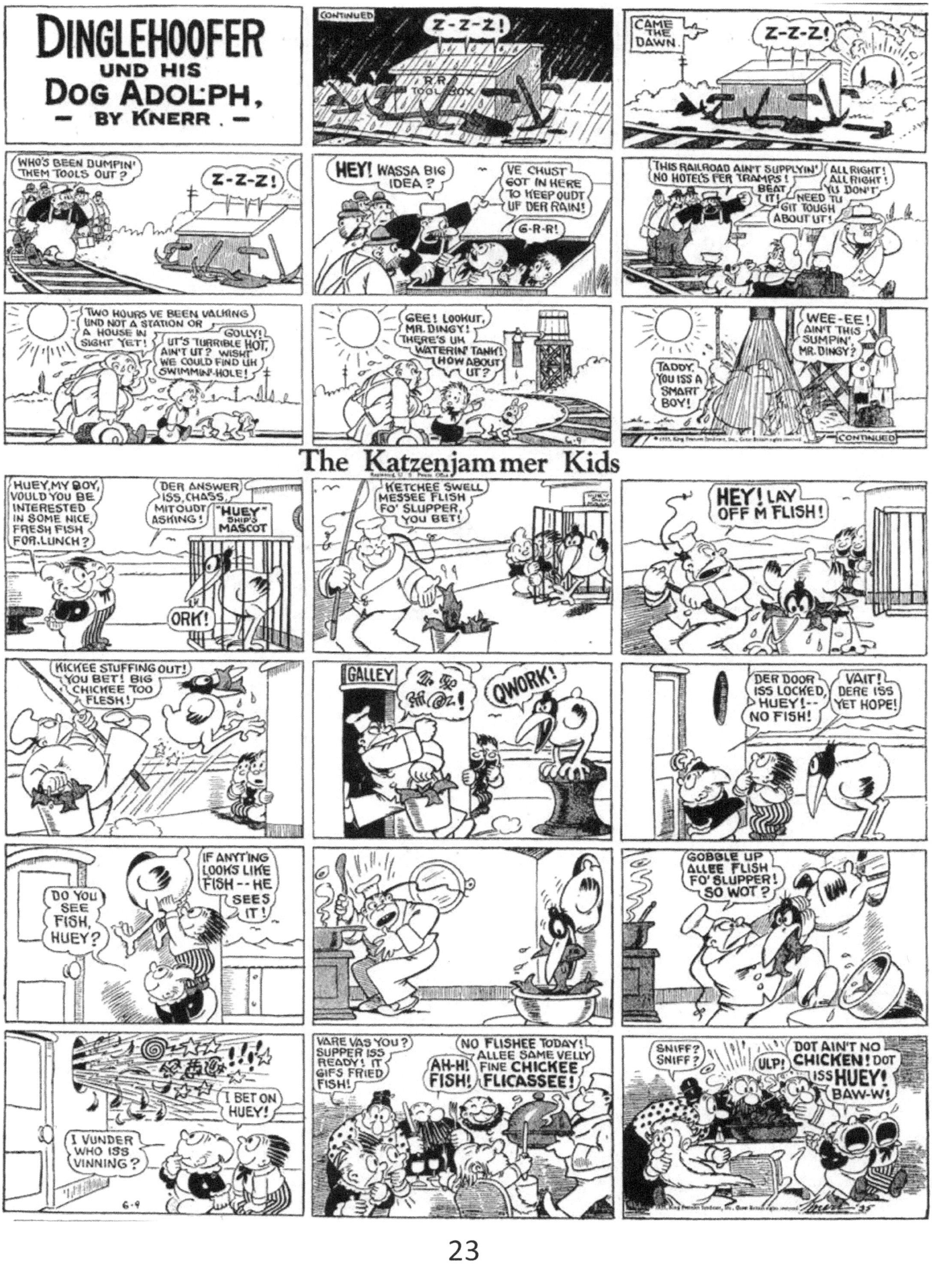

DINGLEHOOFER UND HIS DOG ADOLPH, — BY KNERR. —
CONTINUED
Z-Z-Z!
R.R. TOOL BOX
CAME THE DAWN.
Z-Z-Z!
WHO'S BEEN DUMPIN' THEM TOOLS OUT?
Z-Z-Z!
HEY! WASSA BIG IDEA?
VE CHUST GOT IN HERE TO KEEP OUDT UF DER RAIN!
G-R-R!
THIS RAILROAD AIN'T SUPPLYIN' NO HOTELS FER TRAMPS! BEAT IT!
ALL RIGHT! ALL RIGHT! YU DON'T NEED TU GIT TOUGH ABOUT UT!
TWO HOURS VE BEEN VALKING UND NOT A STATION OR A HOUSE IN SIGHT YET!
GOLLY! UT'S TURRIBLE HOT, AIN'T UT? WISHT WE COULD FIND UH SWIMMIN'-HOLE!
GEE! LOOKUT, MR. DINGY! THERE'S UH WATERIN' TANK! HOW ABOUT UT?
6-9
WEE-EE! AIN'T THIS SUMPIN', MR. DINGY?
TADDY, YOU ISS A SMART BOY!
CONTINUED
The Katzenjammer Kids
HUEY, MY BOY, VOULD YOU BE INTERESTED IN SOME NICE, FRESH FISH FOR LUNCH?
DER ANSWER ISS, CHASS, MITOUDT ASKING!
"HUEY" SHIP'S MASCOT
ORK!
KETCHEE SWELL MESSEE FLISH FO' SLUPPER, YOU BET!
HEY! LAY OFF M FLISH!
KICKEE STUFFING OUT! YOU BET! BIG CHICHEE TOO FLESH!
GALLEY
QWORK!
DER DOOR ISS LOCKED, HUEY!-- NO FISH!
VAIT! DERE ISS YET HOPE!
DO YOU SEE FISH, HUEY?
IF ANYT'ING LOOKS LIKE FISH -- HE SEES IT!
GOBBLE UP ALLEE FLISH FO' SLUPPER! SO WOT?
I BET ON HUEY!
I VUNDER WHO ISS VINNING?
6-9
VARE VAS YOU? SUPPER ISS READY! IT GIFS FRIED FISH!
AH-H! FISH!
NO FLISHEE TODAY! ALLEE SAME VELLY FINE CHICKEE FLICASSEE!
SNIFF? SNIFF?
ULP!
DOT AIN'T NO CHICKEN! DOT ISS HUEY! BAW-W!

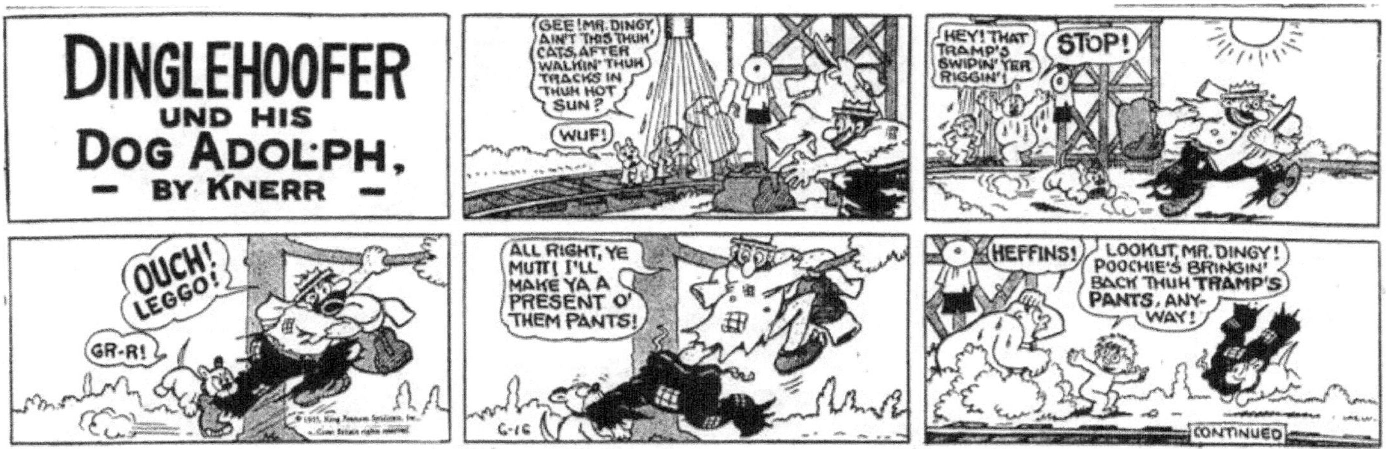

DINGLEHOOFER UND HIS DOG ADOLPH,
— BY KNERR —
GEE! MR. DINGY, AIN'T THIS THUH CATS, AFTER WALKIN' THUH TRACKS IN THUH HOT SUN?
WUF!
HEY! THAT TRAMP'S SWIPIN' YER RIGGIN'!
STOP!
OUCH! LEGGO!
GR-R!
ALL RIGHT, YE MUTT! I'LL MAKE YA A PRESENT O' THEM PANTS!
HEFFINS!
LOOKIT, MR. DINGY! POOCHIE'S BRINGIN' BACK THUH TRAMP'S PANTS, ANY-WAY!
CONTINUED

The Katzenjammer Kids

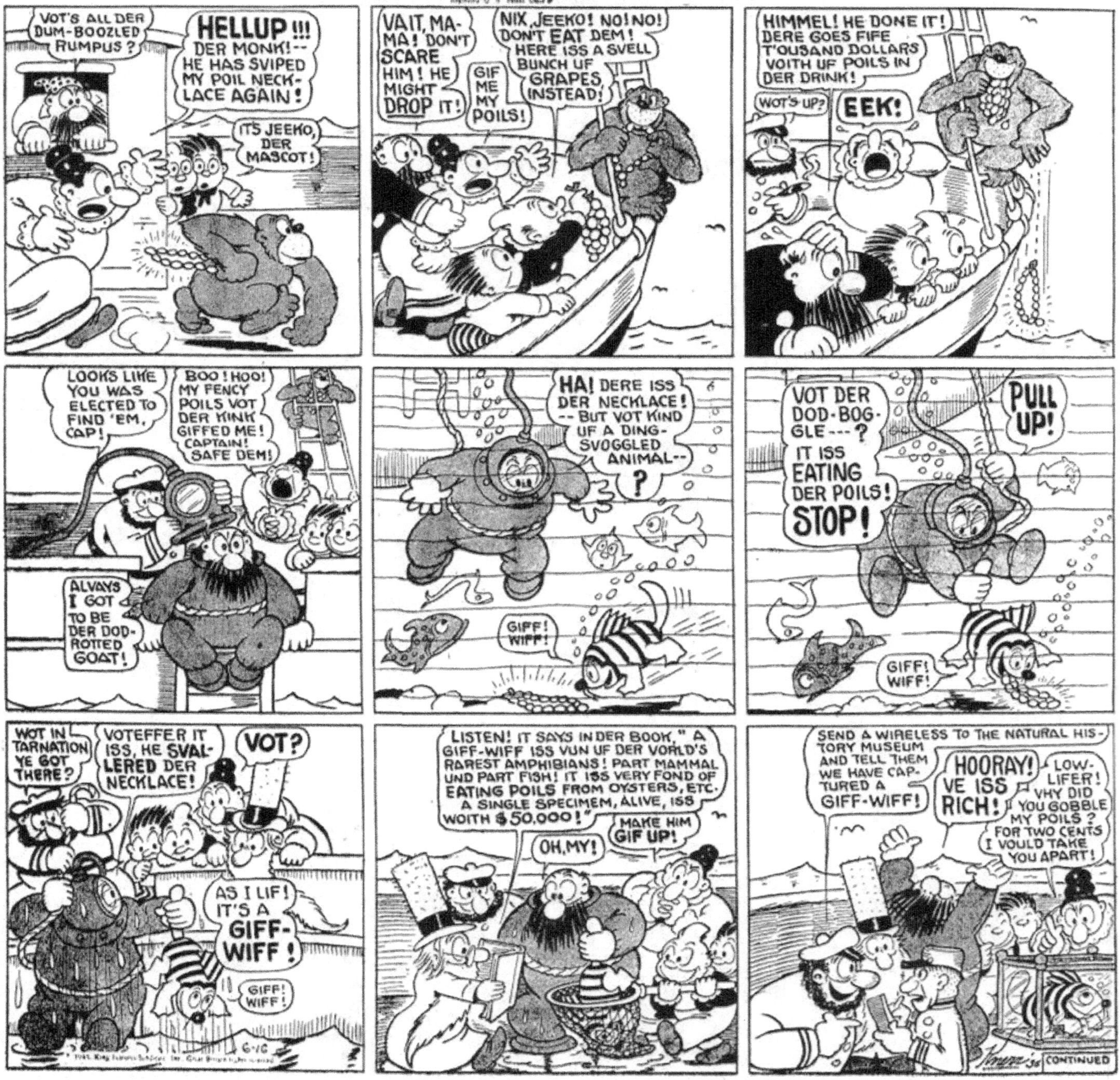

VOT'S ALL DER DUM-BOOZLED RUMPUS?
HELLUP!!! DER MONK! -- HE HAS SVIPED MY POIL NECK-LACE AGAIN!
IT'S JEEKO, DER MASCOT!
VAIT, MA-MA! DON'T SCARE HIM! HE MIGHT DROP IT!
GIF ME MY POILS!
NIX, JEEKO! NO! NO! DON'T EAT DEM! HERE ISS A SVELL BUNCH OF GRAPES, INSTEAD!
HIMMEL! HE DONE IT! DERE GOES FIFE T'OUSAND DOLLARS VOITH UF POILS IN DER DRINK!
WOT'S UP?
EEK!
LOOKS LIKE YOU WAS ELECTED TO FIND 'EM, CAP!
BOO! HOO! MY FENCY POILS VOT DER KINK GIFFED ME! CAPTAIN! SAFE DEM!
ALVAYS I GOT TO BE DER DOD-ROTTED GOAT!
HA! DERE ISS DER NECKLACE! -- BUT VOT KIND UF A DING-SVOGGLED ANIMAL--?
GIFF! WIFF!
VOT DER DOD-BOG-GLE---? IT ISS EATING DER POILS! STOP!
PULL UP!
GIFF! WIFF!
WOT IN TARNATION YE GOT THERE?
VOTEFFER IT ISS, HE SVAL-LERED DER NECKLACE!
VOT?
AS I LIF! IT'S A GIFF-WIFF!
GIFF! WIFF!
LISTEN! IT SAYS IN DER BOOK, " A GIFF-WIFF ISS VUN UF DER VORLD'S RAREST AMPHIBIANS! PART MAMMAL UND PART FISH! IT ISS VERY FOND OF EATING POILS FROM OYSTERS, ETC. A SINGLE SPECIMEN, ALIVE, ISS WOITH $50,000!"
MAKE HIM GIF UP!
OH, MY!
SEND A WIRELESS TO THE NATURAL HIS-TORY MUSEUM AND TELL THEM WE HAVE CAP-TURED A GIFF-WIFF!
HOORAY! VE ISS RICH!
LOW-LIFER! VHY DID YOU GOBBLE MY POILS? FOR TWO CENTS I VOULD TAKE YOU APART!
CONTINUED

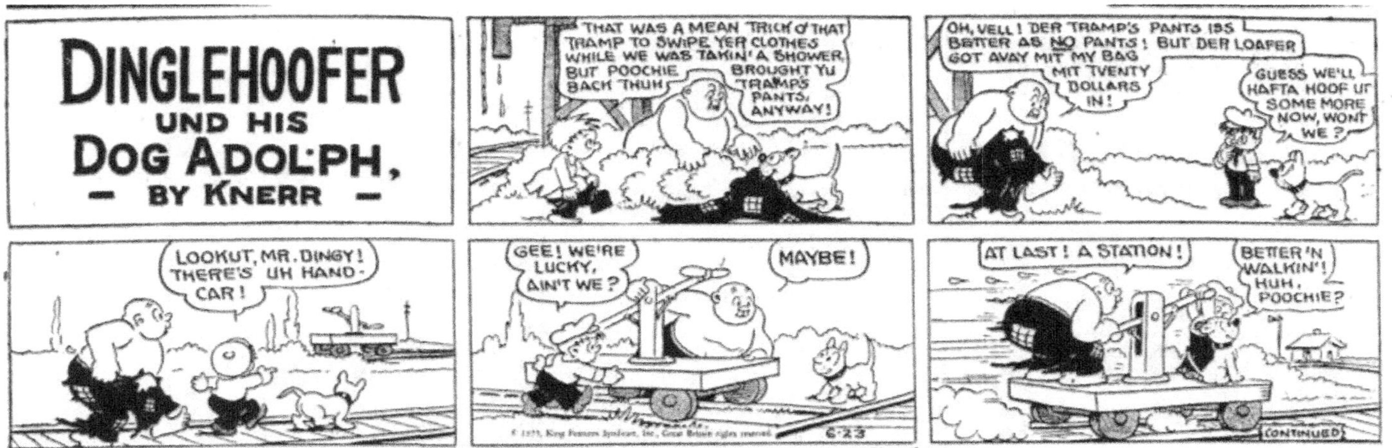
DINGLEHOOFER UND HIS DOG ADOLPH, — BY KNERR —
THAT WAS A MEAN TRICK O' THAT TRAMP TO SWIPE YER CLOTHES WHILE WE WAS TAKIN' A SHOWER.
BUT POOCHIE BRUGHT YU BACK THUH TRAMP'S PANTS, ANYWAY!
OH, VELL! DER TRAMP'S PANTS ISS BETTER AS NO PANTS! BUT DER LOAFER GOT AVAY MIT MY BAG MIT TVENTY DOLLARS IN!
GUESS WE'LL HAFTA HOOF UP SOME MORE NOW, WONT WE?
LOOKUT, MR. DINGY! THERE'S UH HAND-CAR!
GEE! WE'RE LUCKY, AIN'T WE?
MAYBE!
AT LAST! A STATION!
BETTER'N WALKIN'! HUH, POOCHIE?
6·23
CONTINUED

The Katzenjammer Kids

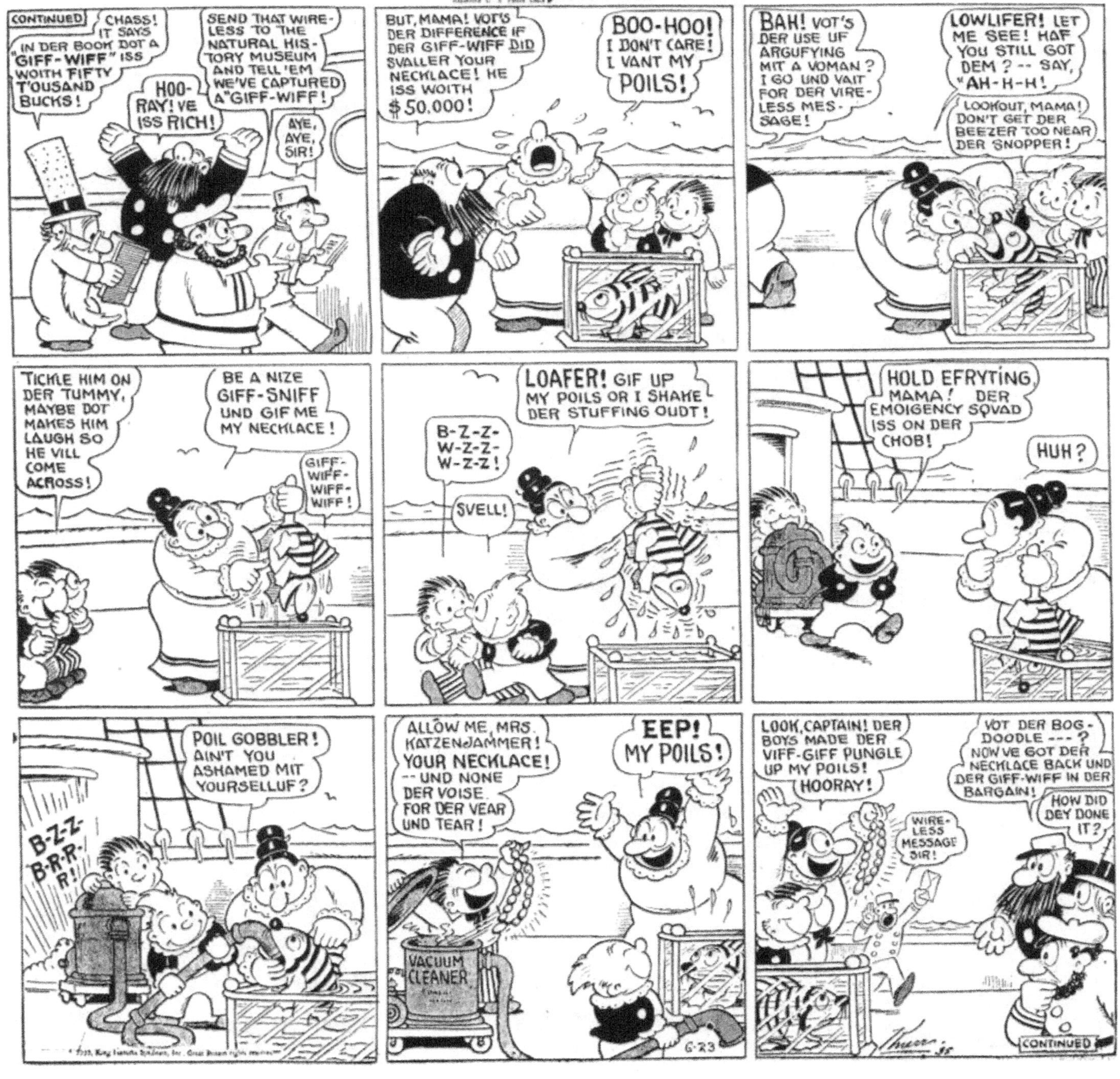
CONTINUED
CHASS! IT SAYS IN DER BOOK DOT A "GIFF-WIFF" ISS WOITH FIFTY T'OUSAND BUCKS!
SEND THAT WIRELESS TO THE NATURAL HISTORY MUSEUM AND TELL 'EM WE'VE CAPTURED A "GIFF-WIFF"!
HOO-RAY! VE ISS RICH!
AYE, AYE, SIR!
BUT, MAMA! VOT'S DER DIFFERENCE IF DER GIFF-WIFF DID SVALLER YOUR NECKLACE! HE ISS WOITH $50,000!
BOO-HOO! I DON'T CARE! I VANT MY POILS!
BAH! VOT'S DER USE UF ARGUFYING MIT A VOMAN? I GO UND VAIT FOR DER VIRELESS MESSAGE!
LOWLIFER! LET ME SEE! HAF YOU STILL GOT DEM? -- SAY, "AH-H-H!
LOOKOUT, MAMA! DON'T GET DER BEEZER TOO NEAR DER SNOPPER!
TICKLE HIM ON DER TUMMY, MAYBE DOT MAKES HIM LAUGH SO HE VILL COME ACROSS!
BE A NIZE GIFF-SNIFF UND GIF ME MY NECKLACE!
GIFF-WIFF-WIFF-WIFF!
LOAFER! GIF UP MY POILS OR I SHAKE DER STUFFING OUDT!
B-Z-Z-W-Z-Z-W-Z-Z!
SVELL!
HOLD EFRYTING, MAMA! DER EMOIGENCY SQVAD ISS ON DER CHOB!
HUH?
POIL GOBBLER! AIN'T YOU ASHAMED MIT YOURSELLUF?
B-Z-Z-B-R-R-R!
ALLOW ME, MRS. KATZENJAMMER! YOUR NECKLACE! -- UND NONE DER VOISE FOR DER VEAR UND TEAR!
EEP! MY POILS!
VACUUM CLEANER
LOOK, CAPTAIN! DER BOYS MADE DER VIFF-GIFF PUNGLE UP MY POILS! HOORAY!
VOT DER BOG-DOODLE ---? NOW VE GOT DER NECKLACE BACK UND DER GIFF-WIFF IN DER BARGAIN!
WIRE-LESS MESSAGE SIR!
HOW DID DEY DONE IT?
6·23
CONTINUED

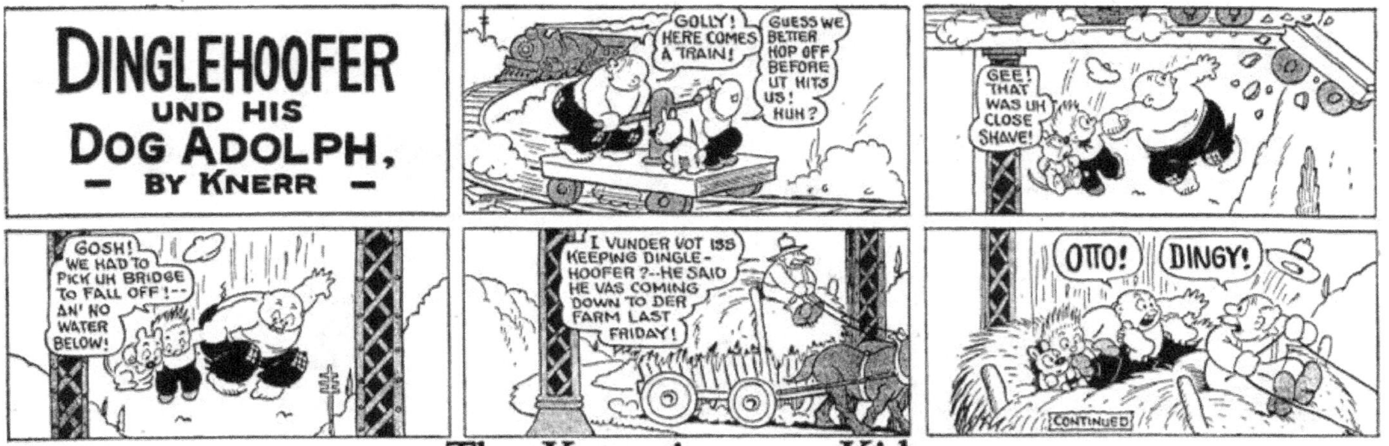
DINGLEHOOFER UND HIS DOG ADOLPH,
— BY KNERR —
GOLLY! HERE COMES A TRAIN!
GUESS WE BETTER HOP OFF BEFORE UT HITS US! HUH?
GEE! THAT WAS UH CLOSE SHAVE!
GOSH! WE HAD TO PICK UH BRIDGE TO FALL OFF!-- AN' NO WATER BELOW!
I VUNDER VOT ISS KEEPING DINGLE-HOOFER?--HE SAID HE VAS COMING DOWN TO DER FARM LAST FRIDAY!
OTTO!
DINGY!
CONTINUED

The Katzenjammer Kids

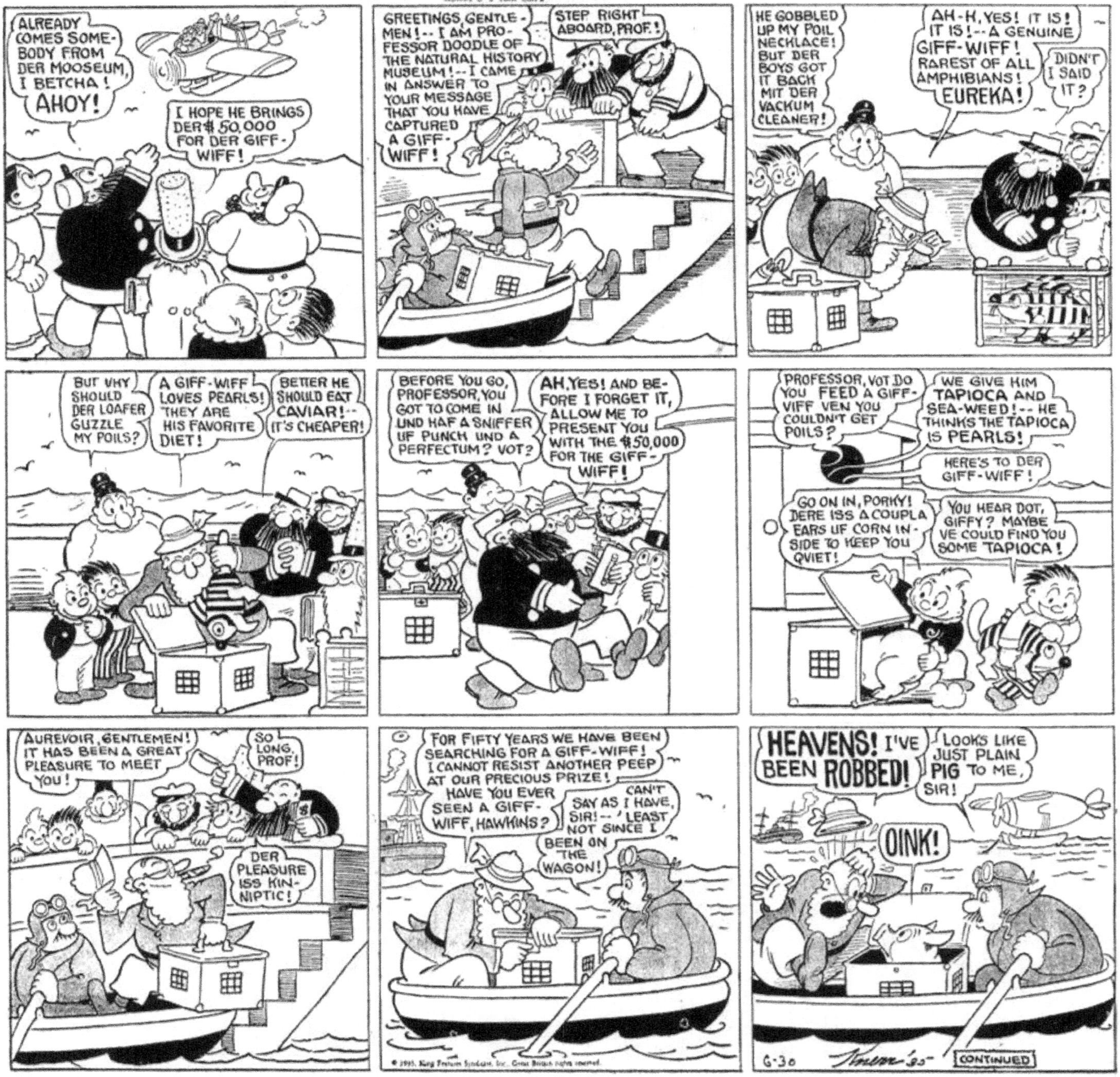
ALREADY COMES SOMEBODY FROM DER MOOSEUM, I BETCHA! AHOY!
I HOPE HE BRINGS DER $50,000 FOR DER GIFF-WIFF!
GREETINGS, GENTLEMEN!-- I AM PROFESSOR DOODLE OF THE NATURAL HISTORY MUSEUM!-- I CAME IN ANSWER TO YOUR MESSAGE THAT YOU HAVE CAPTURED A GIFF-WIFF!
STEP RIGHT ABOARD, PROF.!
HE GOBBLED UP MY POIL NECKLACE! BUT DER BOYS GOT IT BACK MIT DER VACKUM CLEANER!
AH-H, YES! IT IS! IT IS!-- A GENUINE GIFF-WIFF! RAREST OF ALL AMPHIBIANS! EUREKA!
DIDN'T I SAID IT?
BUT VHY SHOULD DER LOAFER GUZZLE MY POILS?
A GIFF-WIFF LOVES PEARLS! THEY ARE HIS FAVORITE DIET!
BETTER HE SHOULD EAT CAVIAR!-- IT'S CHEAPER!
BEFORE YOU GO, PROFESSOR, YOU GOT TO COME IN UND HAF A SNIFFER UF PUNCH UND A PERFECTUM? VOT?
AH, YES! AND BEFORE I FORGET IT, ALLOW ME TO PRESENT YOU WITH THE $50,000 FOR THE GIFF-WIFF!
PROFESSOR, VOT DO YOU FEED A GIFF-VIFF VEN YOU COULDN'T GET POILS?
WE GIVE HIM TAPIOCA AND SEA-WEED!-- HE THINKS THE TAPIOCA IS PEARLS!
HERE'S TO DER GIFF-WIFF!
GO ON IN, PORKY! DERE ISS A COUPLA EARS UF CORN INSIDE TO KEEP YOU QVIET!
YOU HEAR DOT, GIFFY? MAYBE VE COULD FIND YOU SOME TAPIOCA!
AUREVOIR, GENTLEMEN! IT HAS BEEN A GREAT PLEASURE TO MEET YOU!
SO LONG, PROF!
DER PLEASURE ISS KINNIPTIC!
FOR FIFTY YEARS WE HAVE BEEN SEARCHING FOR A GIFF-WIFF! I CANNOT RESIST ANOTHER PEEP AT OUR PRECIOUS PRIZE! HAVE YOU EVER SEEN A GIFF-WIFF, HAWKINS?
CAN'T SAY AS I HAVE, SIR!--'LEAST NOT SINCE I BEEN ON THE WAGON!
HEAVENS! I'VE BEEN ROBBED!
LOOKS LIKE JUST PLAIN PIG TO ME, SIR!
OINK!
CONTINUED

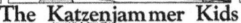

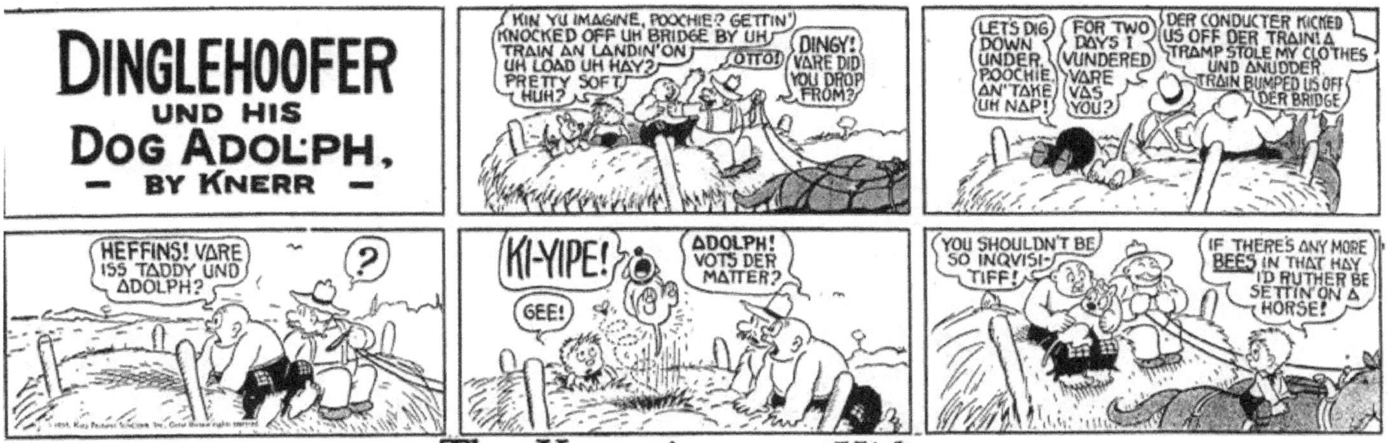
DINGLEHOOFER UND HIS DOG ADOLPH, — BY KNERR —
KIN YU IMAGINE, POOCHIE? GETTIN' KNOCKED OFF UH BRIDGE BY UH TRAIN AN LANDIN' ON UH LOAD UH HAY? PRETTY SOFT, HUH?
OTTO!
DINGY! VARE DID YOU DROP FROM?
LET'S DIG DOWN UNDER, POOCHIE, AN' TAKE UH NAP!
FOR TWO DAYS I VUNDERED VARE VAS YOU?
DER CONDUCTER KICKED US OFF DER TRAIN! A TRAMP STOLE MY CLOTHES UND ANUDDER TRAIN BUMPED US OFF DER BRIDGE
HEFFINS! VARE ISS TADDY UND ADOLPH?
?
KI-YIPE!
ADOLPH! VOTS DER MATTER?
GEE!
YOU SHOULDN'T BE SO INQVISI-TIFF!
IF THERE'S ANY MORE BEES IN THAT HAY I'D RUTHER BE SETTIN' ON A HORSE!

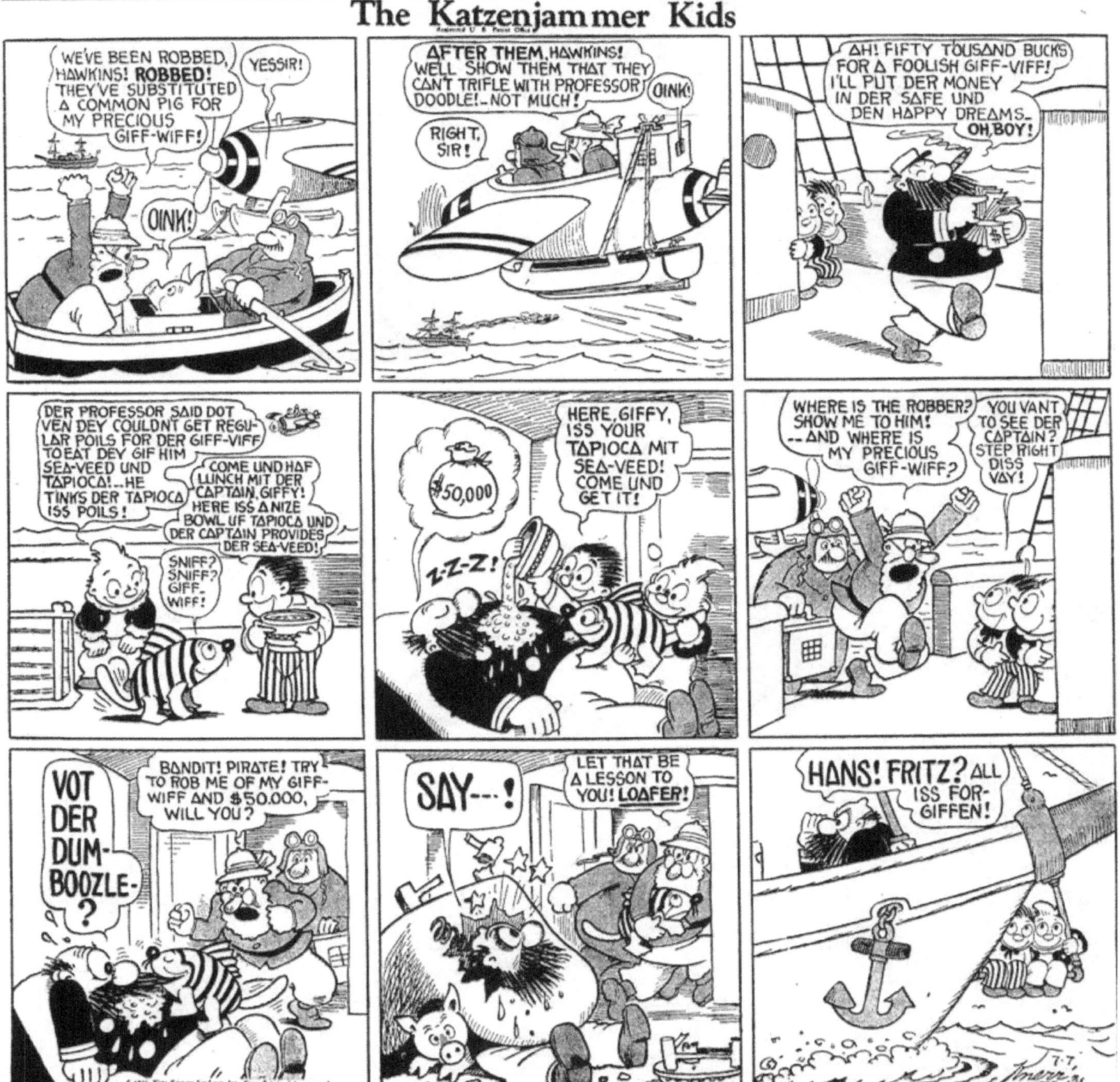
The Katzenjammer Kids
WE'VE BEEN ROBBED, HAWKINS! ROBBED! THEY'VE SUBSTITUTED A COMMON PIG FOR MY PRECIOUS GIFF-WIFF!
YESSIR!
OINK!
AFTER THEM, HAWKINS! WE'LL SHOW THEM THAT THEY CAN'T TRIFLE WITH PROFESSOR DOODLE! – NOT MUCH!
OINK!
RIGHT, SIR!
AH! FIFTY TOUSAND BUCKS FOR A FOOLISH GIFF-VIFF! I'LL PUT DER MONEY IN DER SAFE UND DEN HAPPY DREAMS – OH, BOY!
DER PROFESSOR SAID DOT VEN DEY COULDN'T GET REGU-LAR POILS FOR DER GIFF-VIFF TO EAT DEY GIF HIM SEA-VEED UND TAPIOCA! – HE TINKS DER TAPIOCA ISS POILS!
COME UND HAF LUNCH MIT DER CAPTAIN, GIFFY! HERE ISS A NIZE BOWL UF TAPIOCA UND DER CAPTAIN PROVIDES DER SEA-VEED!
SNIFF? SNIFF? GIFF-WIFF!
$50,000
Z-Z-Z!
HERE, GIFFY, ISS YOUR TAPIOCA MIT SEA-VEED! COME UND GET IT!
WHERE IS THE ROBBER? SHOW ME TO HIM! – AND WHERE IS MY PRECIOUS GIFF-WIFF?
YOU VANT TO SEE DER CAPTAIN? STEP RIGHT DISS VAY!
VOT DER DUM-BOOZLE-?
BANDIT! PIRATE! TRY TO ROB ME OF MY GIFF-WIFF AND $50,000, WILL YOU?
SAY---!
LET THAT BE A LESSON TO YOU! LOAFER!
HANS! FRITZ? ALL ISS FOR-GIFFEN!
Knerr 7-7 '35

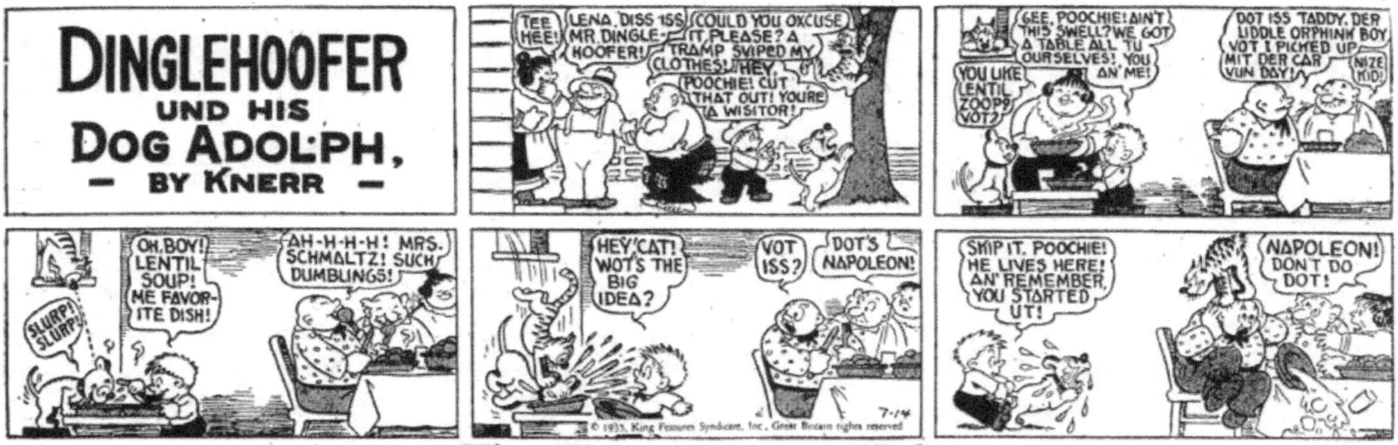
DINGLEHOOFER UND HIS DOG ADOLPH, — BY KNERR —
TEE HEE!
LENA, DISS ISS MR. DINGLEHOOFER!
COULD YOU OXCUSE IT PLEASE? A TRAMP SVIPED MY CLOTHES!
HEY, POOCHIE! CUT THAT OUT! YOU'RE A WISITOR!
YOU LIKE LENTIL ZOOP? VOT?
GEE, POOCHIE! AIN'T THIS SWELL? WE GOT A TABLE ALL TU OURSELVES! YOU AN' ME!
DOT ISS TADDY, DER LIDDLE ORPHINK BOY VOT I PICKED UP MIT DER CAR VUN DAY!
NIZE KID!
SLURP! SLURP!
OH, BOY! LENTIL SOUP! ME FAVORITE DISH!
AH-H-H-H! MRS. SCHMALTZ! SUCH DUMBLINGS!
HEY, CAT! WOT'S THE BIG IDEA?
VOT ISS?
DOT'S NAPOLEON!
7-14
© 1935, King Features Syndicate, Inc., Great Britain rights reserved
SKIP IT, POOCHIE! HE LIVES HERE! AN' REMEMBER, YOU STARTED UT!
NAPOLEON! DON'T DO DOT!

The Katzenjammer Kids

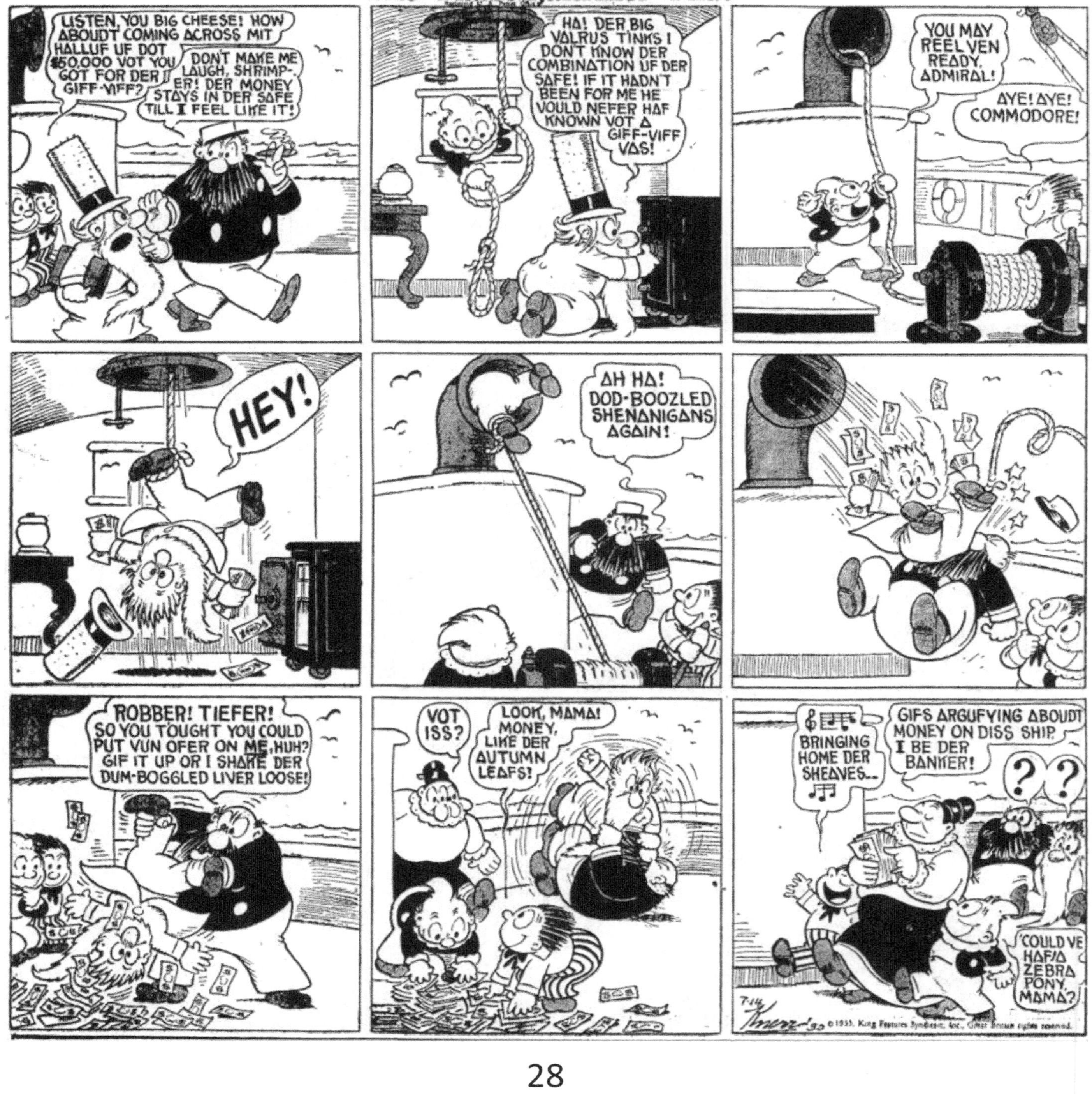
LISTEN, YOU BIG CHEESE! HOW ABOUDT COMING ACROSS MIT HALLUF UF DOT $50,000 VOT YOU GOT FOR DER GIFF-VIFF?
DON'T MAKE ME LAUGH, SHRIMPER! DER MONEY STAYS IN DER SAFE TILL I FEEL LIKE IT!
HA! DER BIG VALRUS TINKS I DON'T KNOW DER COMBINATION UF DER SAFE! IF IT HADN'T BEEN FOR ME HE VOULD NEFER HAF KNOWN VOT A GIFF-VIFF VAS!
YOU MAY REEL VEN READY, ADMIRAL!
AYE! AYE! COMMODORE!
HEY!
AH HA! DOD-BOOZLED SHENANIGANS AGAIN!
ROBBER! TIEFER! SO YOU TOUGHT YOU COULD PUT VUN OFER ON ME, HUH? GIF IT UP OR I SHAKE DER DUM-BOGGLED LIVER LOOSE!
VOT ISS?
LOOK, MAMA! MONEY, LIKE DER AUTUMN LEAFS!
BRINGING HOME DER SHEAVES...
GIFS ARGUFYING ABOUDT MONEY ON DISS SHIP, I BE DER BANKER!
? ?
COULD VE HAF A ZEBRA PONY, MAMA?
7-14
Knerr '35
© 1935, King Features Syndicate, Inc., Great Britain rights reserved.

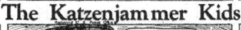

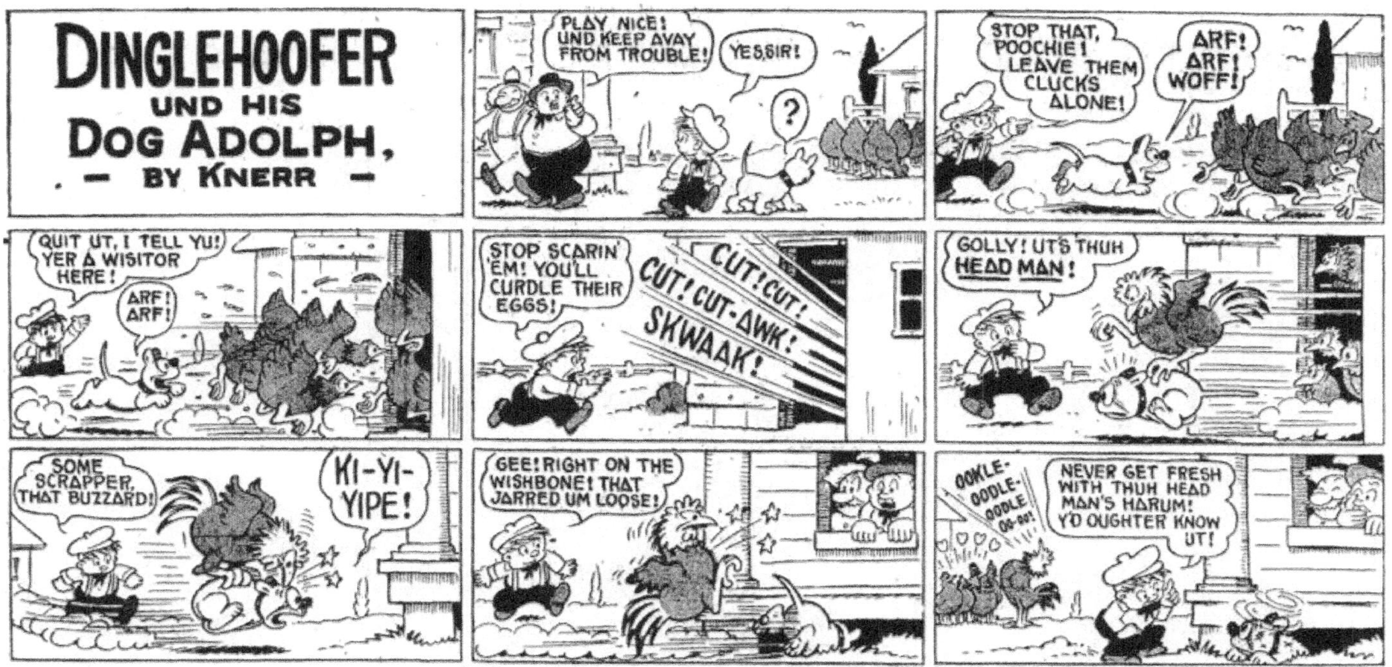
DINGLEHOOFER UND HIS DOG ADOLPH,
— BY KNERR —
PLAY NICE! UND KEEP AVAY FROM TROUBLE!
YES, SIR!
?
STOP THAT, POOCHIE! LEAVE THEM CLUCKS ALONE!
ARF! ARF! WOFF!
QUIT UT, I TELL YU! YER A WISITOR HERE!
ARF! ARF!
STOP SCARIN' 'EM! YOU'LL CURDLE THEIR EGGS!
CUT! CUT!
CUT! CUT-AWK!
SKWAAK!
GOLLY! UT'S THUH HEAD MAN!
SOME SCRAPPER, THAT BUZZARD!
KI-YI-YIPE!
GEE! RIGHT ON THE WISHBONE! THAT JARRED UM LOOSE!
OOKLE-OODLE-OODLE OO-OO!
NEVER GET FRESH WITH THUH HEAD MAN'S HARUM! Y'D OUGHTER KNOW UT!

The Katzenjammer Kids

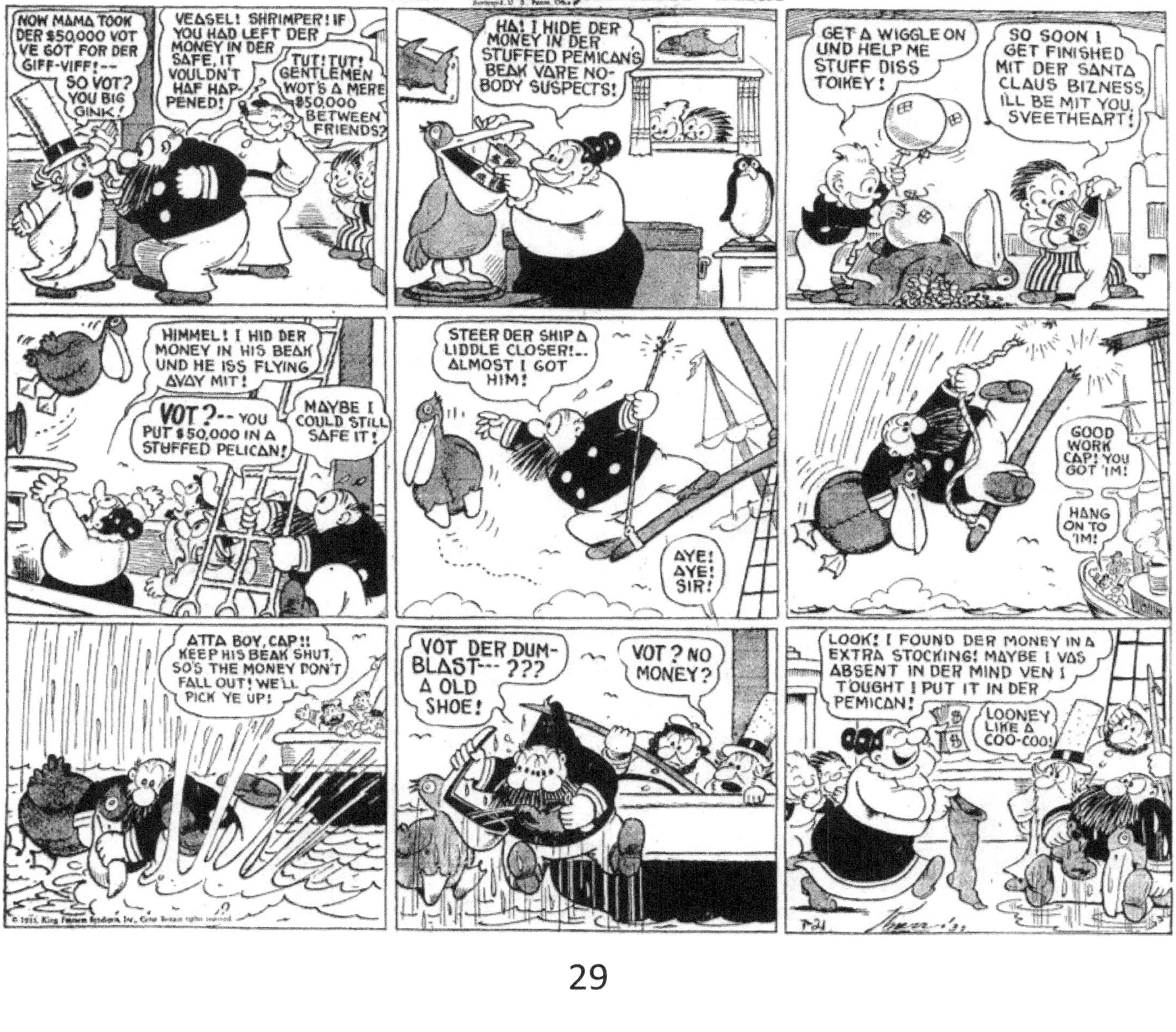
NOW MAMA TOOK DER $50,000 VOT VE GOT FOR DER GIFF-VIFF!--
VEASEL! SHRIMPER! IF YOU HAD LEFT DER MONEY IN DER SAFE, IT VOULDN'T HAF HAPPENED!
SO VOT? YOU BIG GINK!
TUT! TUT! GENTLEMEN WOT'S A MERE $50,000 BETWEEN FRIENDS?
HA! I HIDE DER MONEY IN DER STUFFED PEMICAN'S BEAK VARE NOBODY SUSPECTS!
GET A WIGGLE ON UND HELP ME STUFF DISS TOIKEY!
SO SOON I GET FINISHED MIT DER SANTA CLAUS BIZNESS, I'LL BE MIT YOU, SVEETHEART!
HIMMEL! I HID DER MONEY IN HIS BEAK UND HE ISS FLYING AVAY MIT!
VOT?-- YOU PUT $50,000 IN A STUFFED PELICAN!
MAYBE I COULD STILL SAFE IT!
STEER DER SHIP A LIDDLE CLOSER!-- ALMOST I GOT HIM!
AYE! AYE! SIR!
GOOD WORK CAP! YOU GOT 'IM!
HANG ON TO 'IM!
ATTA BOY, CAP!! KEEP HIS BEAK SHUT, SO'S THE MONEY DON'T FALL OUT! WE'LL PICK YE UP!
VOT DER DUM-BLAST--- ??? A OLD SHOE!
VOT? NO MONEY?
LOOK! I FOUND DER MONEY IN A EXTRA STOCKING! MAYBE I VAS ABSENT IN DER MIND VEN I TOUGHT I PUT IT IN DER PEMICAN!
LOONEY LIKE A COO-COO!

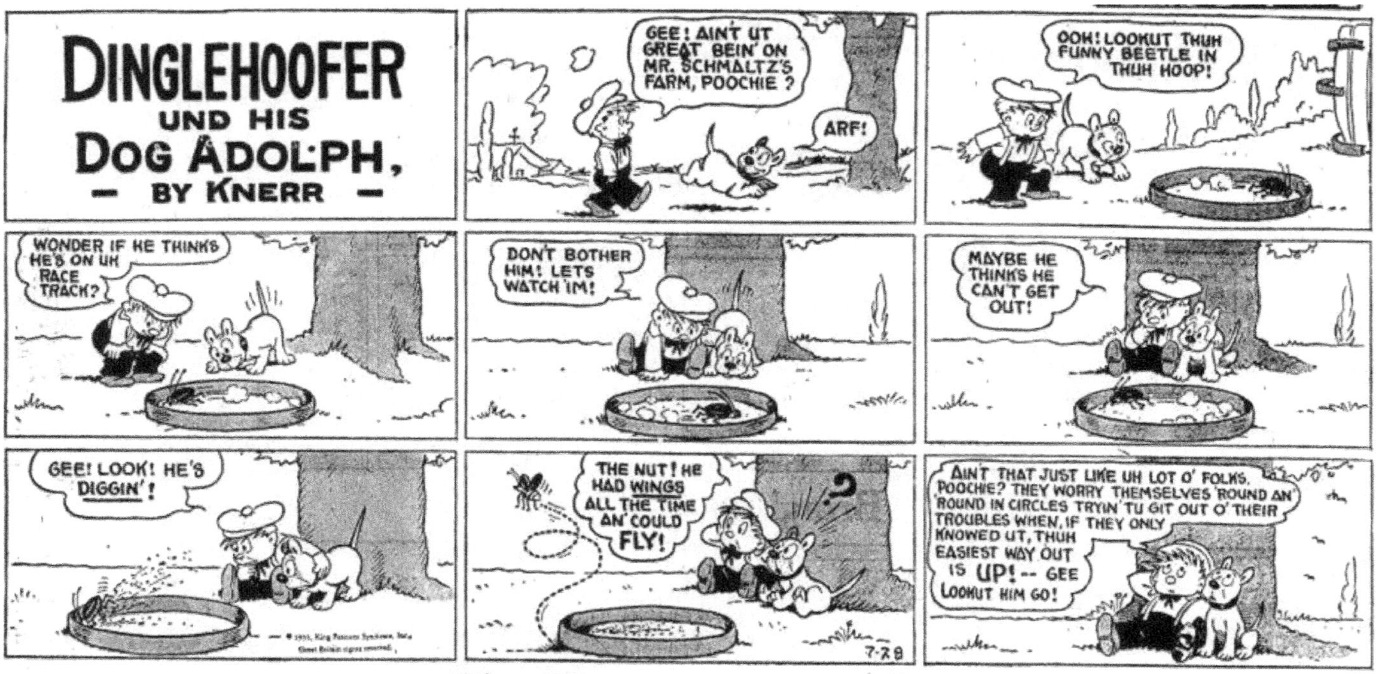
DINGLEHOOFER UND HIS DOG ADOLPH, — BY KNERR —
GEE! AIN'T UT GREAT BEIN' ON MR. SCHMALTZ'S FARM, POOCHIE ?
ARF!
OOH! LOOKUT THUH FUNNY BEETLE IN THUH HOOP!
WONDER IF HE THINKS HE'S ON UH RACE TRACK?
DON'T BOTHER HIM! LETS WATCH 'IM!
MAYBE HE THINKS HE CAN'T GET OUT!
GEE! LOOK! HE'S DIGGIN'!
THE NUT! HE HAD WINGS ALL THE TIME AN' COULD FLY!
AIN'T THAT JUST LIKE UH LOT O' FOLKS, POOCHIE? THEY WORRY THEMSELVES 'ROUND AN' 'ROUND IN CIRCLES TRYIN' TU GIT OUT O' THEIR TROUBLES WHEN, IF THEY ONLY KNOWED UT, THUH EASIEST WAY OUT IS UP! -- GEE LOOKUT HIM GO!
7-28

The Katzenjammer Kids

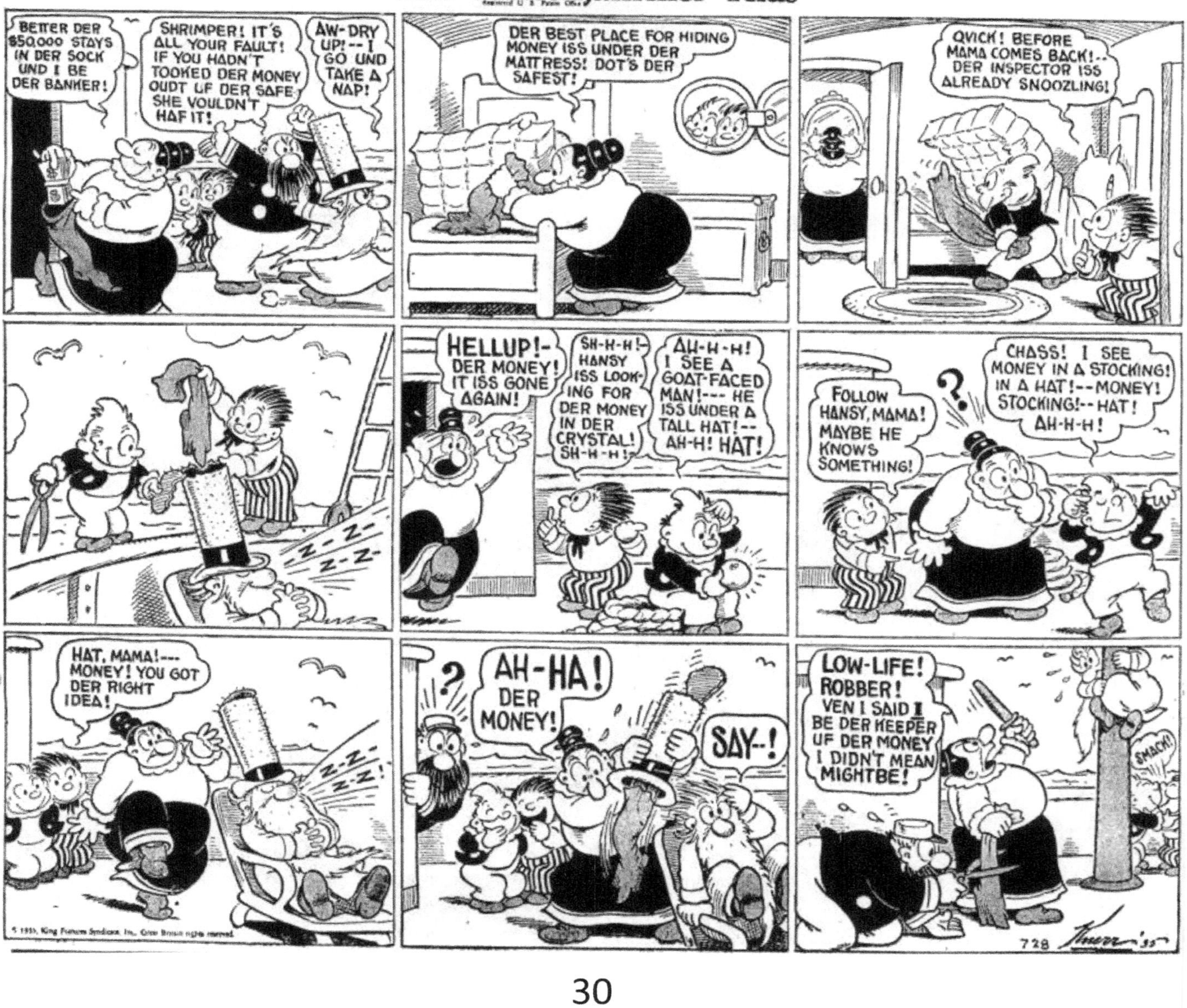
BETTER DER $50,000 STAYS IN DER SOCK UND I BE DER BANKER!
SHRIMPER! IT'S ALL YOUR FAULT! IF YOU HADN'T TOOKED DER MONEY OUDT UF DER SAFE SHE VOULDN'T HAF IT!
AW-DRY UP!-- I GO UND TAKE A NAP!
DER BEST PLACE FOR HIDING MONEY ISS UNDER DER MATTRESS! DOT'S DER SAFEST!
QVICK! BEFORE MAMA COMES BACK!-- DER INSPECTOR ISS ALREADY SNOOZLING!
Z-Z-Z-Z-
HELLUP!- DER MONEY! IT ISS GONE AGAIN!
SH-H-H!- HANSY ISS LOOKING FOR DER MONEY IN DER CRYSTAL! SH-H-H!
AH-H-H! I SEE A GOAT-FACED MAN!--- HE ISS UNDER A TALL HAT!-- AH-H! HAT!
FOLLOW HANSY, MAMA! MAYBE HE KNOWS SOMETHING!
CHASS! I SEE MONEY IN A STOCKING! IN A HAT!--MONEY! STOCKING!--HAT! AH-H-H!
HAT, MAMA!--- MONEY! YOU GOT DER RIGHT IDEA!
Z-Z-Z-Z!
AH-HA! DER MONEY!
SAY--!
LOW-LIFE! ROBBER! VEN I SAID I BE DER KEEPER UF DER MONEY I DIDN'T MEAN MIGHTBE!
SMACK!
7-28
Knerr '35

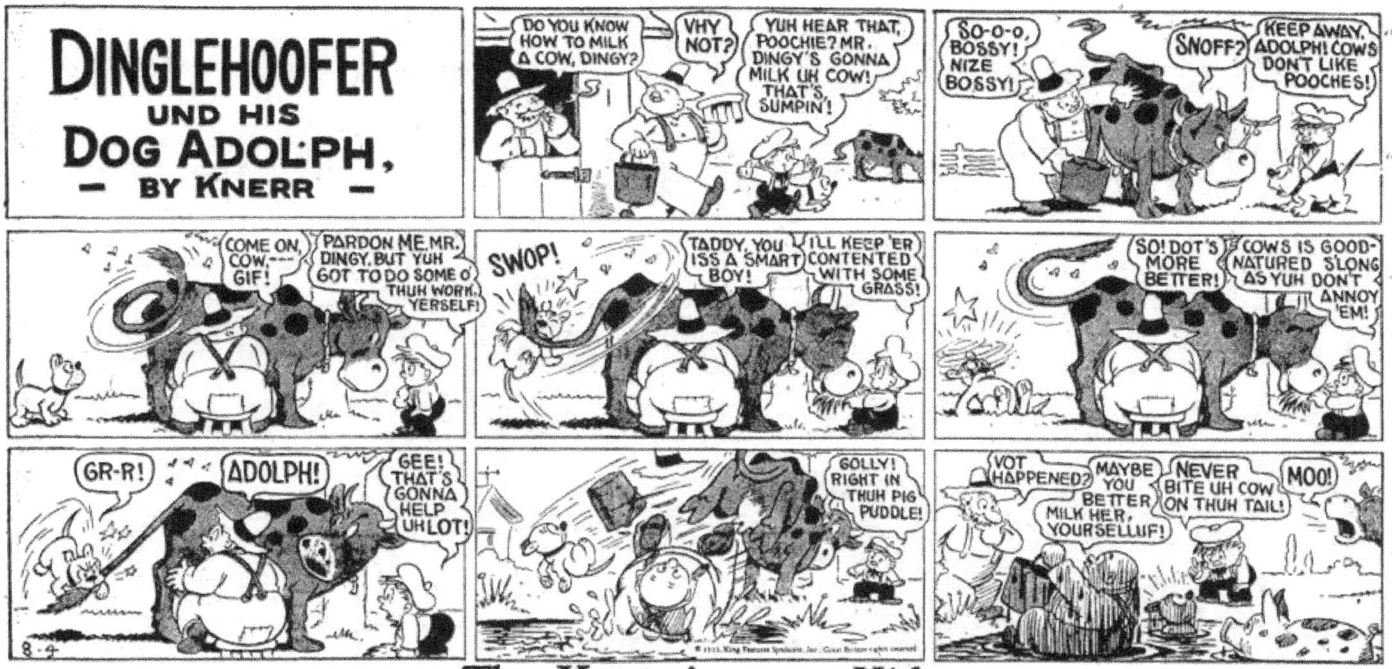
DINGLEHOOFER UND HIS DOG ADOLPH, — BY KNERR —
DO YOU KNOW HOW TO MILK A COW, DINGY?
VHY NOT?
YUH HEAR THAT, POOCHIE? MR. DINGY'S GONNA MILK UH COW! THAT'S SUMPIN'!
SO-O-O, BOSSY! NIZE BOSSY!
SNOFF?
KEEP AWAY, ADOLPH! COWS DON'T LIKE POOCHES!
COME ON, COW,--- GIF!
PARDON ME, MR. DINGY, BUT YUH GOT TO DO SOME O' THUH WORK, YERSELF!
SWOP!
TADDY, YOU ISS A SMART BOY!
I'LL KEEP 'ER CONTENTED WITH SOME GRASS!
SO! DOT'S MORE BETTER!
COWS IS GOOD-NATURED S'LONG AS YUH DON'T ANNOY 'EM!
GR-R!
ADOLPH!
GEE! THAT'S GONNA HELP UH LOT!
GOLLY! RIGHT IN THUH PIG PUDDLE!
VOT HAPPENED?
MAYBE YOU BETTER MILK HER, YOURSELLUF!
NEVER BITE UH COW ON THUH TAIL!
MOO!
8-4

The Katzenjammer Kids

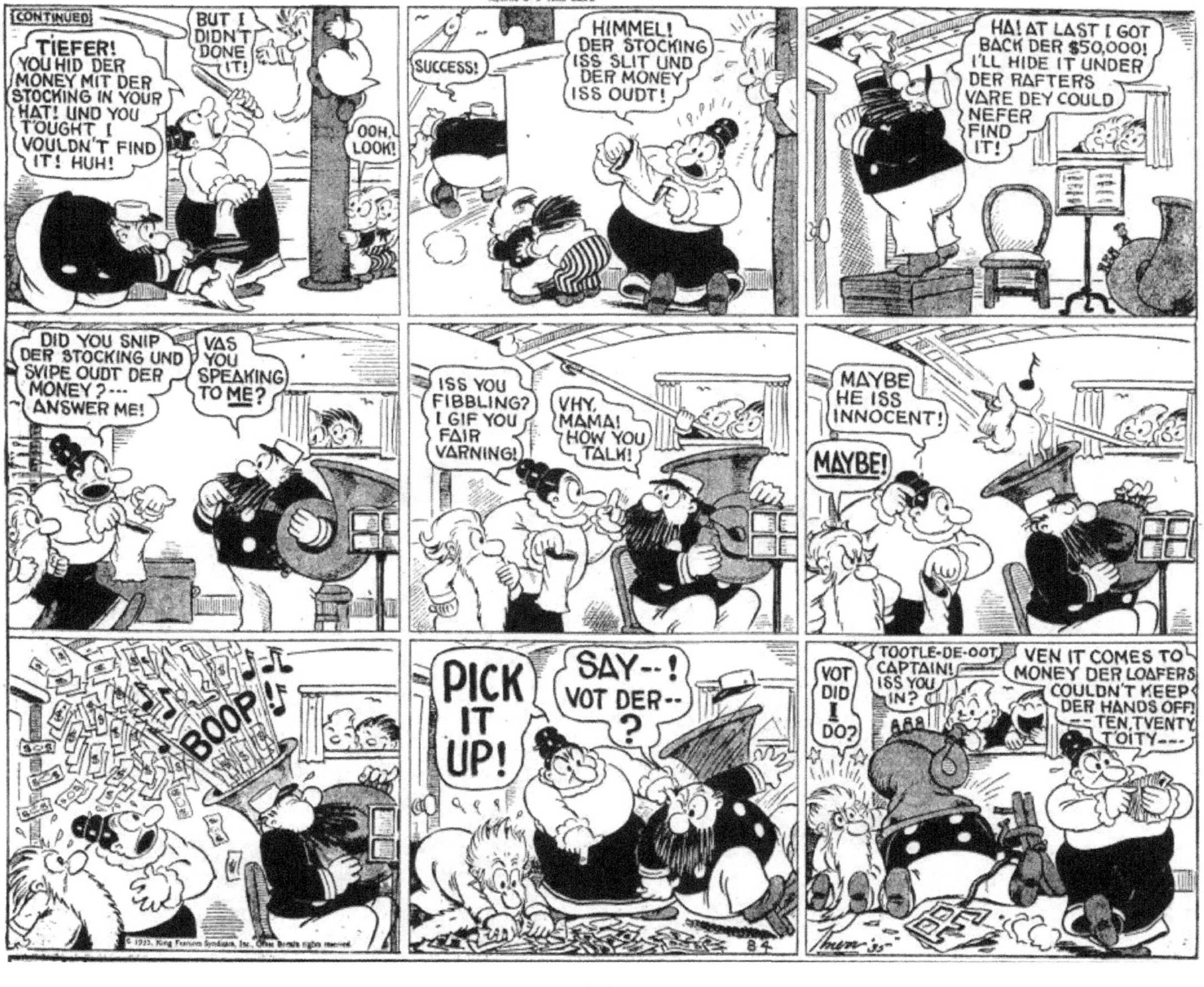
CONTINUED
TIEFER! YOU HID DER MONEY MIT DER STOCKING IN YOUR HAT! UND YOU TOUGHT I VOULDN'T FIND IT! HUH!
BUT I DIDN'T DONE IT!
OOH, LOOK!
SUCCESS!
HIMMEL! DER STOCKING ISS SLIT UND DER MONEY ISS OUDT!
HA! AT LAST I GOT BACK DER $50,000! I'LL HIDE IT UNDER DER RAFTERS VARE DEY COULD NEFER FIND IT!
DID YOU SNIP DER STOCKING UND SVIPE OUDT DER MONEY?--- ANSWER ME!
VAS YOU SPEAKING TO ME?
ISS YOU FIBBLING? I GIF YOU FAIR VARNING!
VHY, MAMA! HOW YOU TALK!
MAYBE HE ISS INNOCENT!
MAYBE!
BOOP!
PICK IT UP!
SAY--! VOT DER--?
VOT DID I DO?
TOOTLE-DE-OOT, CAPTAIN! ISS YOU IN?
VEN IT COMES TO MONEY DER LOAFERS COULDN'T KEEP DER HANDS OFF! --- TEN, TVENTY, TOITY---
8-4
Knerr '35

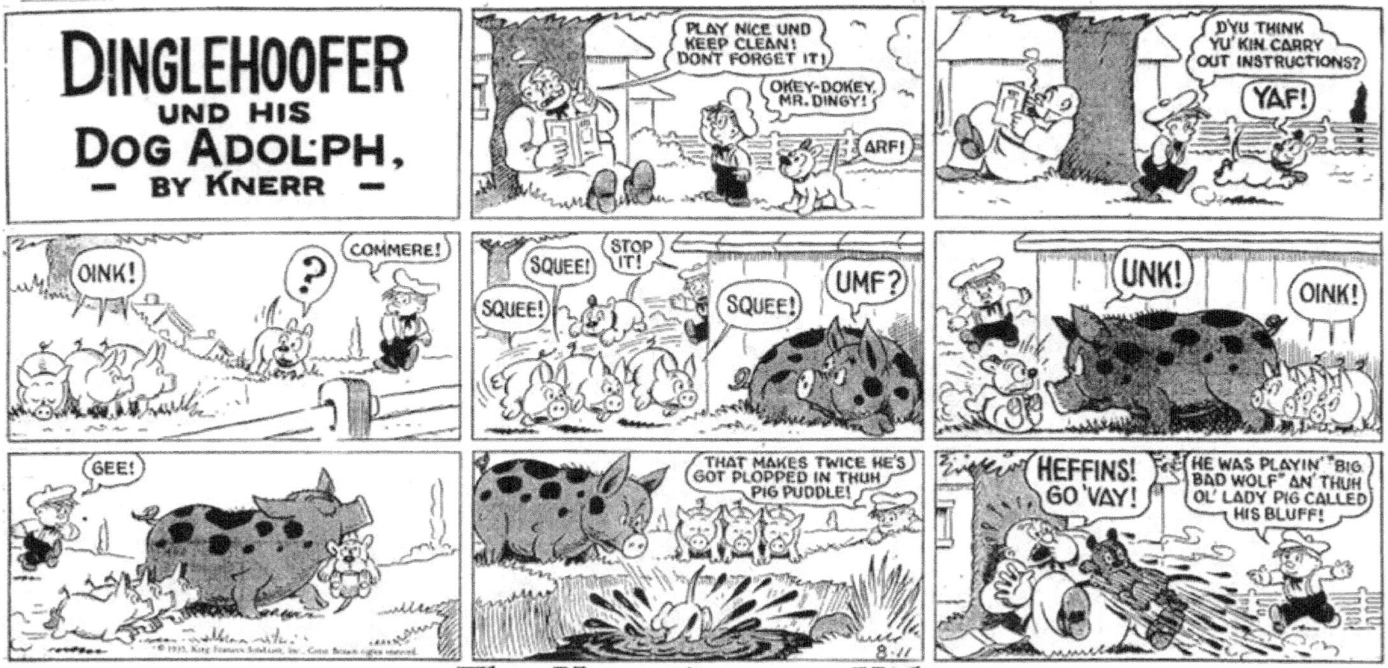
DINGLEHOOFER
UND HIS
DOG ADOLPH,
— BY KNERR —
PLAY NICE UND KEEP CLEAN! DONT FORGET IT!
OKEY-DOKEY, MR. DINGY!
ARF!
D'YU THINK YU' KIN CARRY OUT INSTRUCTIONS?
YAF!
OINK!
?
COMMERE!
SQUEE!
STOP IT!
SQUEE!
SQUEE!
UMF?
UNK!
OINK!
GEE!
THAT MAKES TWICE HE'S GOT PLOPPED IN THUH PIG PUDDLE!
HEFFINS! GO 'VAY!
HE WAS PLAYIN' "BIG BAD WOLF" AN' THUH OL' LADY PIG CALLED HIS BLUFF!
8-11

The Katzenjammer Kids

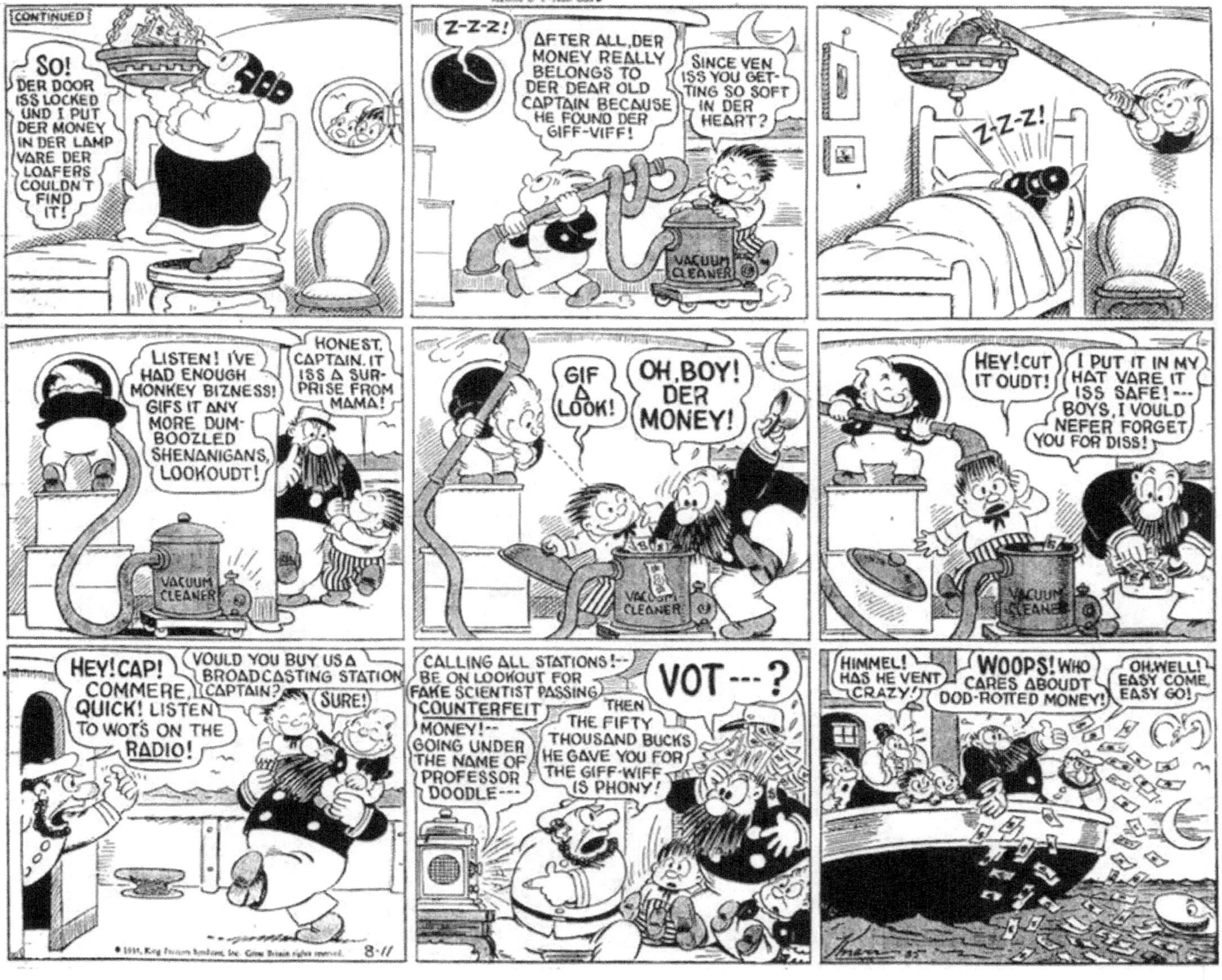
CONTINUED
SO! DER DOOR ISS LOCKED UND I PUT DER MONEY IN DER LAMP VARE DER LOAFERS COULDN'T FIND IT!
Z-Z-Z!
AFTER ALL, DER MONEY REALLY BELONGS TO DER DEAR OLD CAPTAIN BECAUSE HE FOUND DER GIFF-VIFF!
SINCE VEN ISS YOU GETTING SO SOFT IN DER HEART?
VACUUM CLEANER
Z-Z-Z!
LISTEN! I'VE HAD ENOUGH MONKEY BIZNESS! GIFS IT ANY MORE DUMBOOZLED SHENANIGANS, LOOKOUDT!
HONEST, CAPTAIN, IT ISS A SURPRISE FROM MAMA!
VACUUM CLEANER
GIF A LOOK!
OH, BOY! DER MONEY!
VACUUM CLEANER
HEY! CUT IT OUDT!
I PUT IT IN MY HAT VARE IT ISS SAFE! --- BOYS, I VOULD NEFER FORGET YOU FOR DISS!
VACUUM CLEANER
HEY! CAP! COMMERE, QUICK! LISTEN TO WOT'S ON THE RADIO!
VOULD YOU BUY US A BROADCASTING STATION CAPTAIN?
SURE!
CALLING ALL STATIONS!-- BE ON LOOKOUT FOR FAKE SCIENTIST PASSING COUNTERFEIT MONEY!-- GOING UNDER THE NAME OF PROFESSOR DOODLE---
VOT---?
THEN THE FIFTY THOUSAND BUCKS HE GAVE YOU FOR THE GIFF-WIFF IS PHONY!
HIMMEL! HAS HE VENT CRAZY?
WOOPS! WHO CARES ABOUDT DOD-ROTTED MONEY!
OH, WELL! EASY COME, EASY GO!
8-11

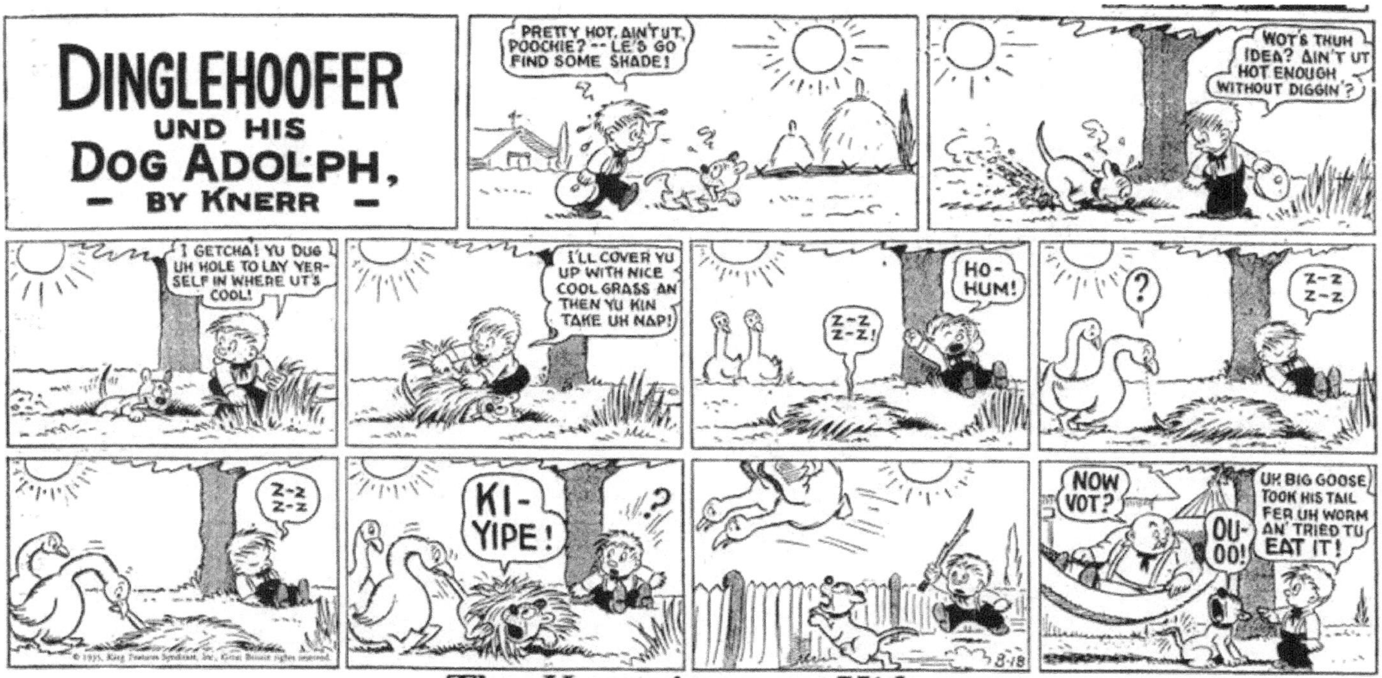
DINGLEHOOFER
UND HIS
DOG ADOLPH,
— BY KNERR —
PRETTY HOT, AIN'T UT, POOCHIE? -- LE'S GO FIND SOME SHADE!
WOT'S THUH IDEA? AIN'T UT HOT ENOUGH WITHOUT DIGGIN'?
I GETCHA! YU DUG UH HOLE TO LAY YERSELF IN WHERE UT'S COOL!
I'LL COVER YU UP WITH NICE COOL GRASS AN' THEN YU KIN TAKE UH NAP!
HO-HUM!
Z-Z Z-Z!
?
Z-Z Z-Z
Z-Z Z-Z
KI-YIPE!
?
NOW VOT?
OU-OO!
UH BIG GOOSE TOOK HIS TAIL FER UH WORM AN' TRIED TU EAT IT!
8-18

The Katzenjammer Kids

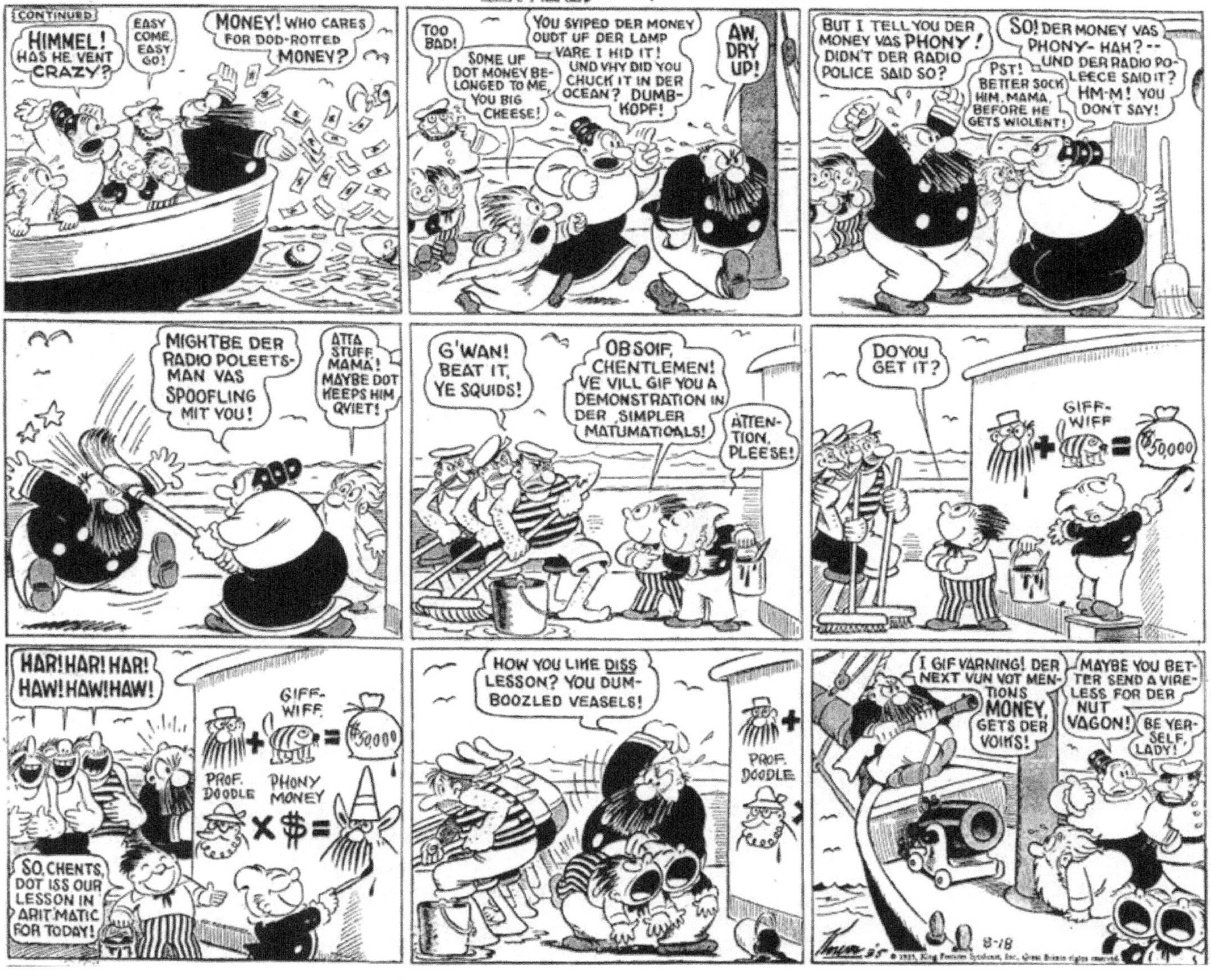
CONTINUED
HIMMEL! HAS HE VENT CRAZY?
EASY COME, EASY GO!
MONEY! WHO CARES FOR DOD-ROTTED MONEY?
TOO BAD!
YOU SVIPED DER MONEY OUDT UF DER LAMP VARE I HID IT!
SOME UF DOT MONEY BELONGED TO ME, YOU BIG CHEESE!
UND VHY DID YOU CHUCK IT IN DER OCEAN? DUMBKOPF!
AW, DRY UP!
BUT I TELL YOU DER MONEY VAS PHONY! DIDN'T DER RADIO POLICE SAID SO?
SO! DER MONEY VAS PHONY- HAH? -- UND DER RADIO POLEECE SAID IT? HM-M! YOU DON'T SAY!
PST! BETTER SOCK HIM, MAMA, BEFORE HE GETS WIOLENT!
MIGHTBE DER RADIO POLEETSMAN VAS SPOOFLING MIT YOU!
ATTA STUFF MAMA! MAYBE DOT KEEPS HIM QVIET!
G'WAN! BEAT IT, YE SQUIDS!
OBSOIF, CHENTLEMEN! VE VILL GIF YOU A DEMONSTRATION IN DER SIMPLER MATUMATICALS!
ATTENTION, PLEESE!
DO YOU GET IT?
GIFF-WIFF
$50,000
HAR! HAR! HAR! HAW! HAW! HAW!
GIFF-WIFF
$50,000
PROF. DOODLE
PHONY MONEY
SO, CHENTS, DOT ISS OUR LESSON IN ARIT'MATIC FOR TODAY!
HOW YOU LIKE DISS LESSON? YOU DUMBOOZLED VEASELS!
PROF. DOODLE
I GIF VARNING! DER NEXT VUN VOT MENTIONS MONEY, GETS DER VOIKS!
MAYBE YOU BETTER SEND A VIRELESS FOR DER NUT VAGON!
BE YERSELF, LADY!
8-18

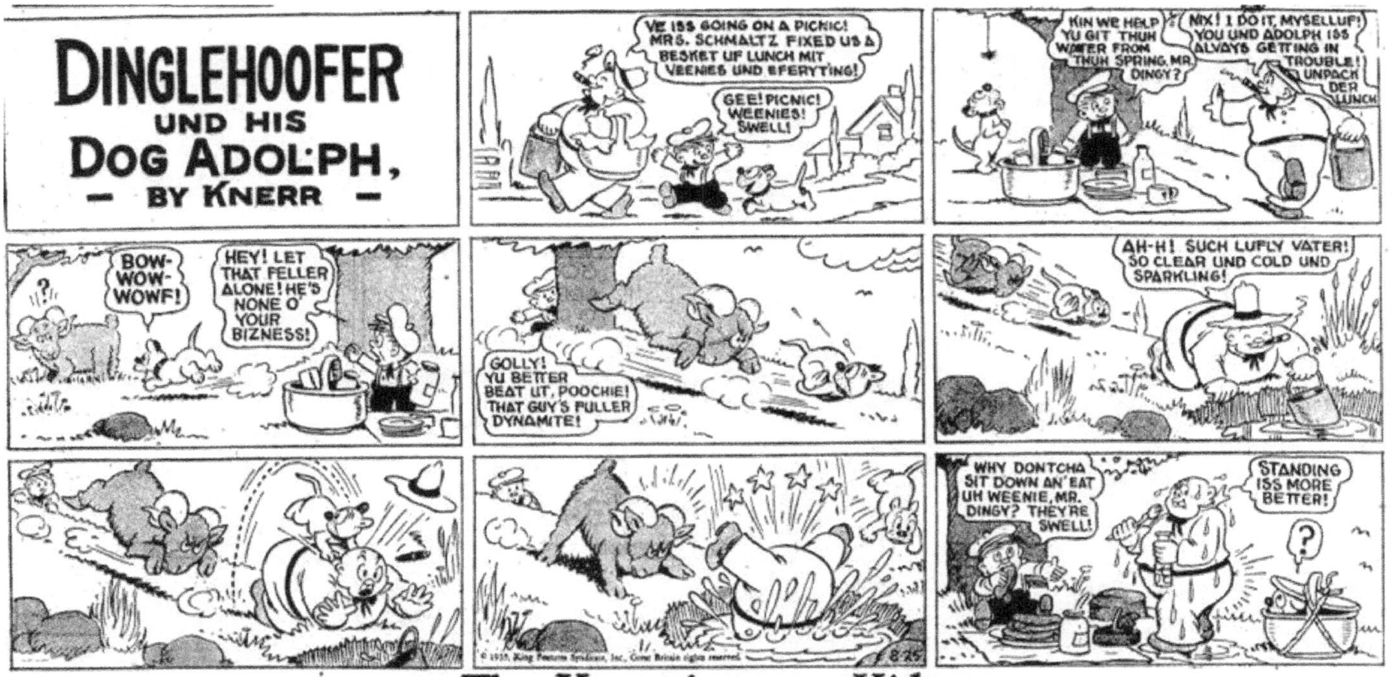
DINGLEHOOFER
UND HIS
DOG ADOLPH,
— BY KNERR —
VE ISS GOING ON A PICNIC! MRS. SCHMALTZ FIXED US A BESKET UF LUNCH MIT VEENIES UND EFERYTING!
GEE! PICNIC! WEENIES! SWELL!
KIN WE HELP YU GIT THUH WATER FROM THUH SPRING, MR. DINGY?
NIX! I DO IT, MYSELLUF! YOU UND ADOLPH ISS ALVAYS GETTING IN TROUBLE! UNPACK DER LUNCH
BOW-WOW-WOWF!
HEY! LET THAT FELLER ALONE! HE'S NONE O' YOUR BIZNESS!
GOLLY! YU BETTER BEAT IT, POOCHIE! THAT GUY'S FULLER DYNAMITE!
AH-H! SUCH LUFLY VATER! SO CLEAR UND COLD UND SPARKLING!
8-25
WHY DONTCHA SIT DOWN AN' EAT UH WEENIE, MR. DINGY? THEY'RE SWELL!
STANDING ISS MORE BETTER!
?

The Katzenjammer Kids

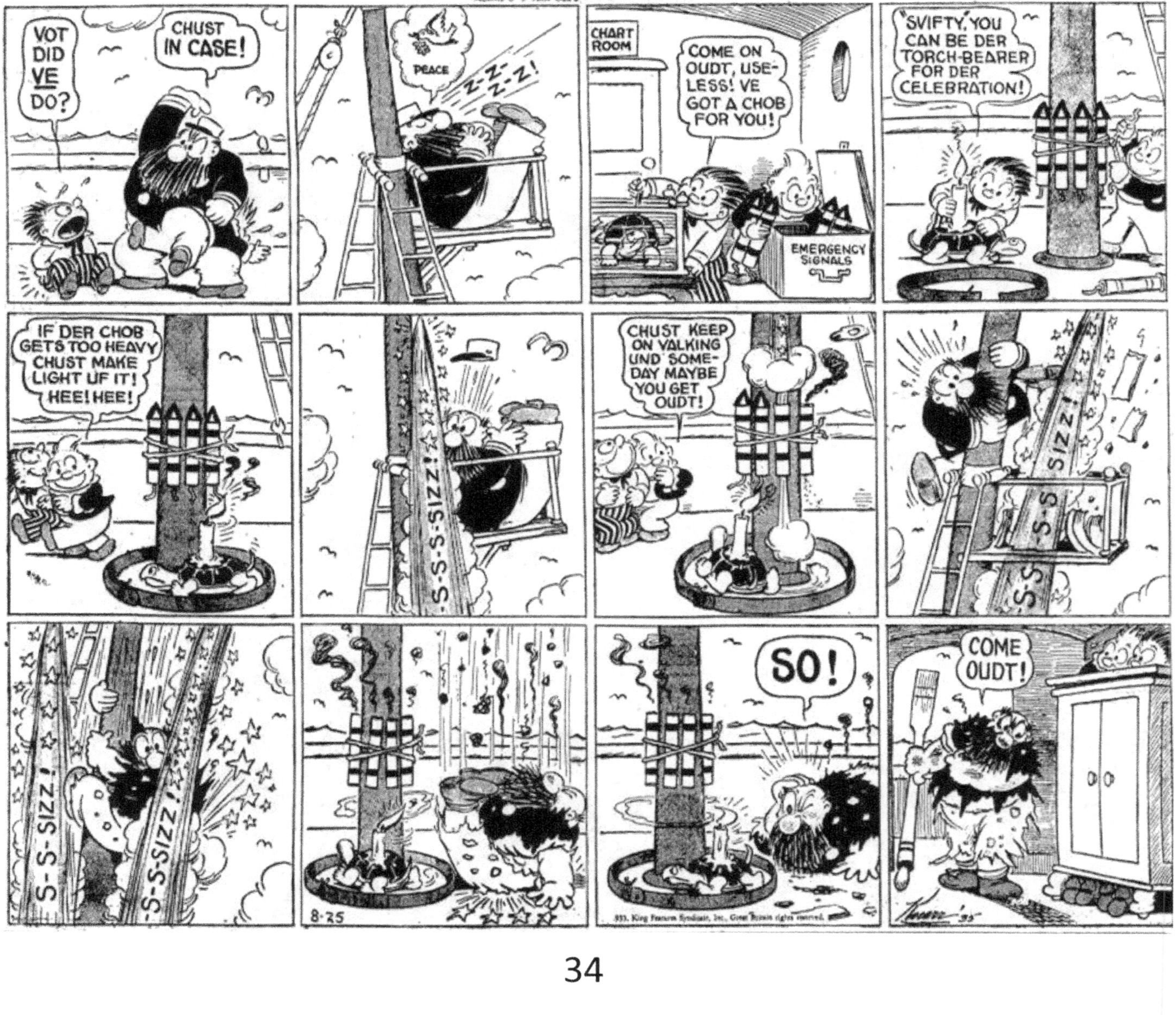
VOT DID VE DO?
CHUST IN CASE!
PEACE
Z-Z-Z-Z!
CHART ROOM
COME ON OUDT, USELESS! VE GOT A CHOB FOR YOU!
EMERGENCY SIGNALS
"SVIFTY," YOU CAN BE DER TORCH-BEARER FOR DER CELEBRATION!
IF DER CHOB GETS TOO HEAVY CHUST MAKE LIGHT UF IT! HEE! HEE!
S-S-S-SIZZ!
CHUST KEEP ON VALKING UND SOMEDAY MAYBE YOU GET OUDT!
S-S-SIZZ!
S-S-SIZZ!
S-S-SIZZ!
8-25
SO!
COME OUDT!

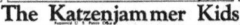

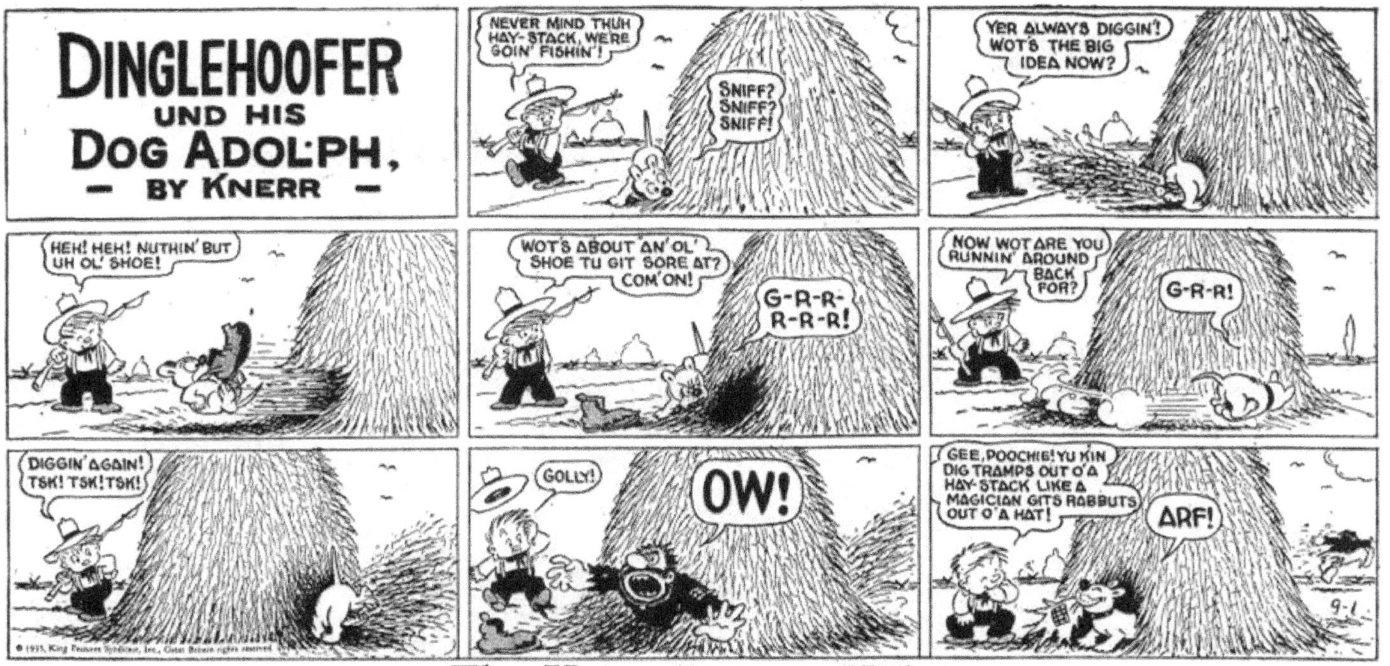
DINGLEHOOFER UND HIS DOG ADOLPH, — BY KNERR —
NEVER MIND THUH HAY-STACK, WE'RE GOIN' FISHIN'!
SNIFF? SNIFF? SNIFF!
YER ALWAYS DIGGIN'! WOT'S THE BIG IDEA NOW?
HEH! HEH! NUTHIN' BUT UH OL' SHOE!
WOT'S ABOUT AN' OL' SHOE TU GIT SORE AT? COM'ON!
G-R-R-R-R-R!
NOW WOT ARE YOU RUNNIN' AROUND BACK FOR?
G-R-R!
DIGGIN' AGAIN! TSK! TSK! TSK!
GOLLY!
OW!
GEE, POOCHIE! YU KIN DIG TRAMPS OUT O'A HAY-STACK LIKE A MAGICIAN GITS RABBUTS OUT O'A HAT!
ARF!
9-1

The Katzenjammer Kids

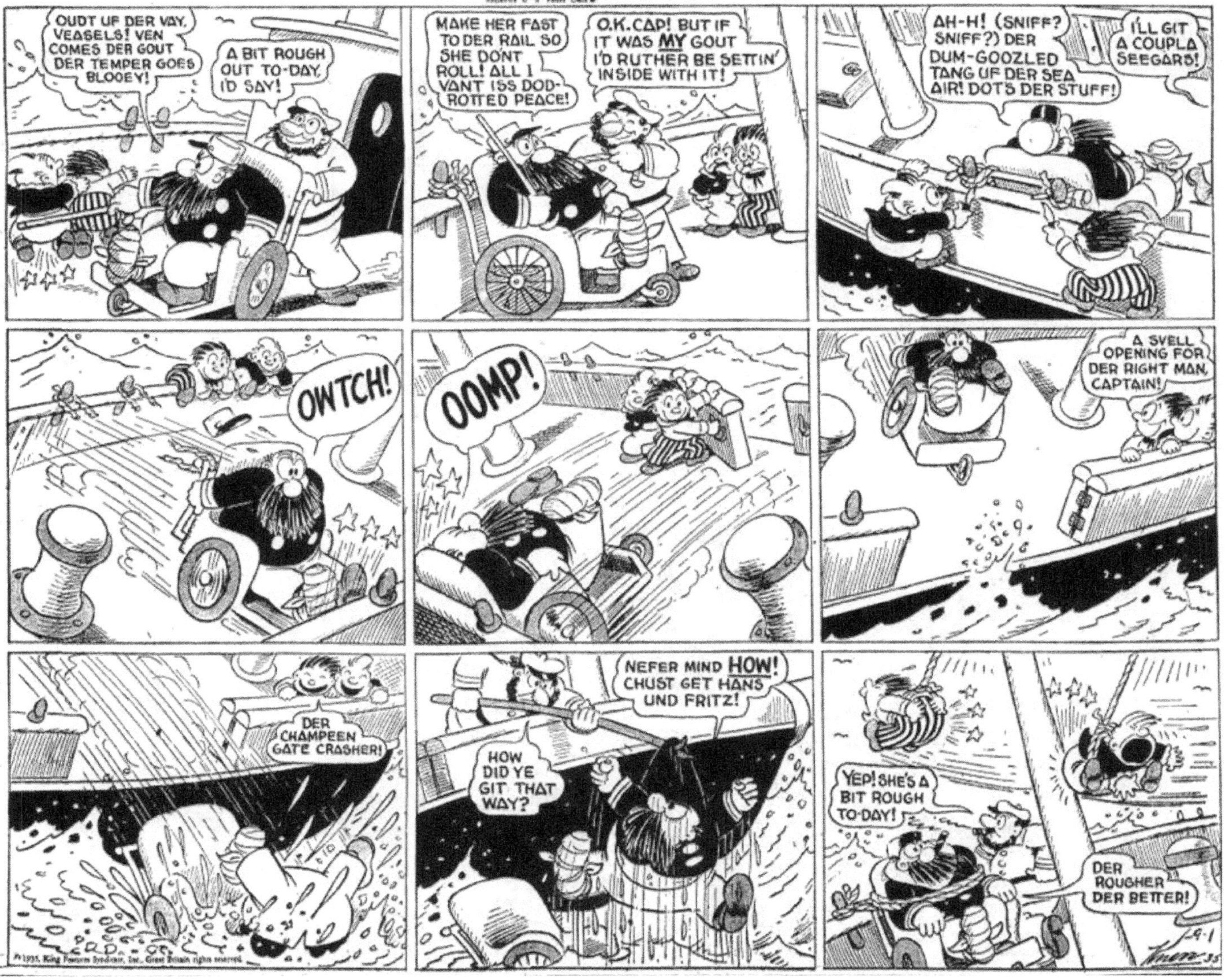
OUDT UF DER VAY, VEASELS! VEN COMES DER GOUT DER TEMPER GOES BLOOEY!
A BIT ROUGH OUT TO-DAY, I'D SAY!
MAKE HER FAST TO DER RAIL SO SHE DON'T ROLL! ALL I VANT ISS DOD-ROTTED PEACE!
O.K. CAP! BUT IF IT WAS MY GOUT I'D RUTHER BE SETTIN' INSIDE WITH IT!
AH-H! (SNIFF? SNIFF?) DER DUM-GOOZLED TANG UF DER SEA AIR! DOTS DER STUFF!
I'LL GIT A COUPLA SEEGARS!
OWTCH!
OOMP!
A SVELL OPENING FOR DER RIGHT MAN, CAPTAIN!
DER CHAMPEEN GATE CRASHER!
NEFER MIND HOW! CHUST GET HANS UND FRITZ!
HOW DID YE GIT THAT WAY?
YEP! SHE'S A BIT ROUGH TO-DAY!
DER ROUGHER DER BETTER!
9-1
Knerr 35

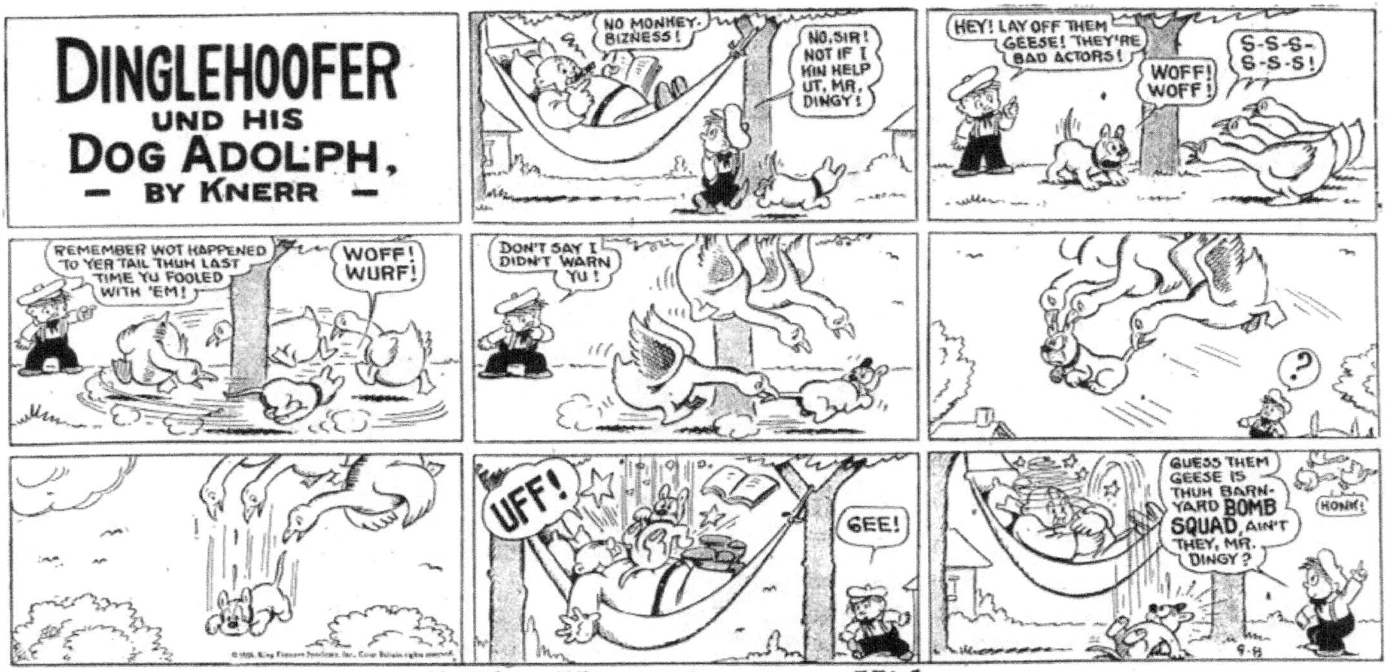
DINGLEHOOFER UND HIS DOG ADOLPH, — BY KNERR —
NO MONKEY-BIZNESS!
NO, SIR! NOT IF I KIN HELP UT, MR. DINGY!
HEY! LAY OFF THEM GEESE! THEY'RE BAD ACTORS!
WOFF! WOFF!
S-S-S-S-S-S!
REMEMBER WOT HAPPENED TO YER TAIL THUH LAST TIME YU FOOLED WITH 'EM!
WOFF! WURF!
DON'T SAY I DIDN'T WARN YU!
?
UFF!
GEE!
GUESS THEM GEESE IS THUH BARN-YARD BOMB SQUAD, AIN'T THEY, MR. DINGY?
HONK!
9-8

The Katzenjammer Kids

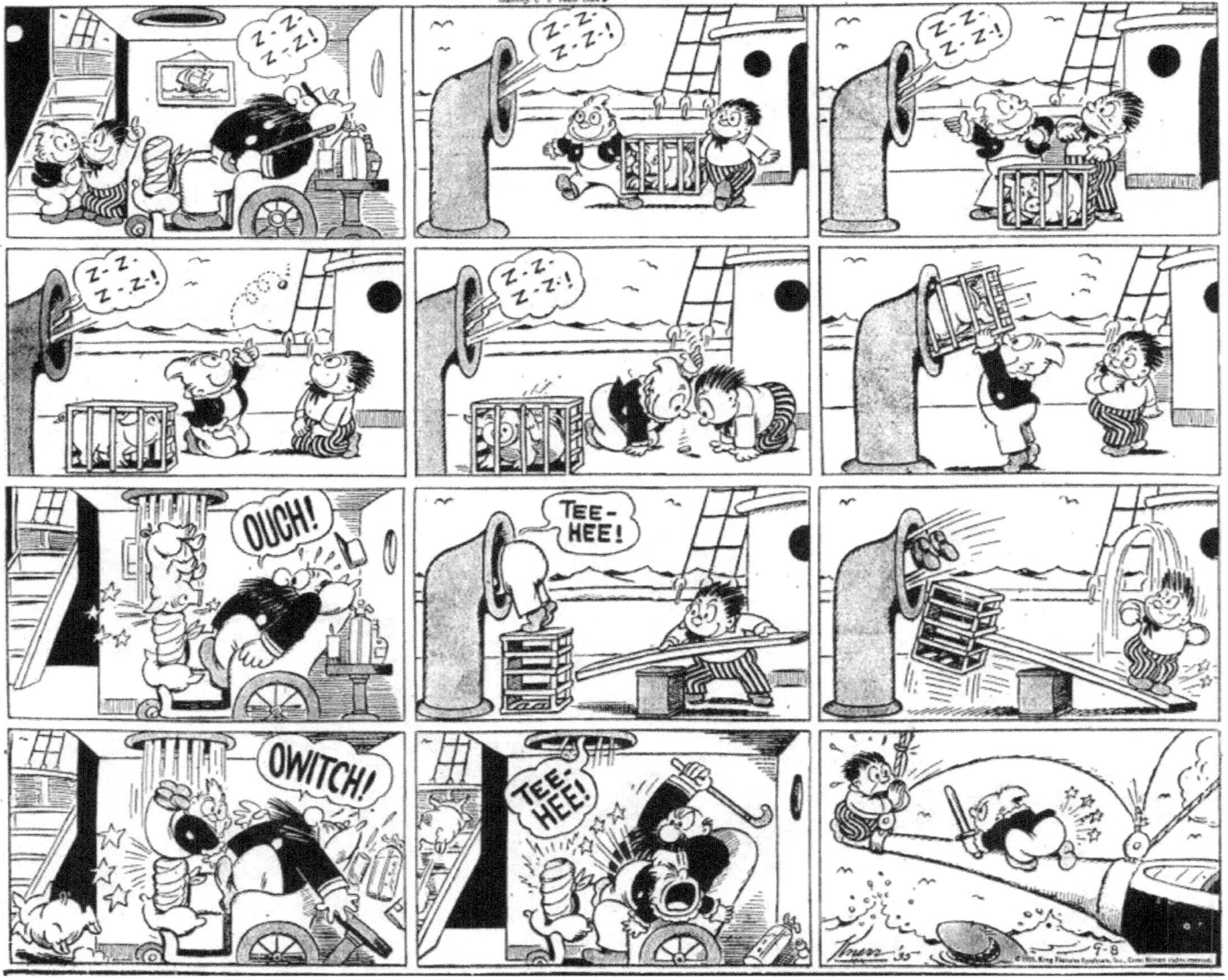
Z-Z-Z-Z-!
Z-Z-Z-Z-!
Z-Z-Z-Z-!
Z-Z-Z-Z-!
Z-Z-Z-Z-!
OUCH!
TEE-HEE!
OWITCH!
TEE-HEE!
Knerr '35
9-8

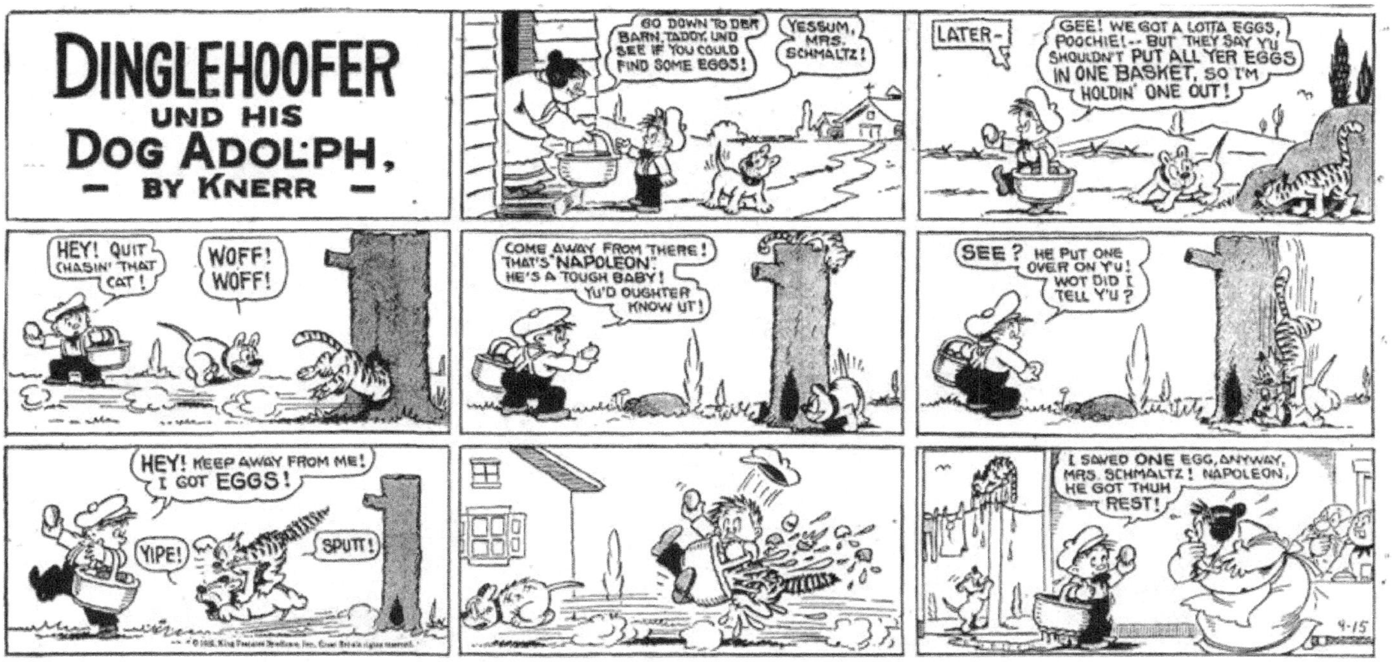

DINGLEHOOFER UND HIS DOG ADOLPH,
— BY KNERR —
GO DOWN TO DER BARN, TADDY, UND SEE IF YOU COULD FIND SOME EGGS!
YESSUM, MRS. SCHMALTZ!
LATER-
GEE! WE GOT A LOTTA EGGS, POOCHIE! -- BUT THEY SAY YU SHOULDN'T PUT ALL YER EGGS IN ONE BASKET, SO I'M HOLDIN' ONE OUT!
HEY! QUIT CHASIN' THAT CAT!
WOFF! WOFF!
COME AWAY FROM THERE! THAT'S "NAPOLEON". HE'S A TOUGH BABY!
YU'D OUGHTER KNOW UT!
SEE? HE PUT ONE OVER ON YU! WOT DID I TELL YU?
HEY! KEEP AWAY FROM ME! I GOT EGGS!
YIPE!
SPUTT!
I SAVED ONE EGG, ANYWAY, MRS. SCHMALTZ! NAPOLEON, HE GOT THUH REST!
9-15

The Katzenjammer Kids

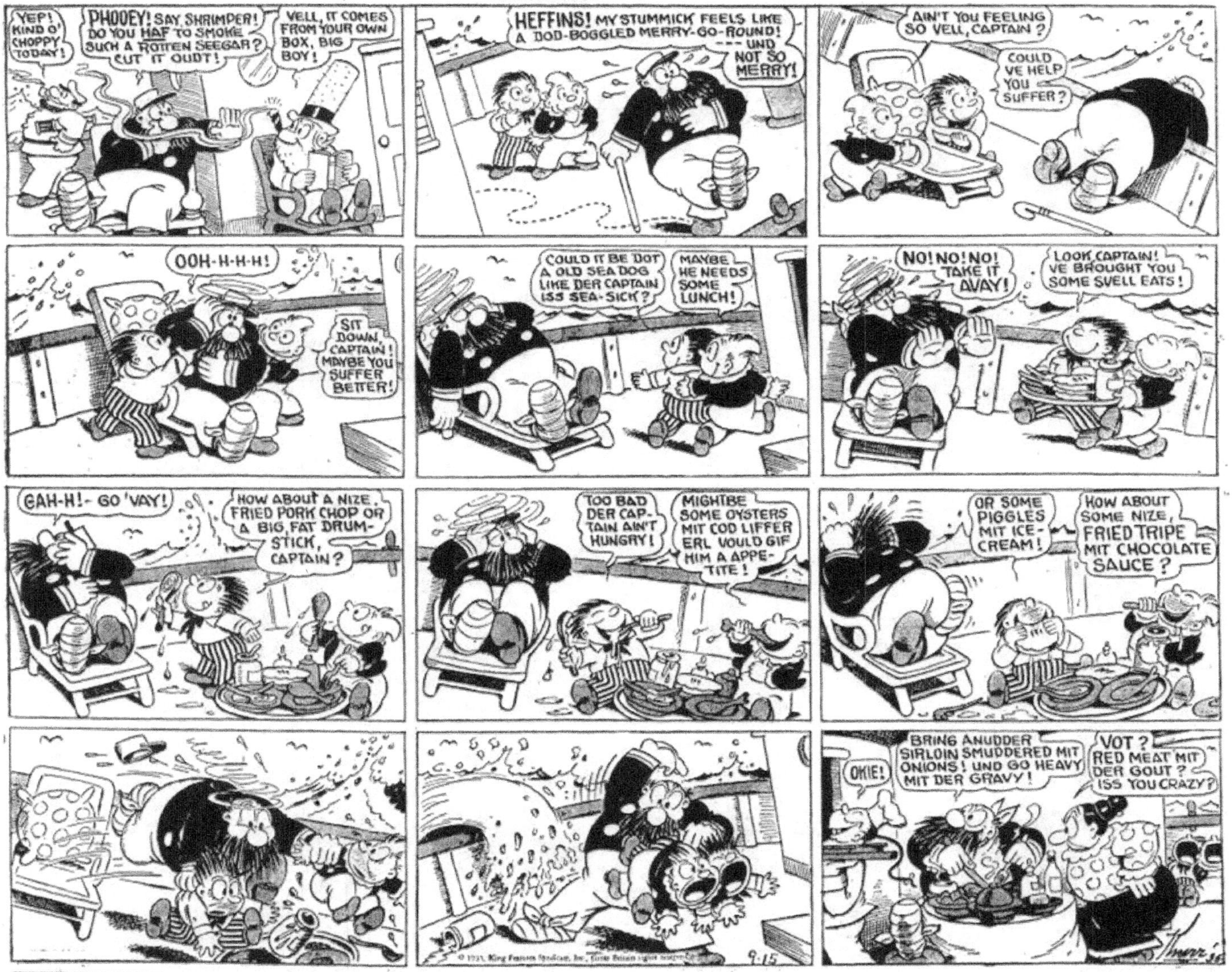

YEP! KIND O' CHOPPY TODAY!
PHOOEY! SAY SHRIMPER! DO YOU HAF TO SMOKE SUCH A ROTTEN SEEGAR? CUT IT OUDT!
VELL, IT COMES FROM YOUR OWN BOX, BIG BOY!
HEFFINS! MY STUMMICK FEELS LIKE A DOB-BOGGLED MERRY-GO-ROUND!
--- UND NOT SO MERRY!
AIN'T YOU FEELING SO VELL, CAPTAIN?
COULD VE HELP YOU SUFFER?
OOH-H-H-H!
SIT DOWN, CAPTAIN! MAYBE YOU SUFFER BETTER!
COULD IT BE DOT A OLD SEA DOG LIKE DER CAPTAIN ISS SEA-SICK?
MAYBE HE NEEDS SOME LUNCH!
NO! NO! NO! TAKE IT AVAY!
LOOK, CAPTAIN! VE BROUGHT YOU SOME SVELL EATS!
GAH-H! - GO 'VAY!
HOW ABOUT A NIZE FRIED PORK CHOP OR A BIG FAT DRUM-STICK, CAPTAIN?
TOO BAD DER CAPTAIN AIN'T HUNGRY!
MIGHTBE SOME OYSTERS MIT COD LIFFER ERL VOULD GIF HIM A APPE-TITE!
OR SOME PIGGLES MIT ICE-CREAM!
HOW ABOUT SOME NIZE, FRIED TRIPE MIT CHOCOLATE SAUCE?
OKIE!
BRING ANUDDER SIRLOIN SMUDDERED MIT ONIONS! UND GO HEAVY MIT DER GRAVY!
VOT? RED MEAT MIT DER GOUT? ISS YOU CRAZY?
9-15
Knerr

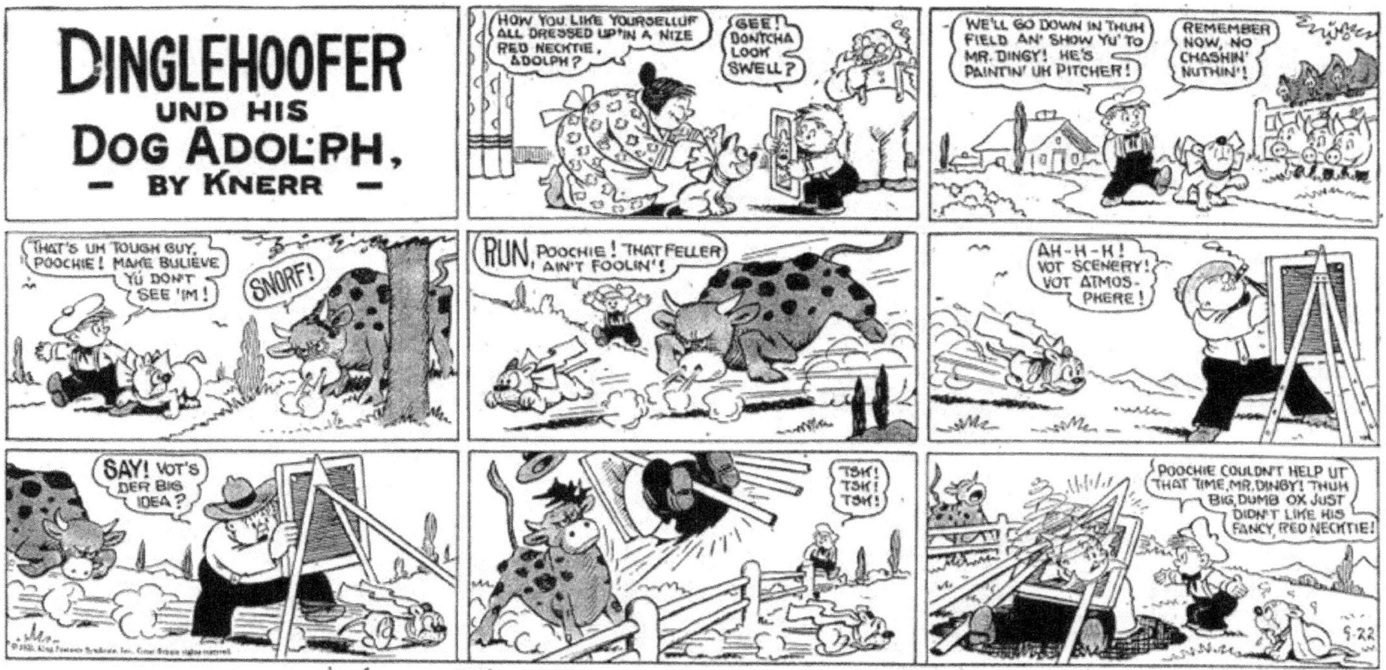
DINGLEHOOFER UND HIS DOG ADOLPH,
— BY KNERR —
HOW YOU LIKE YOURSELLUF ALL DRESSED UP IN A NIZE RED NECKTIE, ADOLPH?
GEE! DONTCHA LOOK SWELL?
WE'LL GO DOWN IN THUH FIELD AN' SHOW YU' TO MR. DINGY! HE'S PAINTIN' UH PITCHER!
REMEMBER NOW, NO CHASHIN' NUTHIN'!
THAT'S UH TOUGH GUY, POOCHIE! MAKE BULIEVE YU DON'T SEE 'IM!
SNORF!
RUN, POOCHIE! THAT FELLER AIN'T FOOLIN'!
AH-H-H! VOT SCENERY! VOT ATMOS-PHERE!
SAY! VOT'S DER BIG IDEA?
TSK! TSK! TSK!
POOCHIE COULDN'T HELP UT THAT TIME, MR. DINGY! THUH BIG, DUMB OX JUST DIDN'T LIKE HIS FANCY, RED NECKTIE!
9-22

The Katzenjammer Kids

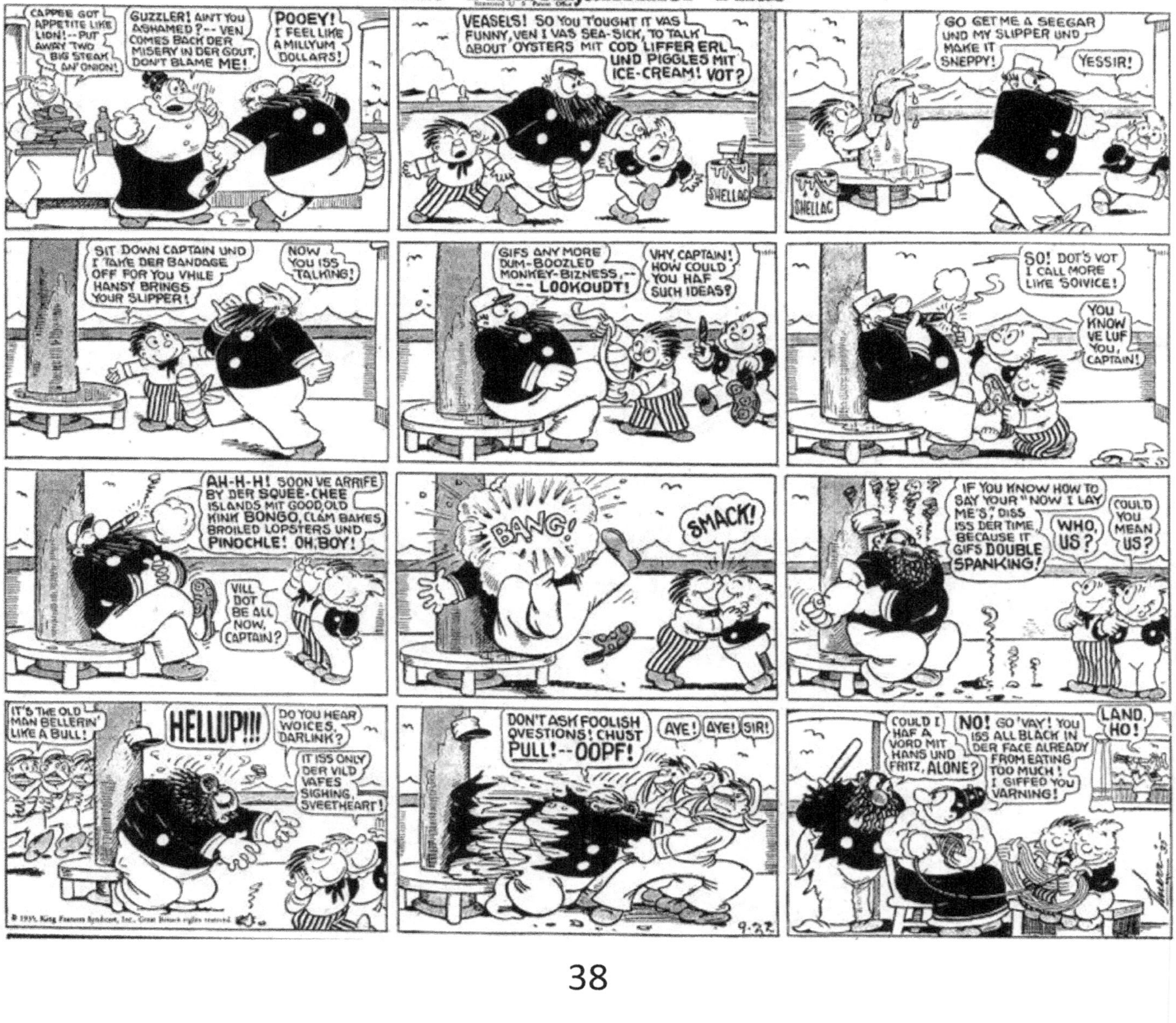
CAPPEE GOT APPETITE LIKE LION!--PUT AWAY TWO BIG STEAK AN' ONION!
GUZZLER! AIN'T YOU ASHAMED?-- VEN COMES BACK DER MISERY IN DER GOUT, DON'T BLAME ME!
POOEY! I FEEL LIKE A MILLYUM DOLLARS!
VEASELS! SO YOU TOUGHT IT VAS FUNNY, VEN I VAS SEA-SICK, TO TALK ABOUT OYSTERS MIT COD LIFFER ERL UND PIGGLES MIT ICE-CREAM! VOT?
SHELLAC
GO GET ME A SEEGAR UND MY SLIPPER UND MAKE IT SNEPPY!
YESSIR!
SHELLAC
SIT DOWN CAPTAIN UND I TAKE DER BANDAGE OFF FOR YOU VHILE HANSY BRINGS YOUR SLIPPER!
NOW YOU ISS TALKING!
GIFS ANY MORE DUM-BOOZLED MONKEY-BIZNESS,-- -- LOOKOUDT!
VHY, CAPTAIN! HOW COULD YOU HAF SUCH IDEAS?
SO! DOT'S VOT I CALL MORE LIKE SOIVICE!
YOU KNOW VE LUF YOU, CAPTAIN!
AH-H-H! SOON VE ARRIFE BY DER SQUEE-CHEE ISLANDS MIT GOOD, OLD KINK BONGO, CLAM BAKES, BROILED LOPSTERS UND PINOCHLE! OH, BOY!
VILL DOT BE ALL NOW, CAPTAIN?
BANG!
SMACK!
IF YOU KNOW HOW TO SAY YOUR "NOW I LAY ME'S," DISS ISS DER TIME, BECAUSE IT GIFS DOUBLE SPANKING!
WHO, US?
COULD YOU MEAN US?
IT'S THE OLD MAN BELLERIN' LIKE A BULL!
HELLUP!!!
DO YOU HEAR VOICES, DARLINK?
IT ISS ONLY DER VILD VAFES SIGHING, SVEETHEART!
DON'T ASK FOOLISH QVESTIONS! CHUST PULL!--OOPF!
AYE! AYE! SIR!
COULD I HAF A VORD MIT HANS UND FRITZ, ALONE?
NO! GO 'VAY! YOU ISS ALL BLACK IN DER FACE ALREADY FROM EATING TOO MUCH! I GIFFED YOU VARNING!
LAND, HO!
9-22
© 1935, King Features Syndicate, Inc., Great Britain rights reserved.

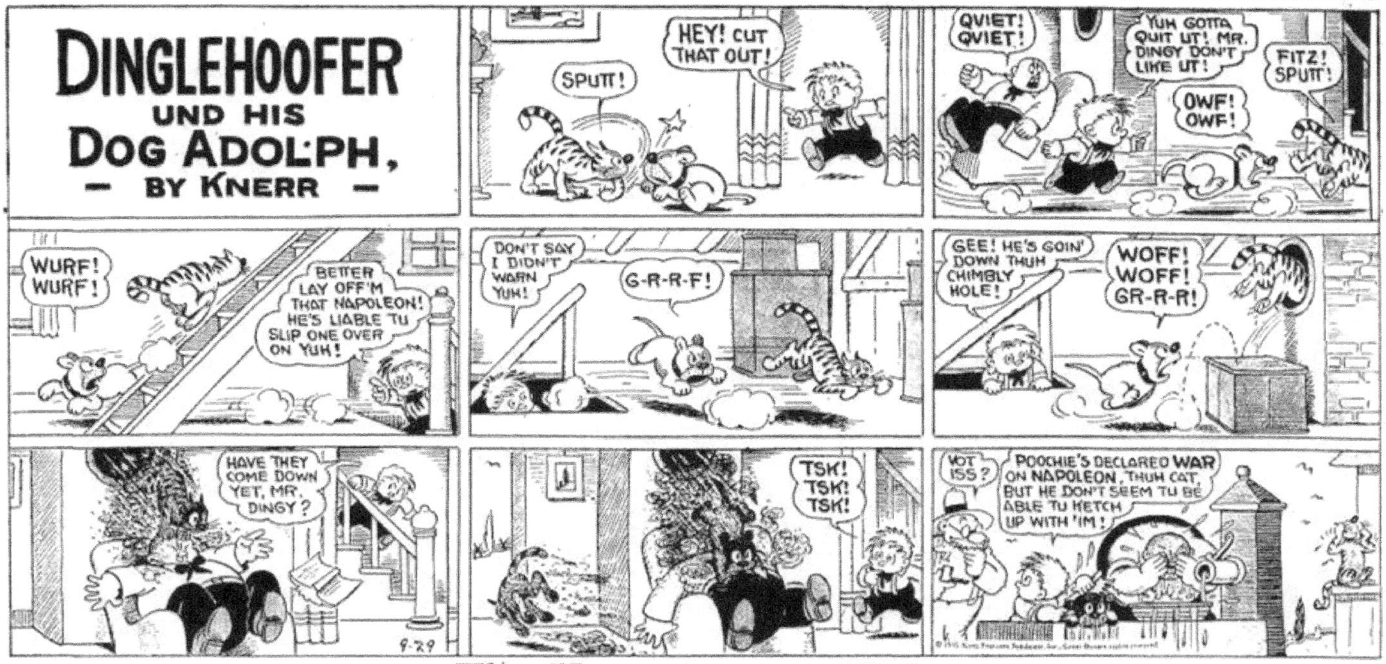
DINGLEHOOFER
UND HIS
DOG ADOLPH,
— BY KNERR —
HEY! CUT THAT OUT!
SPUTT!
QVIET! QVIET!
YUH GOTTA QUIT UT! MR. DINGY DON'T LIKE UT!
OWF! OWF!
FITZ! SPUTT!
WURF! WURF!
BETTER LAY OFF'M THAT NAPOLEON! HE'S LIABLE TU SLIP ONE OVER ON YUH!
DON'T SAY I DIDN'T WARN YUH!
G-R-R-F!
GEE! HE'S GOIN' DOWN THUH CHIMBLY HOLE!
WOFF! WOFF! GR-R-R!
HAVE THEY COME DOWN YET, MR. DINGY?
TSK! TSK! TSK!
VOT ISS?
POOCHIE'S DECLARED WAR ON NAPOLEON, THUH CAT, BUT HE DON'T SEEM TU BE ABLE TU KETCH UP WITH 'IM!
9-29

The Katzenjammer Kids

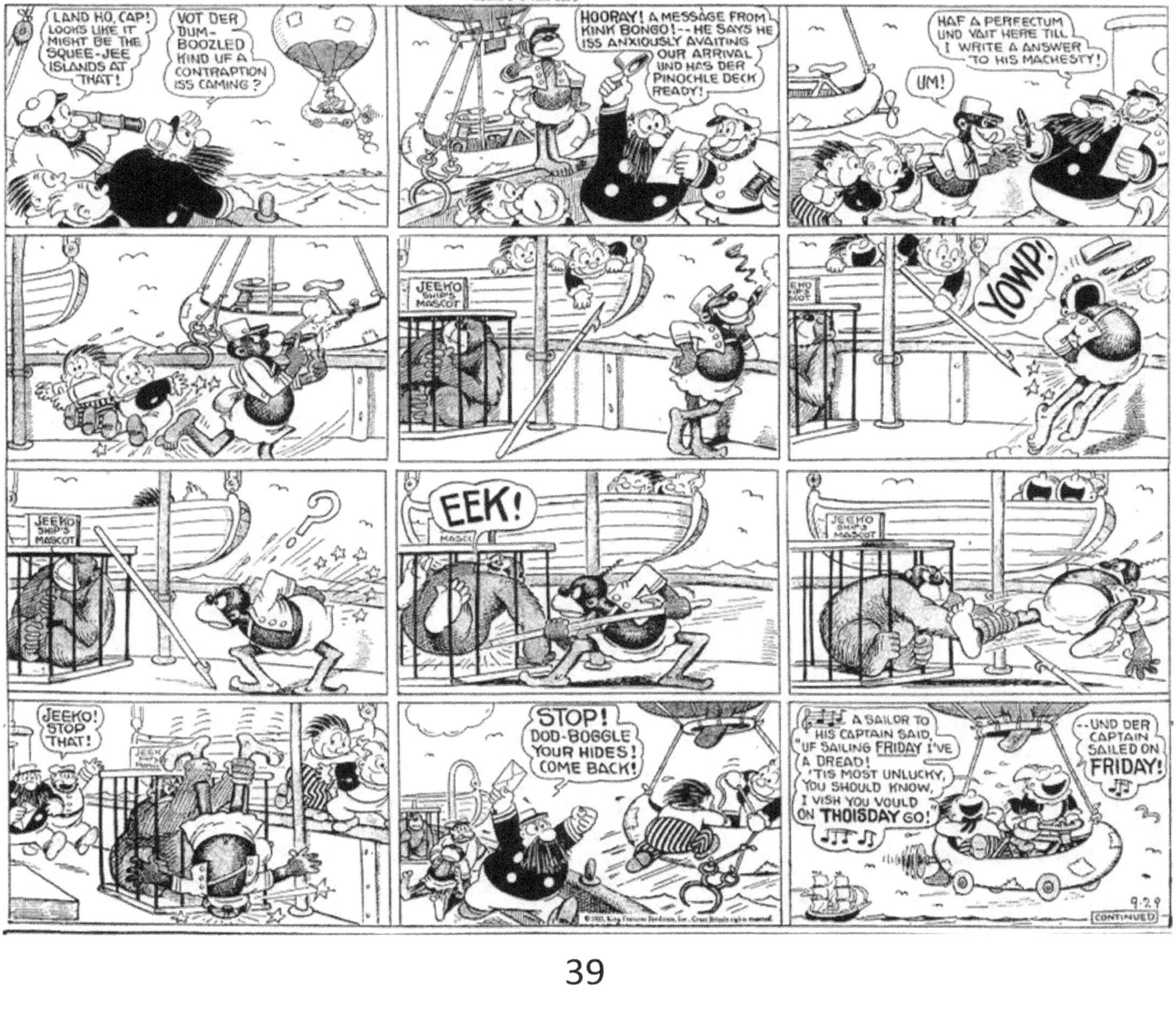
LAND HO, CAP! LOOKS LIKE IT MIGHT BE THE SQUEE-JEE ISLANDS AT THAT!
VOT DER BUM-BOOZLED KIND UF A CONTRAPTION ISS CAMING?
HOORAY! A MESSAGE FROM KINK BONGO!--HE SAYS HE ISS ANXIOUSLY AVAITING OUR ARRIVAL UND HAS DER PINOCHLE DECK READY!
HAF A PERFECTUM UND VAIT HERE TILL I WRITE A ANSWER TO HIS MACHESTY!
UM!
JEEKO SHIP'S MASCOT
YOWP!
EEK!
JEEKO! STOP THAT!
STOP! DOD-BOGGLE YOUR HIDES! COME BACK!
A SAILOR TO HIS CAPTAIN SAID, "UF SAILING FRIDAY I'VE A DREAD! 'TIS MOST UNLUCKY, YOU SHOULD KNOW, I VISH YOU VOULD ON THOISDAY GO!"
--UND DER CAPTAIN SAILED ON FRIDAY!
9-29
CONTINUED

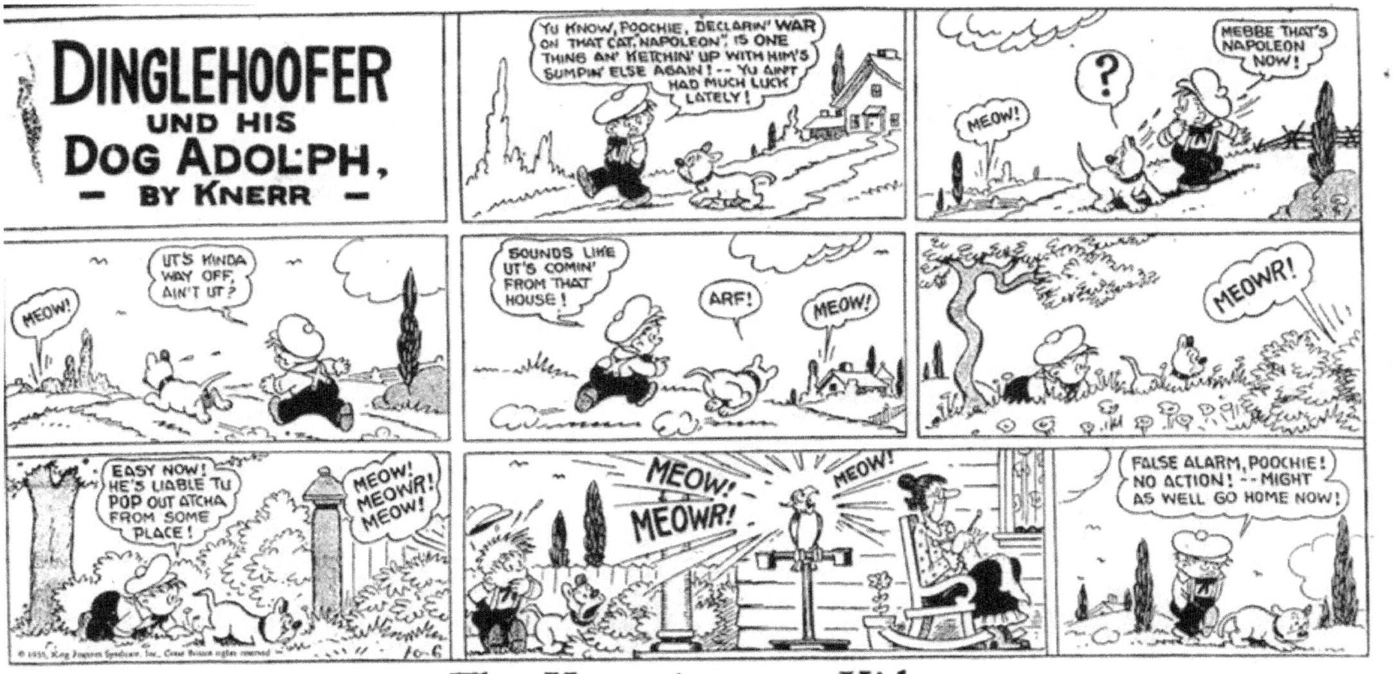
DINGLEHOOFER UND HIS DOG ADOLPH, — BY KNERR —
YU KNOW, POOCHIE, DECLARIN' WAR ON THAT CAT, NAPOLEON" IS ONE THING AN' KETCHIN' UP WITH HIM'S SUMPIN' ELSE AGAIN! -- YU AIN'T HAD MUCH LUCK LATELY!
MEOW!
?
MEBBE THAT'S NAPOLEON NOW!
MEOW!
UT'S KINDA WAY OFF, AIN'T UT?
SOUNDS LIKE UT'S COMIN' FROM THAT HOUSE!
ARF!
MEOW!
MEOWR!
EASY NOW! HE'S LIABLE TU POP OUT ATCHA FROM SOME PLACE!
MEOW! MEOWR! MEOW!
MEOW!
MEOWR!
MEOW!
FALSE ALARM, POOCHIE! NO ACTION! -- MIGHT AS WELL GO HOME NOW!

The Katzenjammer Kids

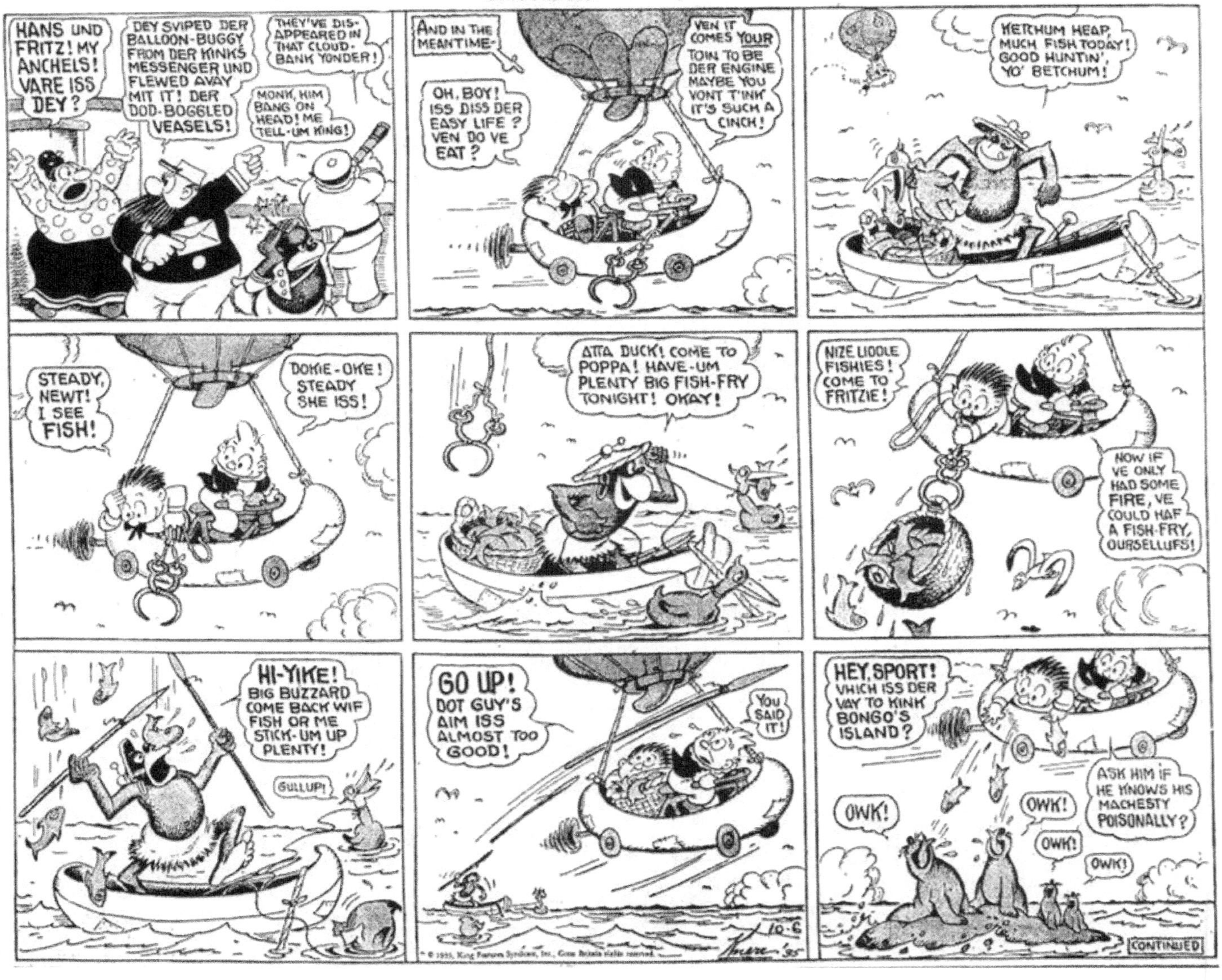
HANS UND FRITZ! MY ANCHELS! VARE ISS DEY?
DEY SVIPED DER BALLOON-BUGGY FROM DER KINKS MESSENGER UND FLEWED AVAY MIT IT! DER DOD-BOGGLED VEASELS!
THEY'VE DISAPPEARED IN THAT CLOUD-BANK YONDER!
MONK, HIM BANG ON HEAD! ME TELL-UM KING!
AND IN THE MEANTIME—
VEN IT COMES YOUR TOIN TO BE DER ENGINE MAYBE YOU VONT T'INK IT'S SUCH A CINCH!
OH, BOY! ISS DISS DER EASY LIFE? VEN DO VE EAT?
KETCHUM HEAP MUCH FISH TODAY! GOOD HUNTIN', YO' BETCHUM!
STEADY, NEWT! I SEE FISH!
DOKIE-OKIE! STEADY SHE ISS!
ATTA DUCK! COME TO POPPA! HAVE-UM PLENTY BIG FISH-FRY TONIGHT! OKAY!
NIZE LIDDLE FISHIES! COME TO FRITZIE!
NOW IF VE ONLY HAD SOME FIRE, VE COULD HAF A FISH-FRY, OURSELLUFS!
HI-YIKE! BIG BUZZARD COME BACK WIF FISH OR ME STICK-UM UP PLENTY!
GULLUP!
GO UP! DOT GUY'S AIM ISS ALMOST TOO GOOD!
YOU SAID IT!
HEY, SPORT! VHICH ISS DER VAY TO KINK BONGO'S ISLAND?
ASK HIM IF HE KNOWS HIS MACHESTY POISONALLY?
OWK!
OWK!
OWK!
OWK!
CONTINUED

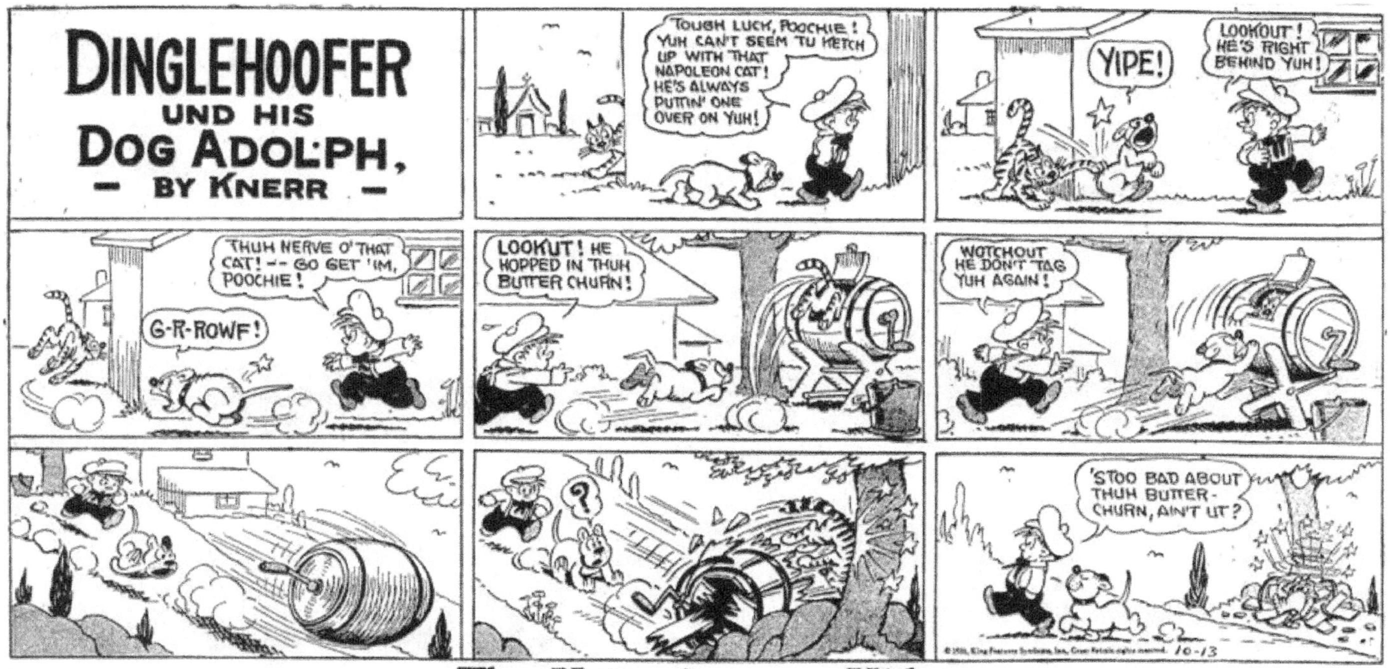
DINGLEHOOFER UND HIS DOG ADOLPH, — BY KNERR —
TOUGH LUCK, POOCHIE! YUH CAN'T SEEM TU KETCH UP WITH THAT NAPOLEON CAT! HE'S ALWAYS PUTTIN' ONE OVER ON YUH!
YIPE!
LOOKOUT! HE'S RIGHT BEHIND YUH!
THUH NERVE O' THAT CAT! -- GO GET 'IM, POOCHIE!
G-R-ROWF!
LOOKUT! HE HOPPED IN THUH BUTTER CHURN!
WOTCHOUT HE DON'T TAG YUH AGAIN!
?
'STOO BAD ABOUT THUH BUTTER-CHURN, AIN'T IT?
10-13

The Katzenjammer Kids

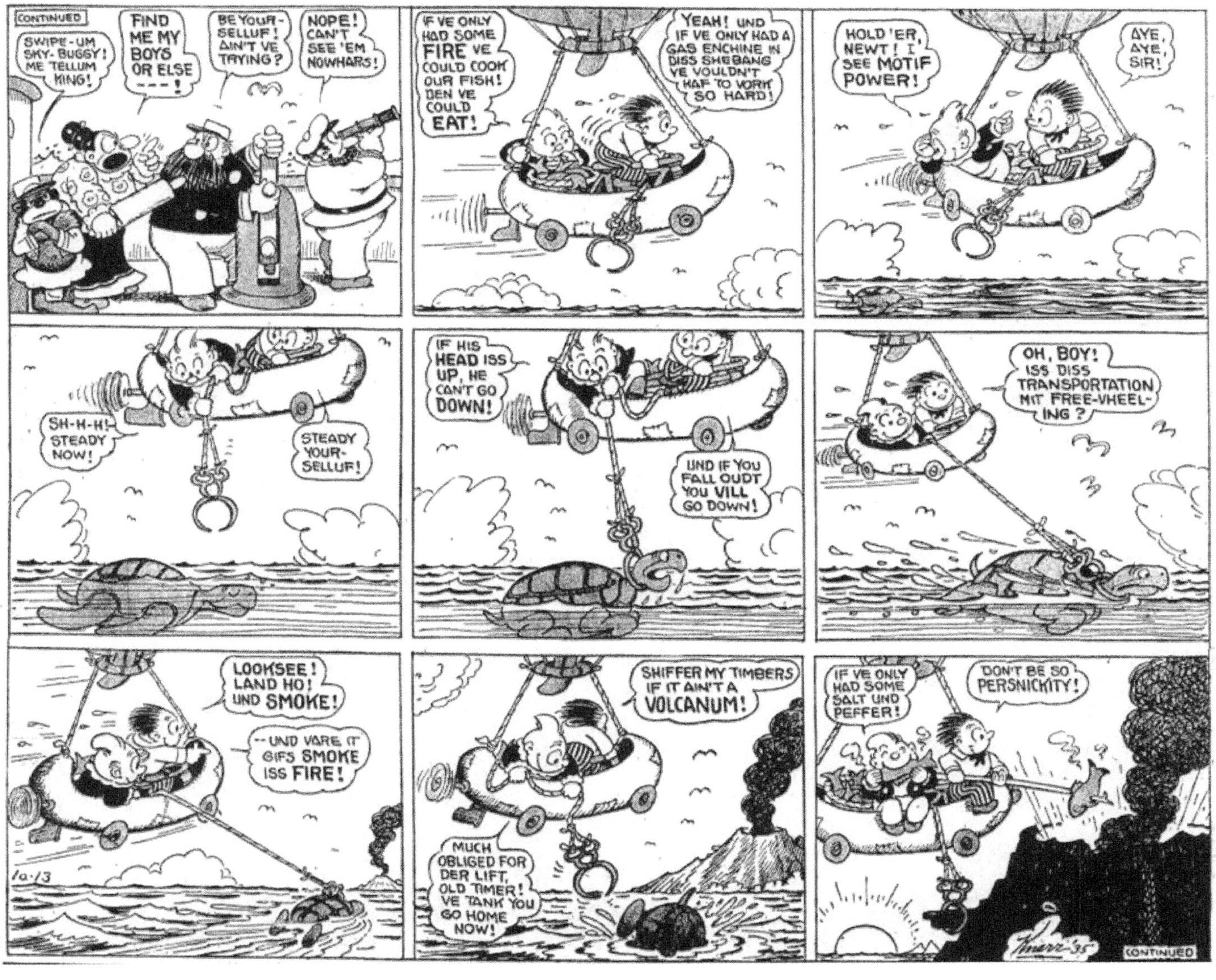
CONTINUED
SWIPE-UM SKY-BUGGY! ME TELLUM KING!
FIND ME MY BOYS OR ELSE ---!
BE YOURSELLUF! AIN'T VE TRYING?
NOPE! CAN'T SEE 'EM NOWHARS!
IF VE ONLY HAD SOME FIRE VE COULD COOK OUR FISH! DEN VE COULD EAT!
YEAH! UND IF VE ONLY HAD A GAS ENCHINE IN DISS SHEBANG VE VOULDN'T HAF TO VORK SO HARD!
HOLD 'ER, NEWT! I SEE MOTIF POWER!
AYE, AYE, SIR!
SH-H-H! STEADY NOW!
STEADY YOURSELLUF!
IF HIS HEAD ISS UP, HE CAN'T GO DOWN!
UND IF YOU FALL OUDT YOU VILL GO DOWN!
OH, BOY! ISS DISS TRANSPORTATION MIT FREE-VHEELING?
LOOKSEE! LAND HO! UND SMOKE!
--UND VARE IT GIFS SMOKE ISS FIRE!
10-13
SHIFFER MY TIMBERS IF IT AIN'T A VOLCANUM!
MUCH OBLIGED FOR DER LIFT, OLD TIMER! VE TANK YOU GO HOME NOW!
IF VE ONLY HAD SOME SALT UND PEFFER!
DON'T BE SO PERSNICKITY!
Knerr '35
CONTINUED

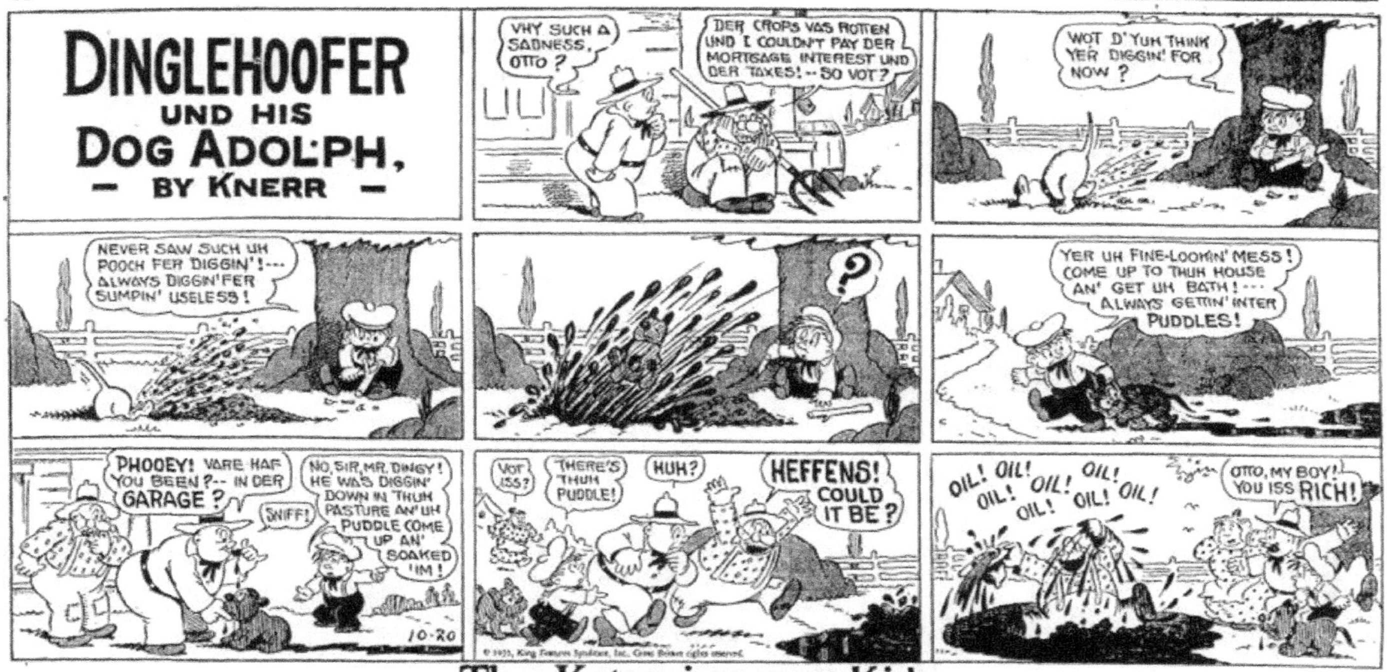
DINGLEHOOFER
UND HIS
DOG ADOLPH,
— BY KNERR —
VHY SUCH A SADNESS, OTTO ?
DER CROPS VAS ROTTEN UND I COULDN'T PAY DER MORTGAGE INTEREST UND DER TAXES! -- SO VOT?
WOT D' YUH THINK YER DIGGIN' FOR NOW ?
NEVER SAW SUCH UH POOCH FER DIGGIN'! --- ALWAYS DIGGIN' FER SUMPIN' USELESS !
?
YER UH FINE-LOOKIN' MESS! COME UP TO THUH HOUSE AN' GET UH BATH! --- ALWAYS GETTIN' INTER PUDDLES!
PHOOEY! VARE HAF YOU BEEN ?-- IN DER GARAGE ?
SNIFF!
NO, SIR, MR. DINGY! HE WAS DIGGIN' DOWN IN THUH PASTURE AN' UH PUDDLE COME UP AN' SOAKED 'IM !
10-20
VOT ISS?
THERE'S THUH PUDDLE!
HUH?
HEFFENS! COULD IT BE ?
OIL! OIL! OIL! OIL! OIL! OIL! OIL! OIL!
OTTO, MY BOY! YOU ISS RICH!

The Katzenjammer Kids

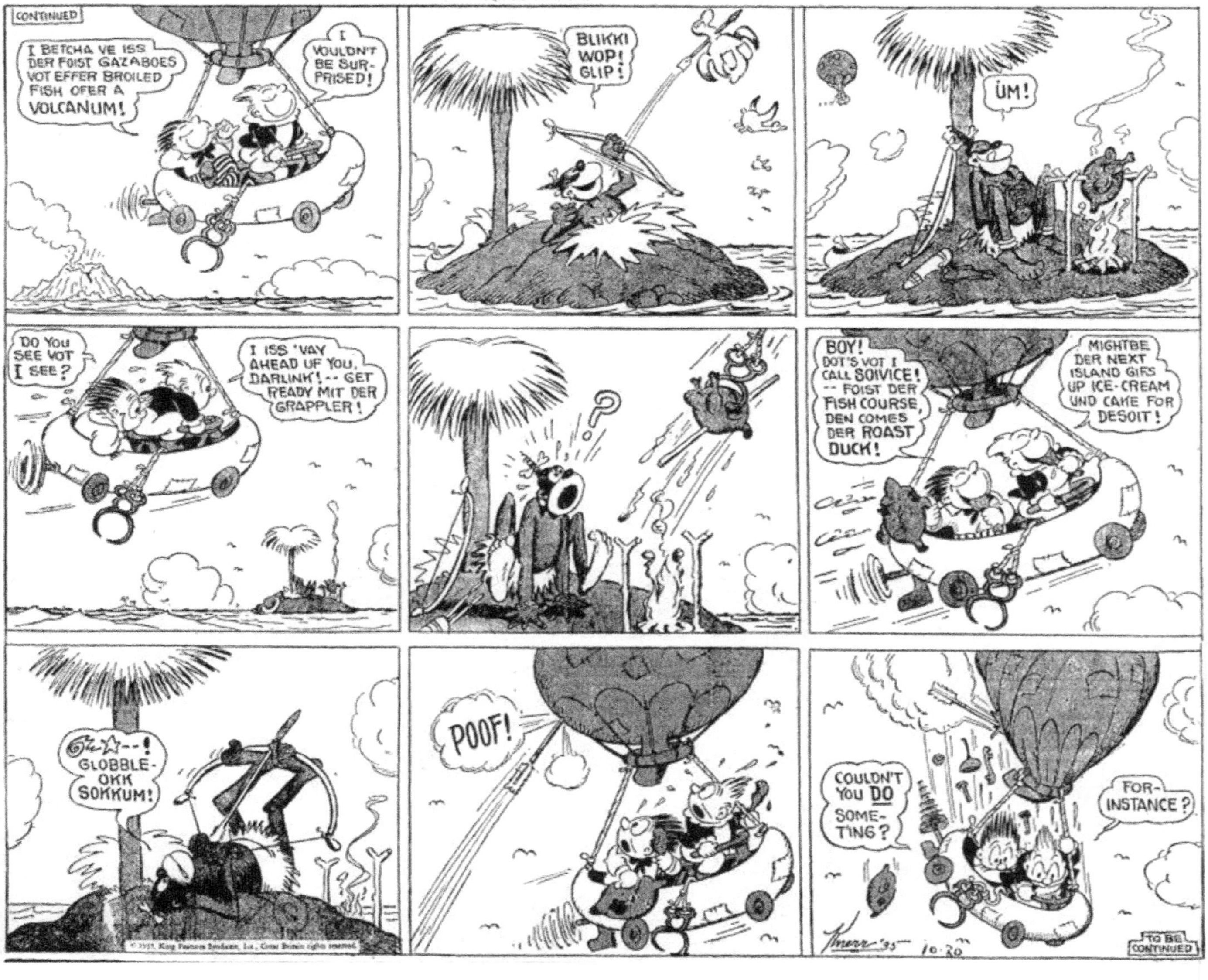
CONTINUED
I BETCHA VE ISS DER FOIST GAZABOES VOT EFFER BROILED FISH OFER A VOLCANUM!
I VOULDN'T BE SUR-PRISED!
BLIKKI WOP! GLIP!
ÜM!
DO YOU SEE VOT I SEE?
I ISS 'VAY AHEAD UF YOU, DARLINK! -- GET READY MIT DER GRAPPLER!
?
BOY! DOT'S VOT I CALL SOIVICE! -- FOIST DER FISH COURSE, DEN COMES DER ROAST DUCK!
MIGHTBE DER NEXT ISLAND GIFS UP ICE-CREAM UND CAKE FOR DESOIT!
--! GLOBBLE-OKK SOKKUM!
POOF!
COULDN'T YOU DO SOME-TING?
FOR-INSTANCE?
Knerr '35 10-20
TO BE CONTINUED

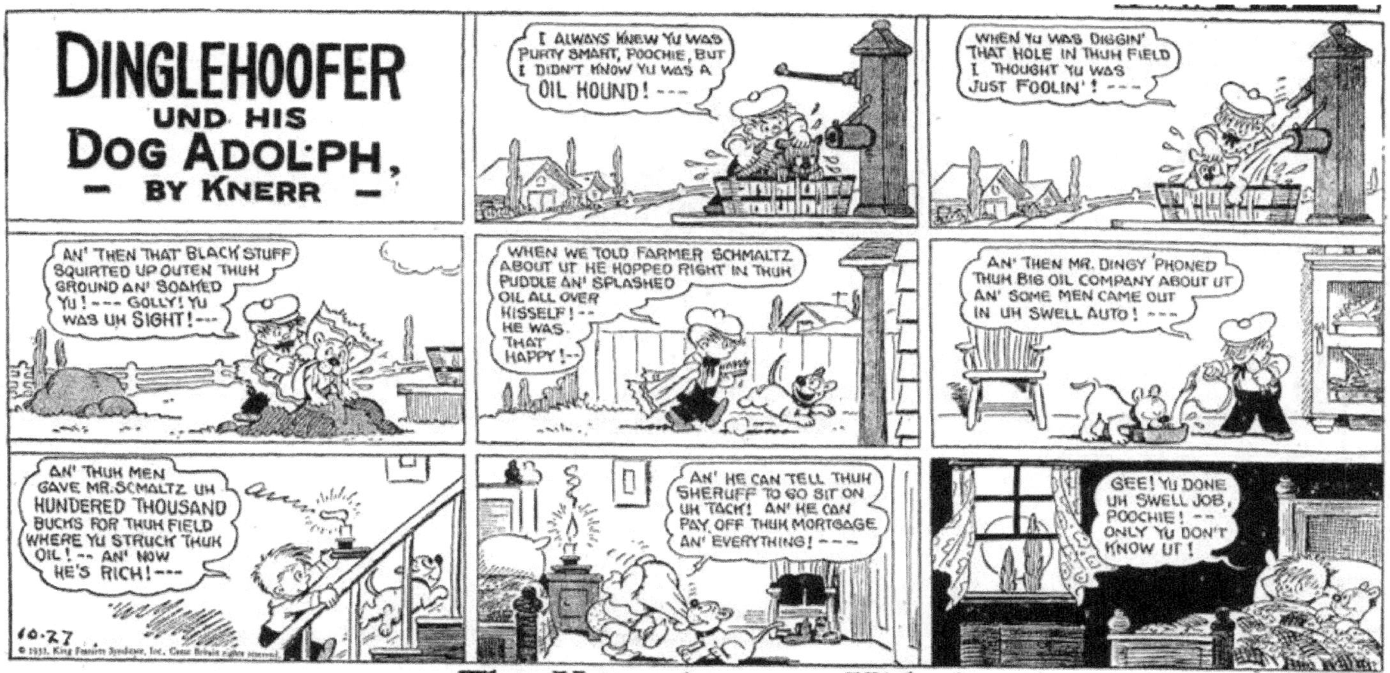
DINGLEHOOFER UND HIS DOG ADOLPH, — BY KNERR —
I ALWAYS KNEW YU WAS PURTY SMART, POOCHIE, BUT I DIDN'T KNOW YU WAS A OIL HOUND! ---
WHEN YU WAS DIGGIN' THAT HOLE IN THUH FIELD I THOUGHT YU WAS JUST FOOLIN'! ---
AN' THEN THAT BLACK STUFF SQUIRTED UP OUTEN THUH GROUND AN' SOAKED YU! --- GOLLY! YU WAS UH SIGHT! ---
WHEN WE TOLD FARMER SCHMALTZ ABOUT UT HE HOPPED RIGHT IN THUH PUDDLE AN' SPLASHED OIL ALL OVER HISSELF! -- HE WAS THAT HAPPY! --
AN' THEN MR. DINGY 'PHONED THUH BIG OIL COMPANY ABOUT UT AN' SOME MEN CAME OUT IN UH SWELL AUTO! ---
AN' THUH MEN GAVE MR. SCHMALTZ UH HUNDRED THOUSAND BUCKS FOR THUH FIELD WHERE YU STRUCK THUH OIL! -- AN' NOW HE'S RICH! ---
AN' HE CAN TELL THUH SHERUFF TO GO SIT ON UH TACK! AN' HE CAN PAY OFF THUH MORTGAGE AN' EVERYTHING! ---
GEE! YU DONE UH SWELL JOB, POOCHIE! -- ONLY YU DON'T KNOW UT!
10-27

The Katzenjammer Kids

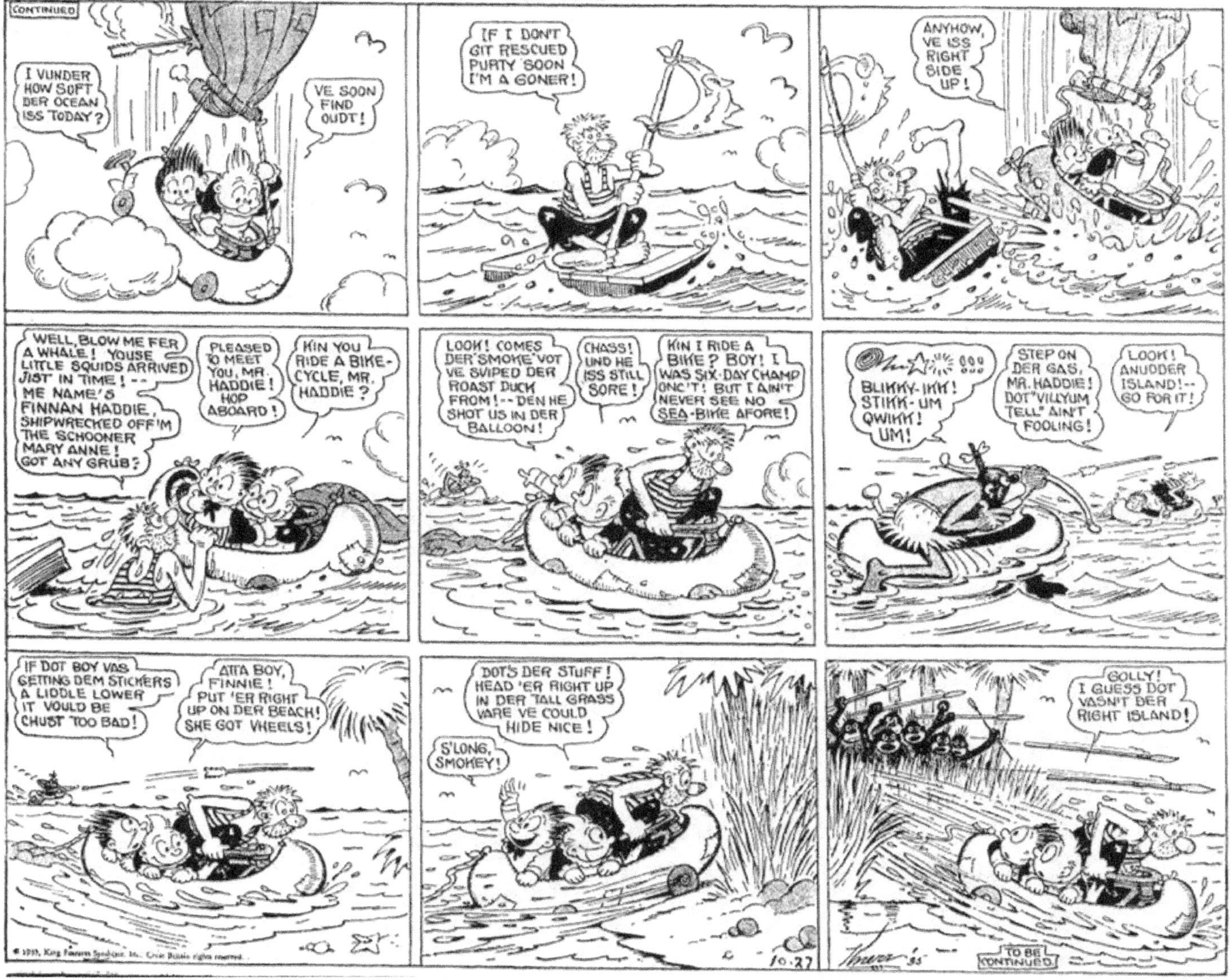
CONTINUED
I VUNDER HOW SOFT DER OCEAN ISS TODAY?
VE SOON FIND OUDT!
IF I DON'T GIT RESCUED PURTY SOON I'M A GONER!
ANYHOW, VE ISS RIGHT SIDE UP!
WELL, BLOW ME FER A WHALE! YOUSE LITTLE SQUIDS ARRIVED JIST IN TIME! -- ME NAME'S FINNAN HADDIE, SHIPWRECKED OFF'M THE SCHOONER MARY ANNE! GOT ANY GRUB?
PLEASED TO MEET YOU, MR. HADDIE! HOP ABOARD!
KIN YOU RIDE A BIKE-CYCLE, MR. HADDIE?
LOOK! COMES DER SMOKE' VOT VE SVIPED DER ROAST DUCK FROM! -- DEN HE SHOT US IN DER BALLOON!
CHASS! UND HE ISS STILL SORE!
KIN I RIDE A BIKE? BOY! I WAS SIX-DAY CHAMP ONC'T! BUT I AIN'T NEVER SEE NO SEA-BIKE AFORE!
BLIKKY-IKK! STIKK-UM QWIKK! UM!
STEP ON DER GAS, MR. HADDIE! DOT "VILLYUM TELL" AIN'T FOOLING!
LOOK! ANUDDER ISLAND! -- GO FOR IT!
IF DOT BOY VAS GETTING DEM STICKERS A LIDDLE LOWER IT VOULD BE CHUST TOO BAD!
ATTA BOY, FINNIE! PUT 'ER RIGHT UP ON DER BEACH! SHE GOT VHEELS!
DOT'S DER STUFF! HEAD 'ER RIGHT UP IN DER TALL GRASS VARE VE COULD HIDE NICE!
S'LONG, SMOKEY!
GOLLY! I GUESS DOT VASN'T DER RIGHT ISLAND!
10-27
Knerr '35
TO BE CONTINUED

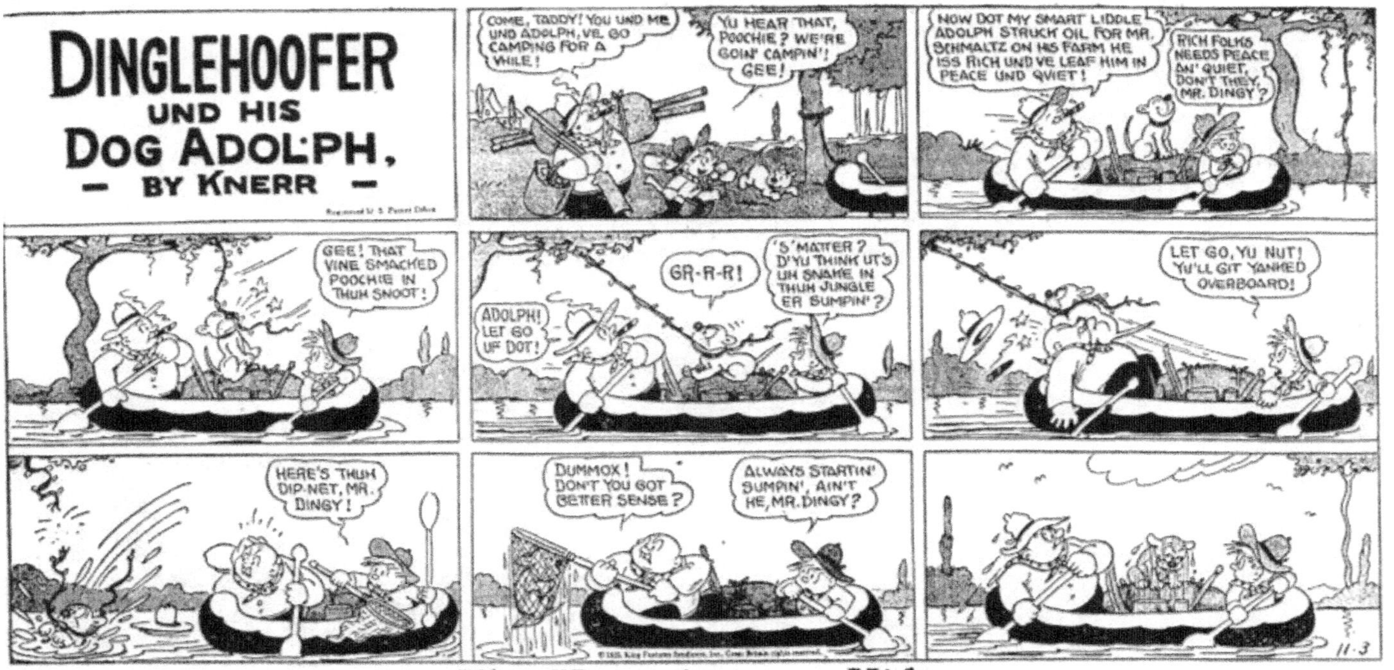
DINGLEHOOFER UND HIS DOG ADOLPH, — BY KNERR —
COME, TADDY! YOU UND ME UND ADOLPH, VE GO CAMPING FOR A VHILE!
YU HEAR THAT, POOCHIE? WE'RE GOIN' CAMPIN'! GEE!
NOW DOT MY SMART LIDDLE ADOLPH STRUCK OIL FOR MR. SCHMALTZ ON HIS FARM HE ISS RICH UND VE LEAF HIM IN PEACE UND QVIET!
RICH FOLKS NEEDS PEACE AN' QUIET, DON'T THEY, MR. DINGY?
GEE! THAT VINE SMACKED POOCHIE IN THUH SNOOT!
GR-R-R!
'S'MATTER? D'YU THINK UT'S UH SNAKE IN THUH JUNGLE ER SUMPIN'?
ADOLPH! LET GO UF DOT!
LET GO, YU NUT! YU'LL GIT YANKED OVERBOARD!
HERE'S THUH DIP-NET, MR. DINGY!
DUMMOX! DON'T YOU GOT BETTER SENSE?
ALWAYS STARTIN' SUMPIN', AIN'T HE, MR. DINGY?
11-3

The Katzenjammer Kids

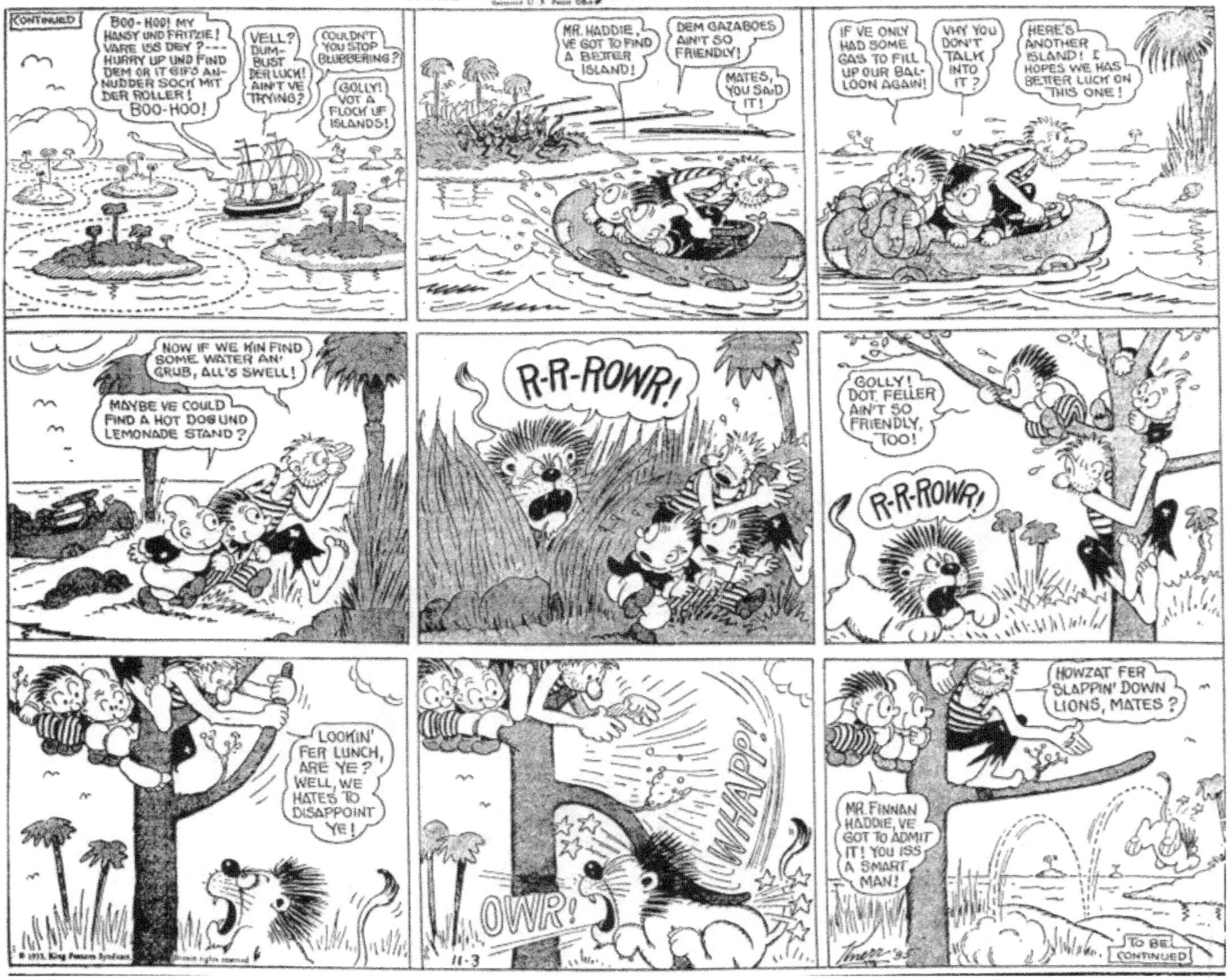
CONTINUED
BOO-HOO! MY HANSY UND FRITZIE! VARE ISS DEY?--- HURRY UP UND FIND DEM OR IT GIFS AN-NUDDER SOCK MIT DER ROLLER! BOO-HOO!
VELL? DUM-BUST DER LUCK! AIN'T VE TRYING?
COULDN'T YOU STOP BLUBBERING?
GOLLY! VOT A FLOCK UF ISLANDS!
MR. HADDIE, VE GOT TO FIND A BETTER ISLAND!
DEM GAZABOES AIN'T SO FRIENDLY!
MATES, YOU SAID IT!
IF VE ONLY HAD SOME GAS TO FILL UP OUR BAL-LOON AGAIN!
VHY YOU DON'T TALK INTO IT?
HERE'S ANOTHER ISLAND! I HOPES WE HAS BETTER LUCK ON THIS ONE!
NOW IF WE KIN FIND SOME WATER AN' GRUB, ALL'S SWELL!
MAYBE VE COULD FIND A HOT DOG UND LEMONADE STAND?
R-R-ROWR!
GOLLY! DOT FELLER AIN'T SO FRIENDLY, TOO!
R-R-ROWR!
LOOKIN' FER LUNCH, ARE YE? WELL, WE HATES TO DISAPPOINT YE!
WHAPP!
OWR!
11-3
HOWZAT FER SLAPPIN' DOWN LIONS, MATES?
MR. FINNAN HADDIE, VE GOT TO ADMIT IT! YOU ISS A SMART MAN!
TO BE CONTINUED

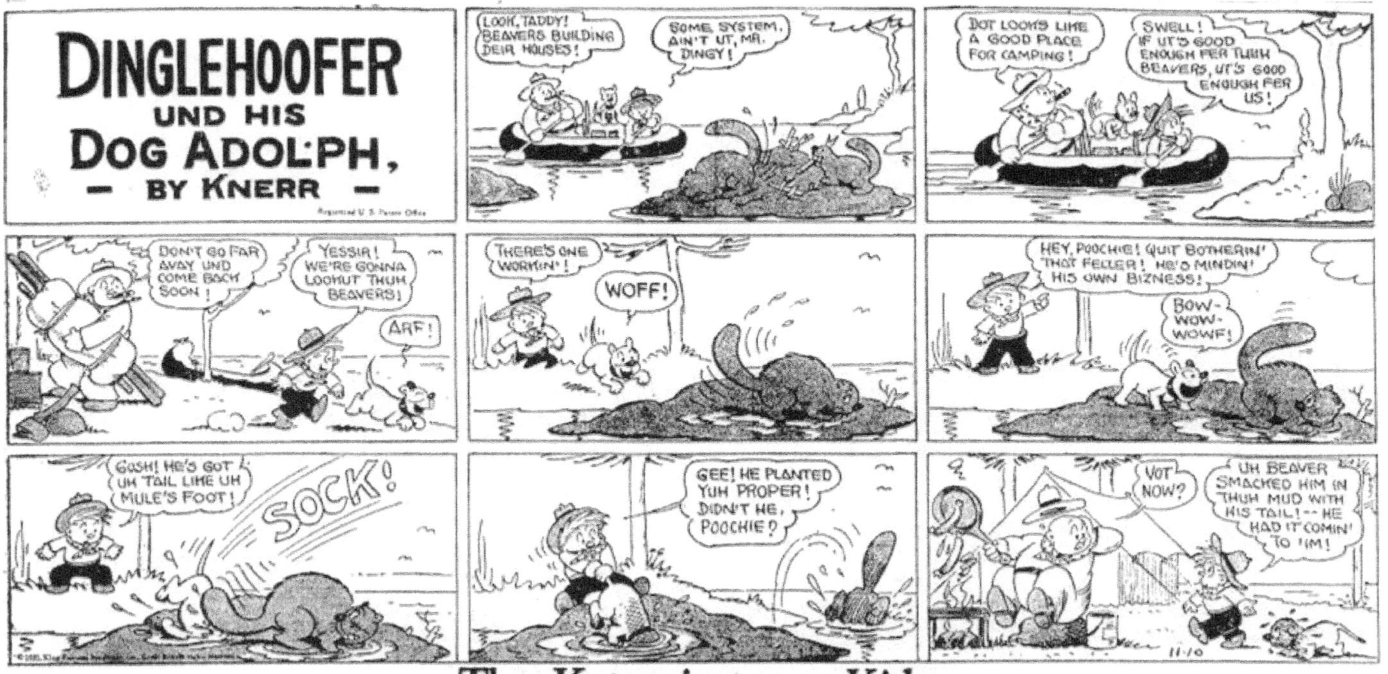
DINGLEHOOFER UND HIS DOG ADOLPH,
— BY KNERR —
LOOK, TADDY! BEAVERS BUILDING DEIR HOUSES!
SOME SYSTEM, AIN'T UT, MR. DINGY!
DOT LOOKS LIKE A GOOD PLACE FOR CAMPING!
SWELL! IF UT'S GOOD ENOUGH FER THUH BEAVERS, UT'S GOOD ENOUGH FER US!
DON'T GO FAR AVAY UND COME BACK SOON!
YESSIR! WE'RE GONNA LOOKUT THUH BEAVERS!
ARF!
THERE'S ONE WORKIN'!
WOFF!
HEY, POOCHIE! QUIT BOTHERIN' THAT FELLER! HE'S MINDIN' HIS OWN BIZNESS!
BOW-WOW-WOWF!
GOSH! HE'S GOT UH TAIL LIKE UH MULE'S FOOT!
SOCK!
GEE! HE PLANTED YUH PROPER! DIDN'T HE, POOCHIE?
VOT NOW?
UH BEAVER SMACKED HIM IN THUH MUD WITH HIS TAIL! -- HE HAD IT COMIN' TO 'IM!
11-10

The Katzenjammer Kids

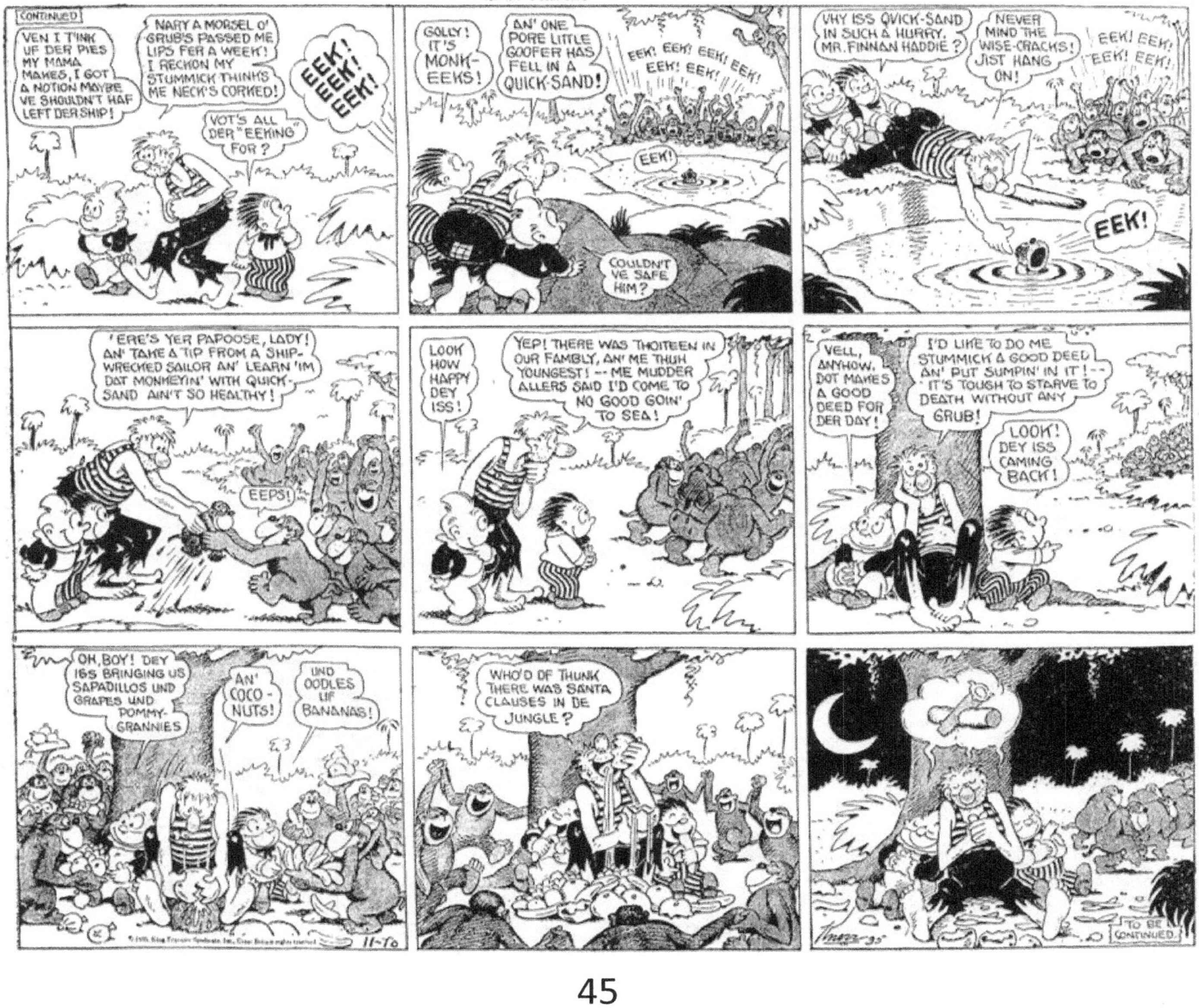
CONTINUED
VEN I T'INK UF DER PIES MY MAMA MAKES, I GOT A NOTION MAYBE VE SHOULDN'T HAF LEFT DER SHIP!
NARY A MORSEL O' GRUB'S PASSED ME LIPS FER A WEEK! I RECKON MY STUMMICK THINKS ME NECK'S CORKED!
EEK! EEK! EEK!
VOT'S ALL DER "EEKING" FOR?
GOLLY! IT'S MONK-EEKS!
AN' ONE PORE LITTLE GOOFER HAS FELL IN A QUICK-SAND!
EEK! EEK! EEK! EEK! EEK! EEK! EEK!
EEK!
COULDN'T VE SAFE HIM?
VHY ISS QVICK-SAND IN SUCH A HURRY, MR. FINNAN HADDIE?
NEVER MIND THE WISE-CRACKS! JUST HANG ON!
EEK! EEK! EEK! EEK!
EEK!
'ERE'S YER PAPOOSE, LADY! AN' TAKE A TIP FROM A SHIP-WRECKED SAILOR AN' LEARN 'IM DAT MONKEYIN' WITH QUICK-SAND AIN'T SO HEALTHY!
EEPS!
LOOK HOW HAPPY DEY ISS!
YEP! THERE WAS THOITEEN IN OUR FAMBLY, AN' ME THUH YOUNGEST! -- ME MUDDER ALLERS SAID I'D COME TO NO GOOD GOIN' TO SEA!
VELL, ANYHOW, DOT MAKES A GOOD DEED FOR DER DAY!
I'D LIKE TO DO ME STUMMICK A GOOD DEED AN' PUT SUMPIN' IN IT! -- IT'S TOUGH TO STARVE TO DEATH WITHOUT ANY GRUB!
LOOK! DEY ISS CAMING BACK!
OH, BOY! DEY ISS BRINGING US SAPADILLOS UND GRAPES UND POMMY-GRANNIES
AN' COCO-NUTS!
UND OODLES UF BANANAS!
11-10
WHO'D OF THUNK THERE WAS SANTA CLAUSES IN DE JUNGLE?
TO BE CONTINUED.

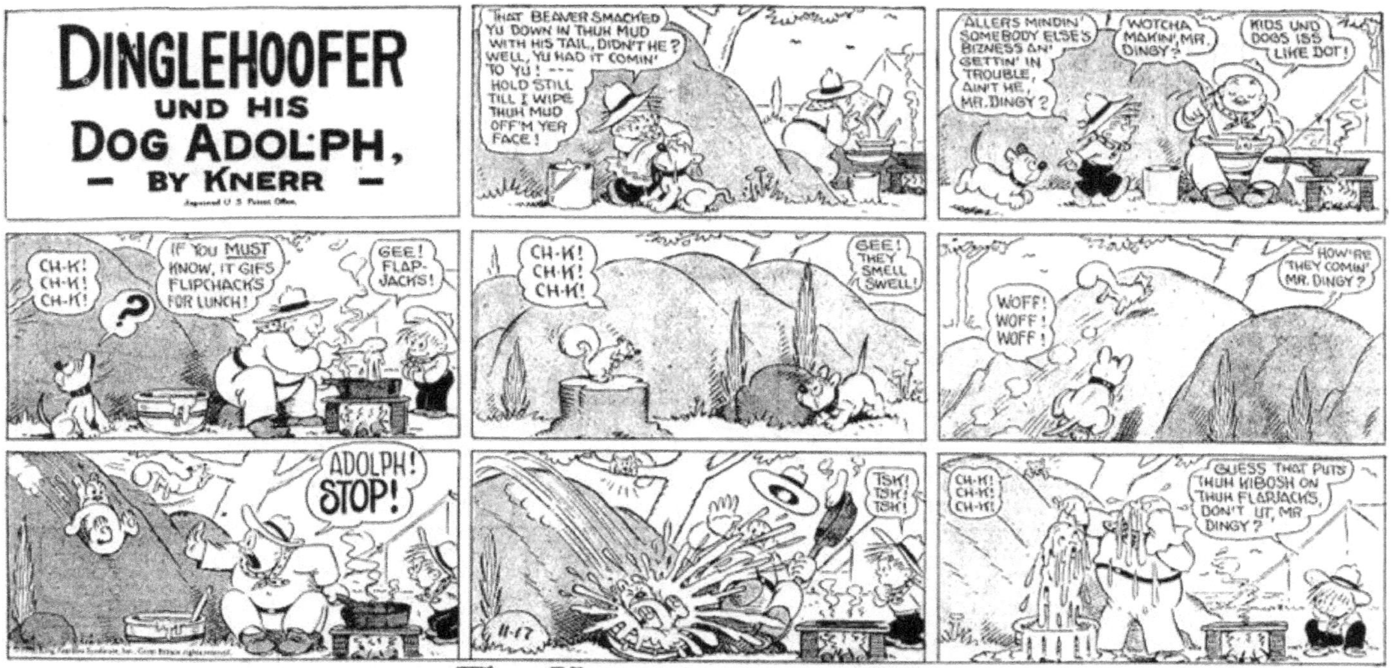
DINGLEHOOFER UND HIS DOG ADOLPH,
— BY KNERR —
THAT BEAVER SMACKED YU DOWN IN THUH MUD WITH HIS TAIL, DIDN'T HE? WELL, YU HAD IT COMIN' TO YU! --- HOLD STILL TILL I WIPE THUH MUD OFF'M YER FACE!
ALLERS MINDIN' SOMEBODY ELSE'S BIZNESS AN' GETTIN' IN TROUBLE, AIN'T HE, MR. DINGY?
WOTCHA MAKIN', MR. DINGY?
KIDS UND DOGS ISS LIKE DOT!
CH-K! CH-K! CH-K!
?
IF YOU MUST KNOW, IT GIFS FLIPCHACKS FOR LUNCH!
GEE! FLAP-JACKS!
CH-K! CH-K! CH-K!
GEE! THEY SMELL SWELL!
WOFF! WOFF! WOFF!
HOW'RE THEY COMIN' MR. DINGY?
ADOLPH! STOP!
TSK! TSK! TSK!
11-17
CH-K! CH-K! CH-K!
GUESS THAT PUTS THUH KIBOSH ON THUH FLAPJACKS, DON'T IT, MR. DINGY?

The Katzenjammer Kids

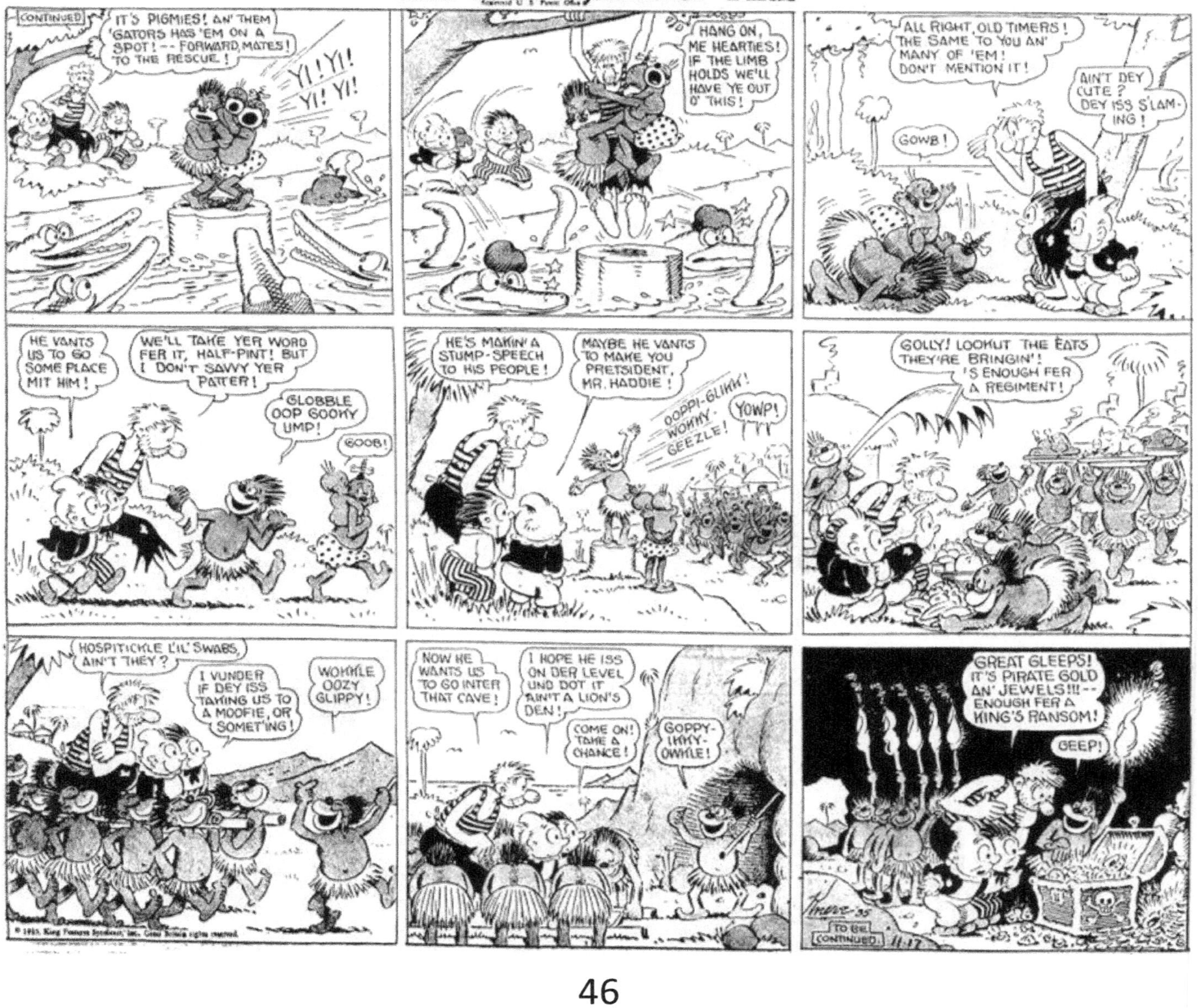
CONTINUED
IT'S PIGMIES! AN' THEM 'GATORS HAS 'EM ON A SPOT! -- FORWARD, MATES! TO THE RESCUE!
YI! YI! YI! YI!
HANG ON, ME HEARTIES! IF THE LIMB HOLDS WE'LL HAVE YE OUT O' THIS!
ALL RIGHT, OLD TIMERS! THE SAME TO YOU AN' MANY OF 'EM! DON'T MENTION IT!
GOWB!
AIN'T DEY CUTE? DEY ISS S'LAM-ING!
HE VANTS US TO GO SOME PLACE MIT HIM!
WE'LL TAKE YER WORD FER IT, HALF-PINT! BUT I DON'T SAVVY YER PATTER!
GLOBBLE OOP GOOKY UMP!
GOOB!
HE'S MAKIN' A STUMP-SPEECH TO HIS PEOPLE!
MAYBE HE VANTS TO MAKE YOU PRETSIDENT, MR. HADDIE!
OOPPI-GLIKK! WOKKY GEEZLE!
YOWP!
GOLLY! LOOKUT THE EATS THEY'RE BRINGIN'!
'S ENOUGH FER A REGIMENT!
HOSPITICKLE LI'L SWABS, AIN'T THEY?
I VUNDER IF DEY ISS TAKING US TO A MOOFIE, OR SOMET'ING!
WOKKLE OOZY GLIPPY!
NOW HE WANTS US TO GO INTER THAT CAVE!
I HOPE HE ISS ON DER LEVEL UND DOT IT AIN'T A LION'S DEN!
COME ON! TAKE A CHANCE!
GOPPY-IKKY-OWKLE!
GREAT GLEEPS! IT'S PIRATE GOLD AN' JEWELS!!! -- ENOUGH FER A KING'S RANSOM!
GEEP!
TO BE CONTINUED.
11-17

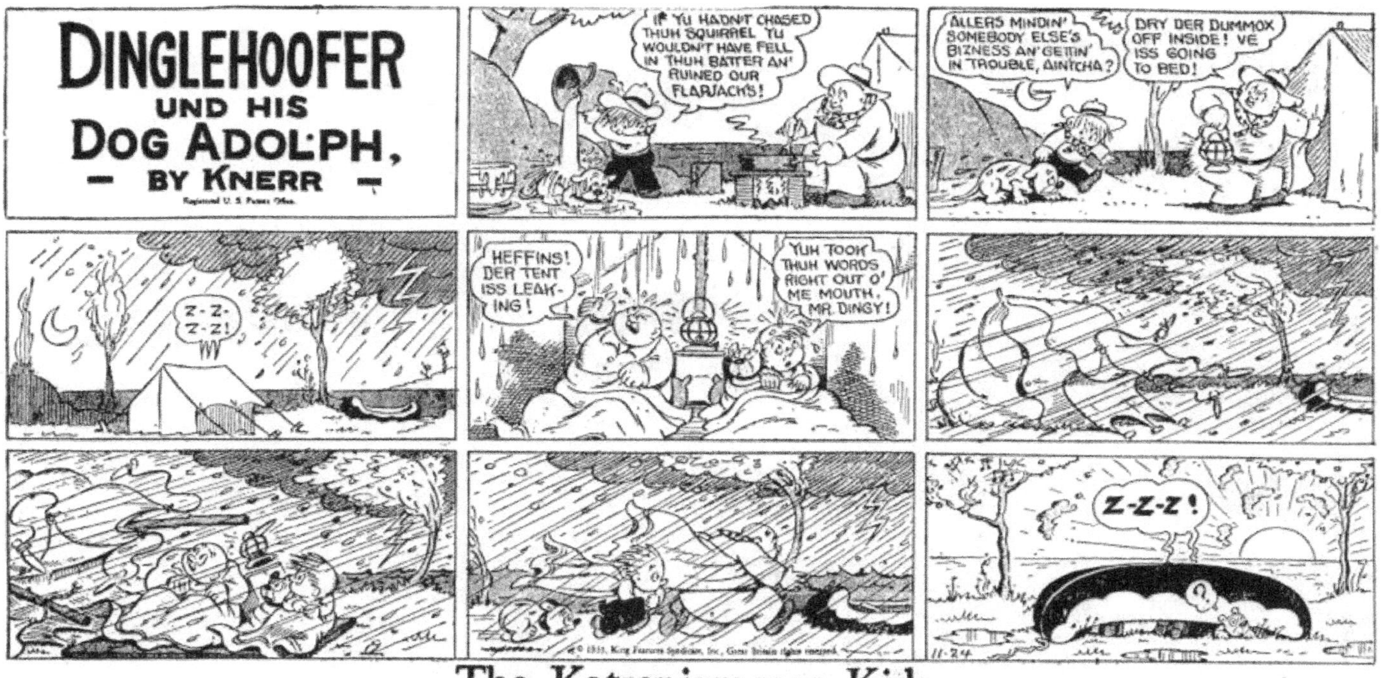
DINGLEHOOFER UND HIS DOG ADOLPH,
BY KNERR
IF YU HADN'T CHASED THUH SQUIRREL TU WOULDN'T HAVE FELL IN THUH BATTER AN' RUINED OUR FLAPJACKS!
ALLERS MINDIN' SOMEBODY ELSE'S BIZNESS AN' GETTIN' IN TROUBLE, AINTCHA?
DRY DER DUMMOX OFF INSIDE! VE ISS GOING TO BED!
Z-Z-Z-Z!
HEFFINS! DER TENT ISS LEAKING!
YUH TOOK THUH WORDS RIGHT OUT O' ME MOUTH, MR. DINGY!
Z-Z-Z!
11-24

The Katzenjammer Kids

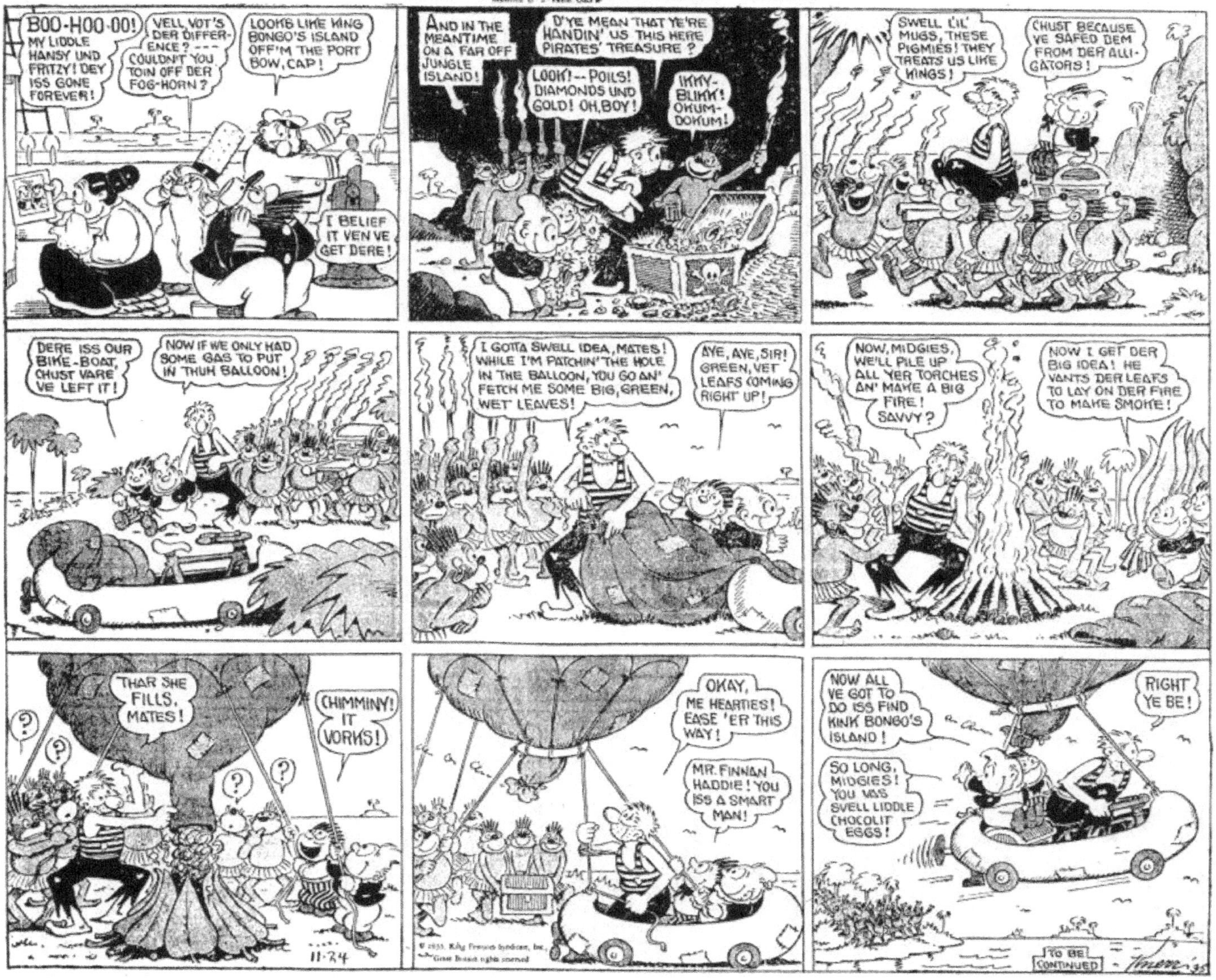
BOO-HOO-OO! MY LIDDLE HANSY UND FRITZY! DEY ISS GONE FOREVER!
VELL, VOT'S DER DIFFERENCE? --- COULDN'T YOU TOIN OFF DER FOG-HORN?
LOOKS LIKE KING BONGO'S ISLAND OFF'M THE PORT BOW, CAP!
I BELIEF IT VEN VE GET DERE!
AND IN THE MEANTIME ON A FAR OFF JUNGLE ISLAND!
D'YE MEAN THAT YE'RE HANDIN' US THIS HERE PIRATES' TREASURE?
LOOK! -- POILS! DIAMONDS UND GOLD! OH, BOY!
IKKY-BLIKK! OKUM-DOKUM!
SWELL LIL' MUGS, THESE PIGMIES! THEY TREATS US LIKE KINGS!
CHUST BECAUSE VE SAFED DEM FROM DER ALLIGATORS!
DERE ISS OUR BIKE-BOAT, CHUST VARE VE LEFT IT!
NOW IF WE ONLY HAD SOME GAS TO PUT IN THUH BALLOON!
I GOTTA SWELL IDEA, MATES! WHILE I'M PATCHIN' THE HOLE IN THE BALLOON, YOU GO AN' FETCH ME SOME BIG, GREEN, WET LEAVES!
AYE, AYE, SIR! GREEN, VET LEAFS COMING RIGHT UP!
NOW, MIDGIES, WE'LL PILE UP ALL YER TORCHES AN' MAKE A BIG FIRE! SAVVY?
NOW I GET DER BIG IDEA! HE VANTS DER LEAFS TO LAY ON DER FIRE TO MAKE SMOKE!
THAR SHE FILLS, MATES!
CHIMMINY! IT VORKS!
?
11-24
OKAY, ME HEARTIES! EASE 'ER THIS WAY!
MR. FINNAN HADDIE! YOU ISS A SMART MAN!
NOW ALL VE GOT TO DO ISS FIND KINK BONGO'S ISLAND!
RIGHT YE BE!
SO LONG, MIDGIES! YOU VAS SVELL LIDDLE CHOCOLIT EGGS!
TO BE CONTINUED

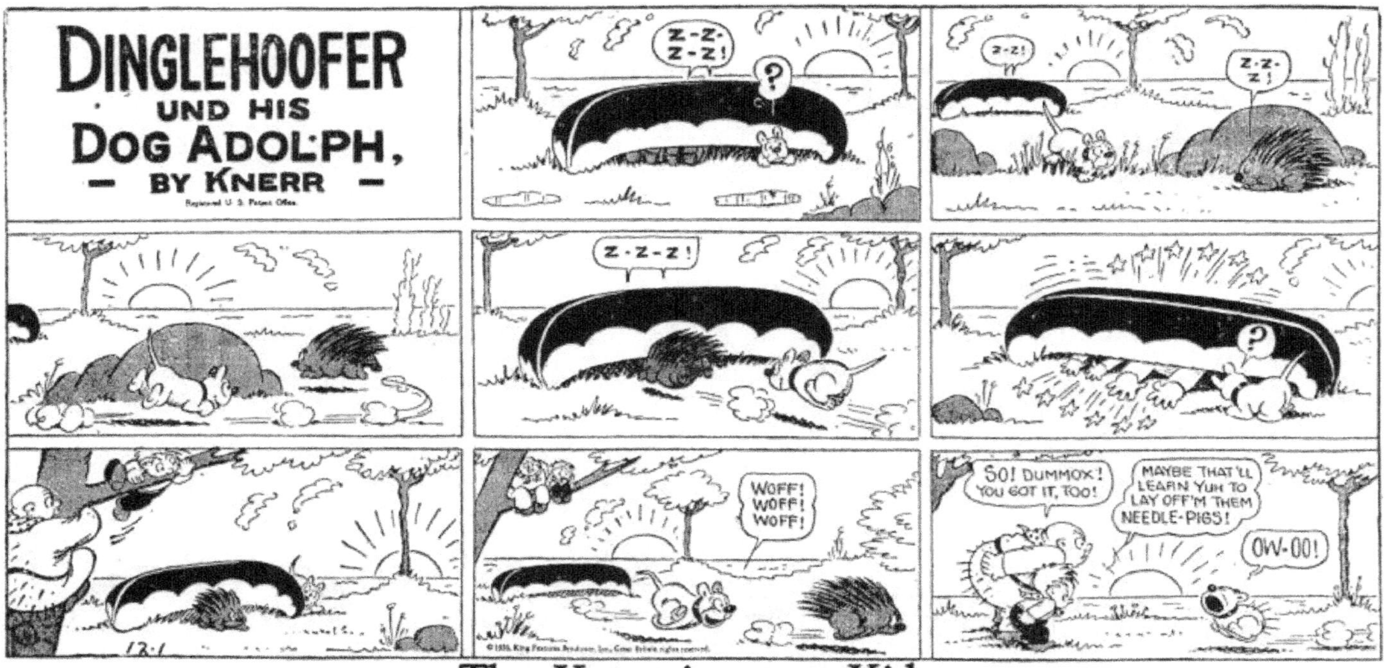
DINGLEHOOFER UND HIS DOG ADOLPH, BY KNERR
Z-Z-Z-Z!
?
Z-Z!
Z-Z-Z!
Z-Z-Z!
?
WOFF! WOFF! WOFF!
SO! DUMMOX! YOU GOT IT, TOO!
MAYBE THAT'LL LEARN YUH TO LAY OFF'M THEM NEEDLE-PIGS!
OW-OO!

The Katzenjammer Kids

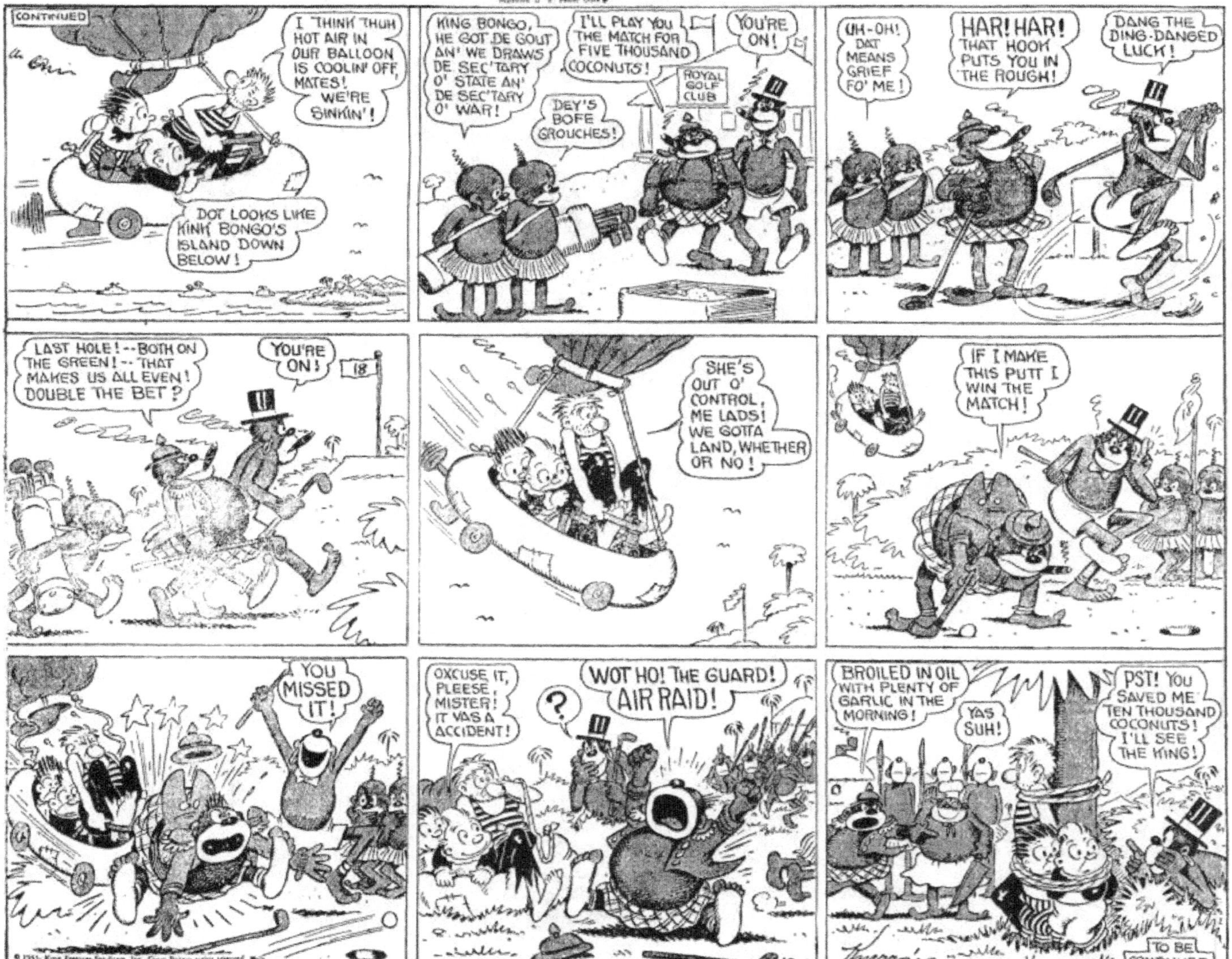
CONTINUED
I THINK THUH HOT AIR IN OUR BALLOON IS COOLIN' OFF, MATES! WE'RE SINKIN'!
DOT LOOKS LIKE KINK BONGO'S ISLAND DOWN BELOW!
KING BONGO, HE GOT DE GOUT AN' WE DRAWS DE SEC'TARY O' STATE AN' DE SEC'TARY O' WAR!
I'LL PLAY YOU THE MATCH FOR FIVE THOUSAND COCONUTS!
YOU'RE ON!
DEY'S BOFE GROUCHES!
ROYAL GOLF CLUB
UH-OH! DAT MEANS GRIEF FO' ME!
HAR! HAR! THAT HOOK PUTS YOU IN THE ROUGH!
DANG THE DING-DANGED LUCK!
LAST HOLE! -- BOTH ON THE GREEN! -- THAT MAKES US ALL EVEN! DOUBLE THE BET?
YOU'RE ON!
18
SHE'S OUT O' CONTROL, ME LADS! WE GOTTA LAND, WHETHER OR NO!
IF I MAKE THIS PUTT I WIN THE MATCH!
YOU MISSED IT!
OXCUSE IT, PLEESE, MISTER! IT VAS A ACCIDENT!
?
WOT HO! THE GUARD! AIR RAID!
BROILED IN OIL WITH PLENTY OF GARLIC IN THE MORNING!
YAS SUH!
PST! YOU SAVED ME TEN THOUSAND COCONUTS! I'LL SEE THE KING!
TO BE CONTINUED

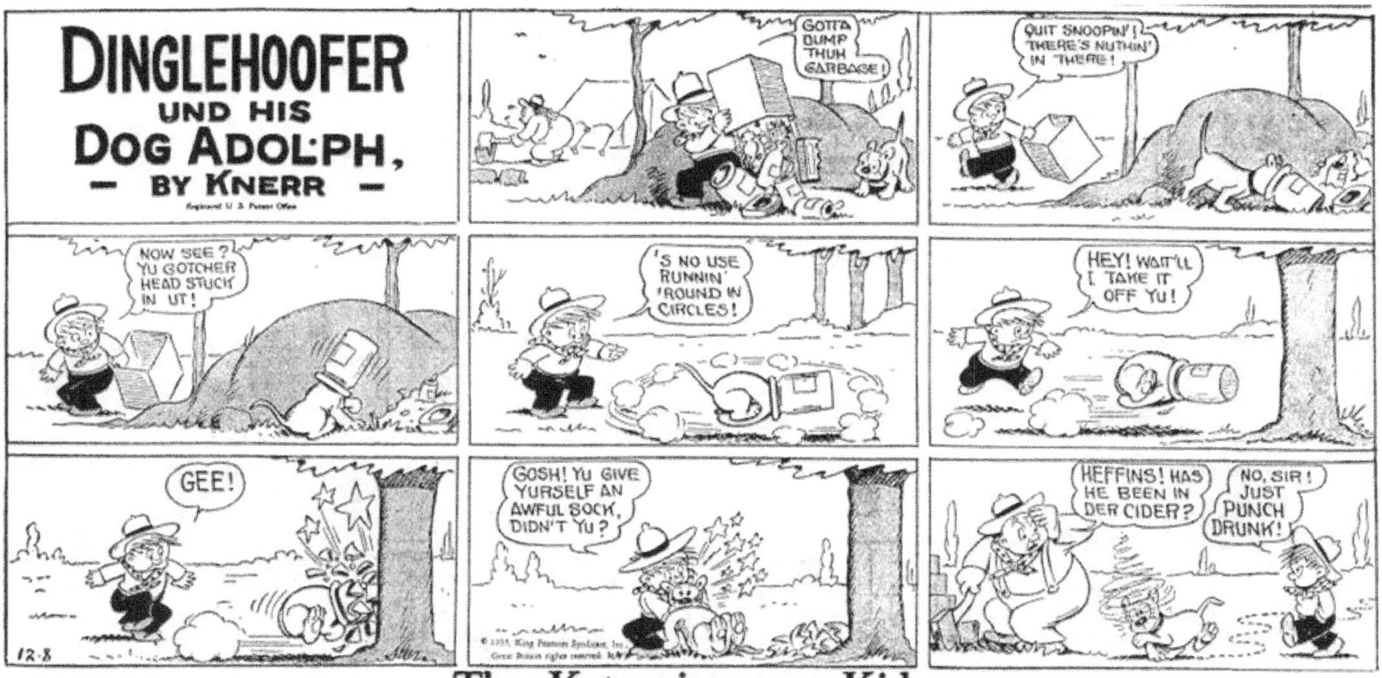
DINGLEHOOFER UND HIS DOG ADOLPH, — BY KNERR —
GOTTA DUMP THUH GARBAGE!
QUIT SNOOPIN'! THERE'S NUTHIN' IN THERE!
NOW SEE? YU GOTCHER HEAD STUCK IN UT!
'S NO USE RUNNIN' 'ROUND IN CIRCLES!
HEY! WAIT'LL I TAKE IT OFF YU!
GEE!
GOSH! YU GIVE YURSELF AN AWFUL SOCK, DIDN'T YU?
HEFFINS! HAS HE BEEN IN DER CIDER?
NO, SIR! JUST PUNCH DRUNK!

The Katzenjammer Kids

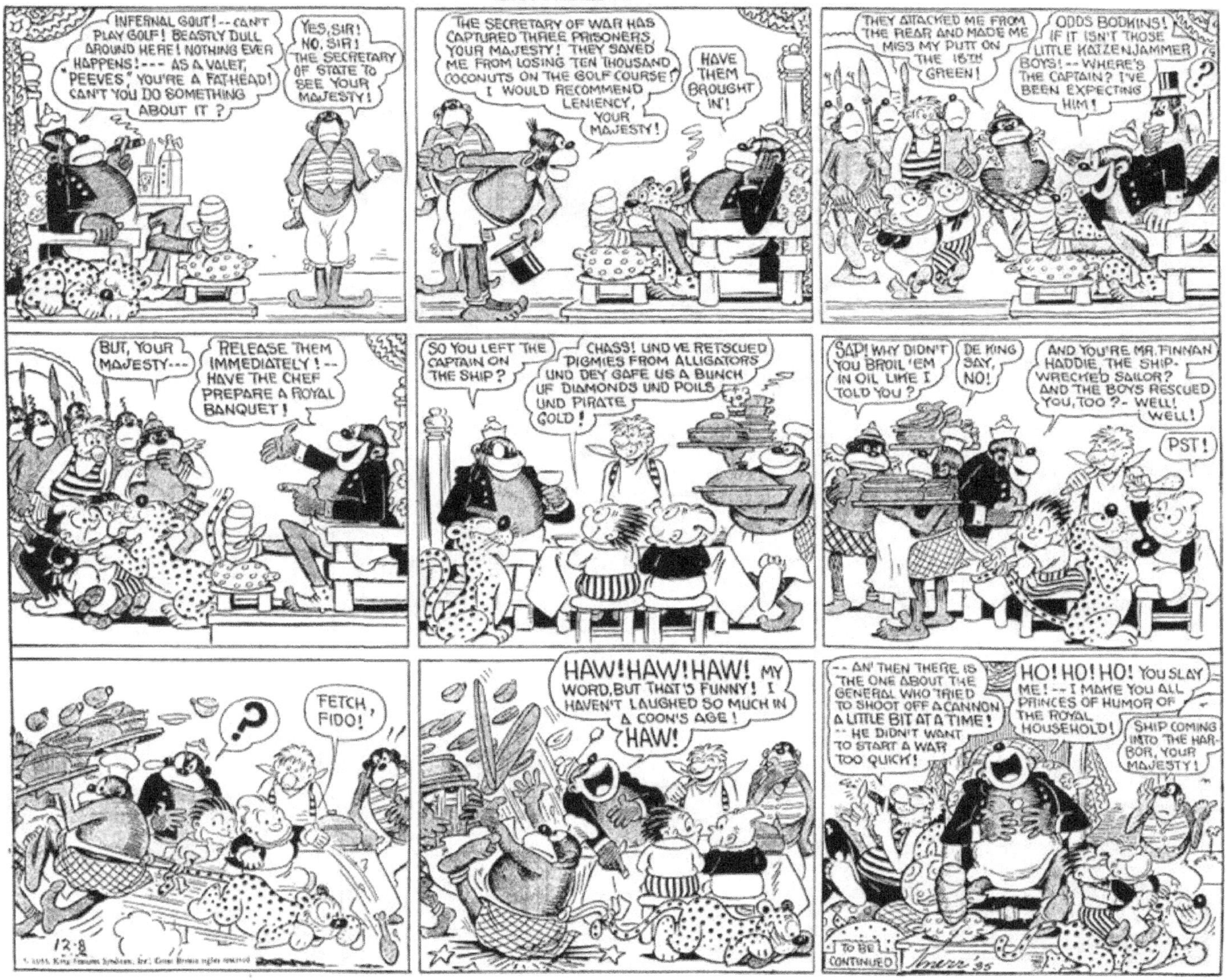
INFERNAL GOUT!--CAN'T PLAY GOLF! BEASTLY DULL AROUND HERE! NOTHING EVER HAPPENS!--- AS A VALET, "PEEVES," YOU'RE A FATHEAD! CAN'T YOU DO SOMETHING ABOUT IT?
YES, SIR! NO, SIR! THE SECRETARY OF STATE TO SEE YOUR MAJESTY!
THE SECRETARY OF WAR HAS CAPTURED THREE PRISONERS, YOUR MAJESTY! THEY SAVED ME FROM LOSING TEN THOUSAND COCONUTS ON THE GOLF COURSE! I WOULD RECOMMEND LENIENCY, YOUR MAJESTY!
HAVE THEM BROUGHT IN'!
THEY ATTACKED ME FROM THE REAR AND MADE ME MISS MY PUTT ON THE 15TH GREEN!
ODDS BODKINS! IF IT ISN'T THOSE LITTLE KATZENJAMMER BOYS!--WHERE'S THE CAPTAIN? I'VE BEEN EXPECTING HIM!
?
BUT, YOUR MAJESTY---
RELEASE THEM IMMEDIATELY!-- HAVE THE CHEF PREPARE A ROYAL BANQUET!
SO YOU LEFT THE CAPTAIN ON THE SHIP?
CHASS! UND VE RETSCUED PIGMIES FROM ALLIGATORS UND DEY GAFE US A BUNCH UF DIAMONDS UND POILS UND PIRATE GOLD!
SAP! WHY DIDN'T YOU BROIL 'EM IN OIL LIKE I TOLD YOU?
DE KING SAY, NO!
AND YOU'RE MR. FINNAN HADDIE, THE SHIP-WRECKED SAILOR? AND THE BOYS RESCUED YOU, TOO?- WELL! WELL!
PST!
?
FETCH, FIDO!
HAW! HAW! HAW! MY WORD, BUT THAT'S FUNNY! I HAVEN'T LAUGHED SO MUCH IN A COON'S AGE!
HAW!
--AN' THEN THERE IS THE ONE ABOUT THE GENERAL WHO TRIED TO SHOOT OFF A CANNON A LITTLE BIT AT A TIME! --HE DIDN'T WANT TO START A WAR TOO QUICK!
HO! HO! HO! YOU SLAY ME!--I MAKE YOU ALL PRINCES OF HUMOR OF THE ROYAL HOUSEHOLD!
SHIP COMING INTO THE HARBOR, YOUR MAJESTY!
TO BE CONTINUED

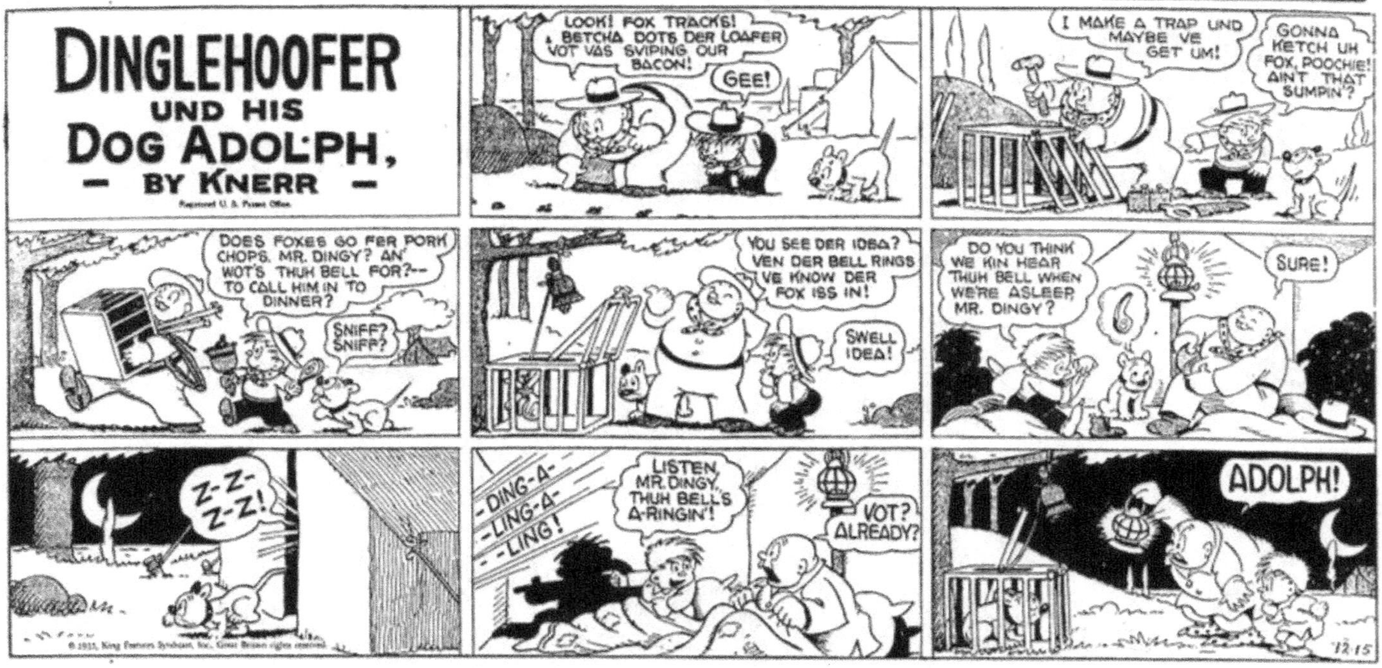
DINGLEHOOFER UND HIS DOG ADOLPH, — BY KNERR —
LOOK! FOX TRACKS! BETCHA DOTS DER LOAFER VOT VAS SVIPING OUR BACON!
GEE!
I MAKE A TRAP UND MAYBE VE GET UM!
GONNA KETCH UH FOX, POOCHIE! AIN'T THAT SUMPIN'?
DOES FOXES GO FER PORK CHOPS, MR. DINGY? AN' WOT'S THUH BELL FOR?-- TO CALL HIM IN TO DINNER?
SNIFF? SNIFF?
YOU SEE DER IDEA? VEN DER BELL RINGS VE KNOW DER FOX ISS IN!
SWELL IDEA!
DO YOU THINK WE KIN HEAR THUH BELL WHEN WE'RE ASLEEP, MR. DINGY?
SURE!
Z-Z-Z-Z!
-DING-A- -LING-A- -LING!
LISTEN, MR. DINGY, THUH BELL'S A-RINGIN'!
VOT? ALREADY?
ADOLPH!

The Katzenjammer Kids

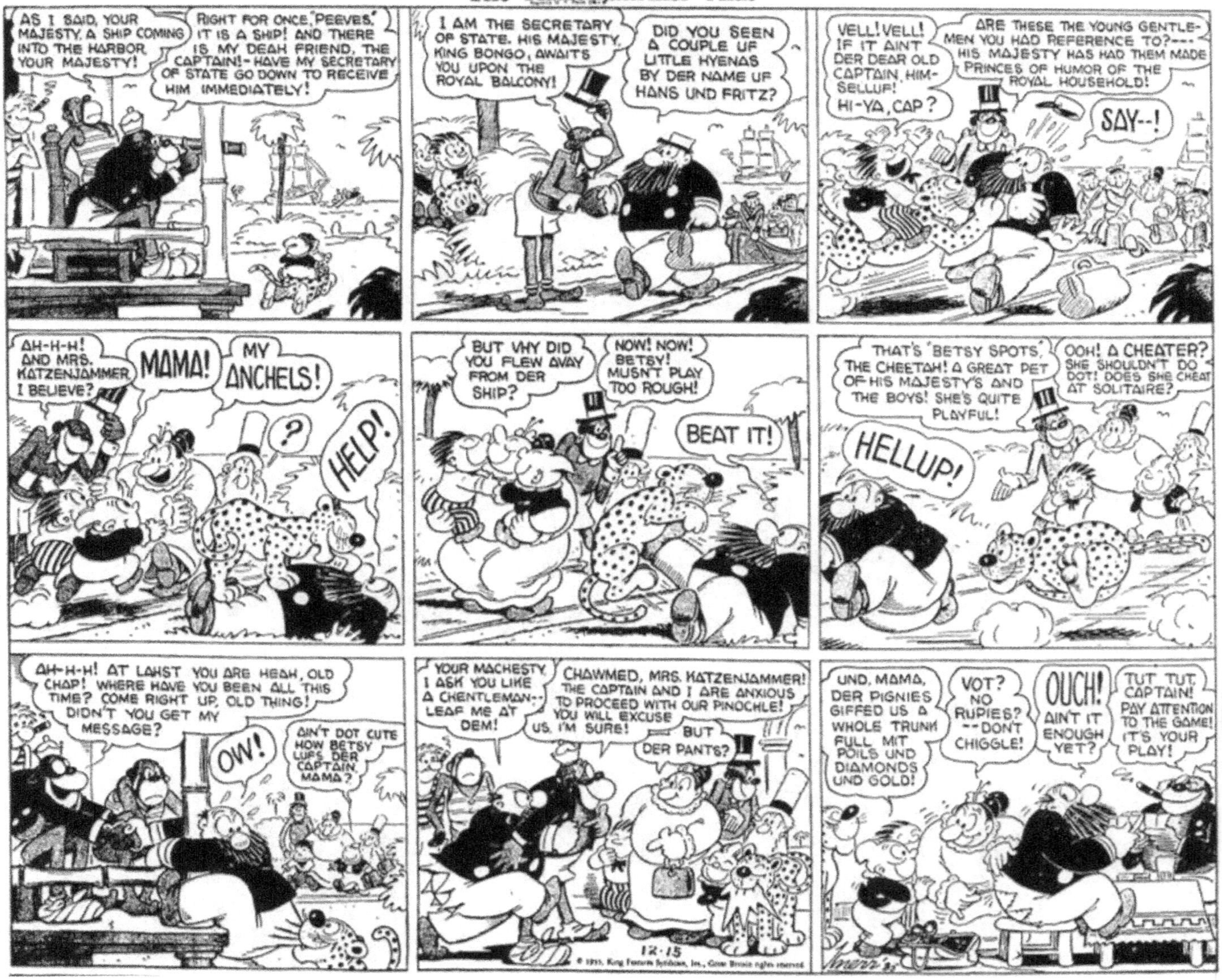
AS I SAID, YOUR MAJESTY, A SHIP COMING INTO THE HARBOR, YOUR MAJESTY!
RIGHT FOR ONCE, "PEEVES." IT IS A SHIP! AND THERE IS MY DEAH FRIEND, THE CAPTAIN!—HAVE MY SECRETARY OF STATE GO DOWN TO RECEIVE HIM IMMEDIATELY!
I AM THE SECRETARY OF STATE. HIS MAJESTY, KING BONGO, AWAITS YOU UPON THE ROYAL BALCONY!
DID YOU SEEN A COUPLE UF LITTLE HYENAS BY DER NAME UF HANS UND FRITZ?
VELL! VELL! IF IT AINT DER DEAR OLD CAPTAIN, HIMSELLUF!
HI-YA, CAP?
ARE THESE THE YOUNG GENTLEMEN YOU HAD REFERENCE TO?--- HIS MAJESTY HAS HAD THEM MADE PRINCES OF HUMOR OF THE ROYAL HOUSEHOLD!
SAY--!
AH-H-H! AND MRS. KATZENJAMMER, I BELIEVE?
MAMA!
MY ANCHELS!
?
HELP!
BUT VHY DID YOU FLEW AVAY FROM DER SHIP?
NOW! NOW! BETSY! MUSN'T PLAY TOO ROUGH!
BEAT IT!
THAT'S "BETSY SPOTS," THE CHEETAH! A GREAT PET OF HIS MAJESTY'S AND THE BOYS! SHE'S QUITE PLAYFUL!
OOH! A CHEATER? SHE SHOULDN'T DO DOT! DOES SHE CHEAT AT SOLITAIRE?
HELLUP!
AH-H-H! AT LAHST YOU ARE HEAH, OLD CHAP! WHERE HAVE YOU BEEN ALL THIS TIME? COME RIGHT UP, OLD THING! DIDN'T YOU GET MY MESSAGE?
OW!
AIN'T DOT CUTE HOW BETSY LUFS DER CAPTAIN, MAMA?
YOUR MACHESTY, I ASK YOU LIKE A CHENTLEMAN-- LEAF ME AT DEM!
CHAWMED, MRS. KATZENJAMMER! THE CAPTAIN AND I ARE ANXIOUS TO PROCEED WITH OUR PINOCHLE! YOU WILL EXCUSE US, I'M SURE!
BUT DER PANTS?
UND, MAMA, DER PIGNIES GIFFED US A WHOLE TRUNK FULL MIT POILS UND DIAMONDS UND GOLD!
VOT? NO RUPIES? --DON'T CHIGGLE!
OUCH! AIN'T IT ENOUGH YET?
TUT TUT, CAPTAIN! PAY ATTENTION TO THE GAME! IT'S YOUR PLAY!

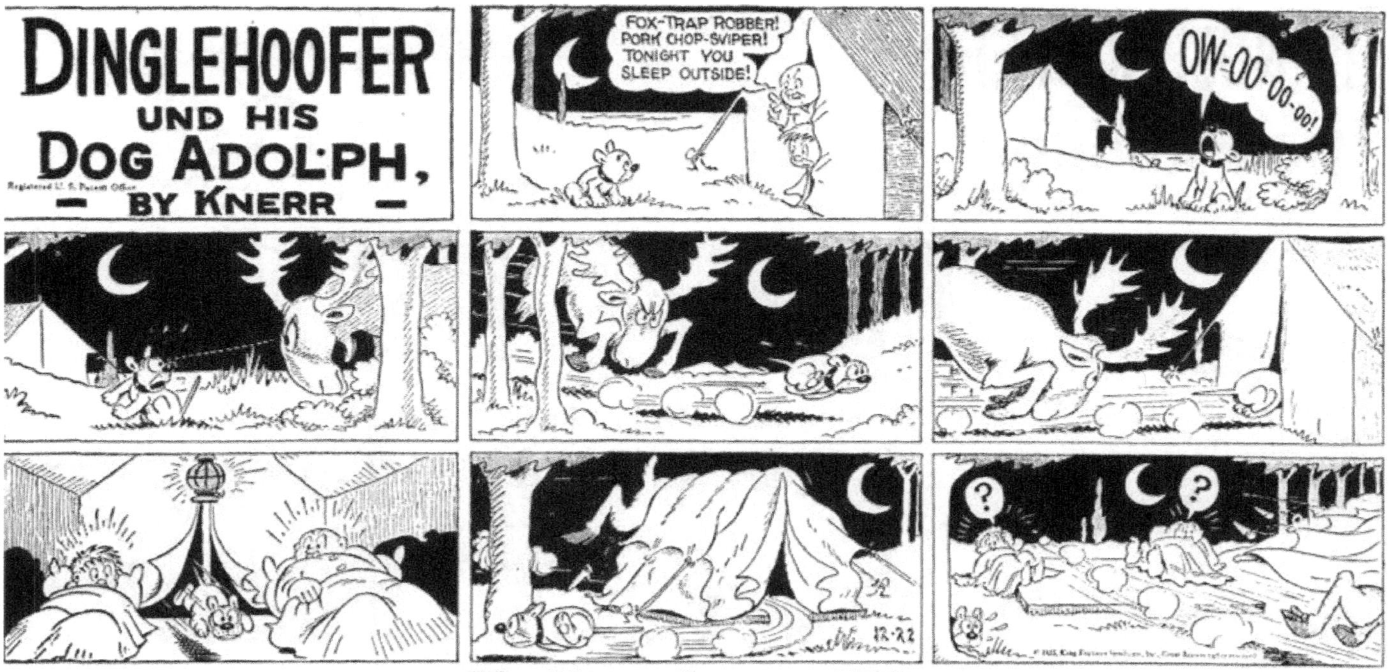
DINGLEHOOFER UND HIS DOG ADOLPH,
Registered U. S. Patent Office
— BY KNERR —
FOX-TRAP ROBBER! PORK CHOP-SVIPER! TONIGHT YOU SLEEP OUTSIDE!
OW-OO-OO-OO!
12-22

The Katzenjammer Kids

Registered U. S. Patent Office

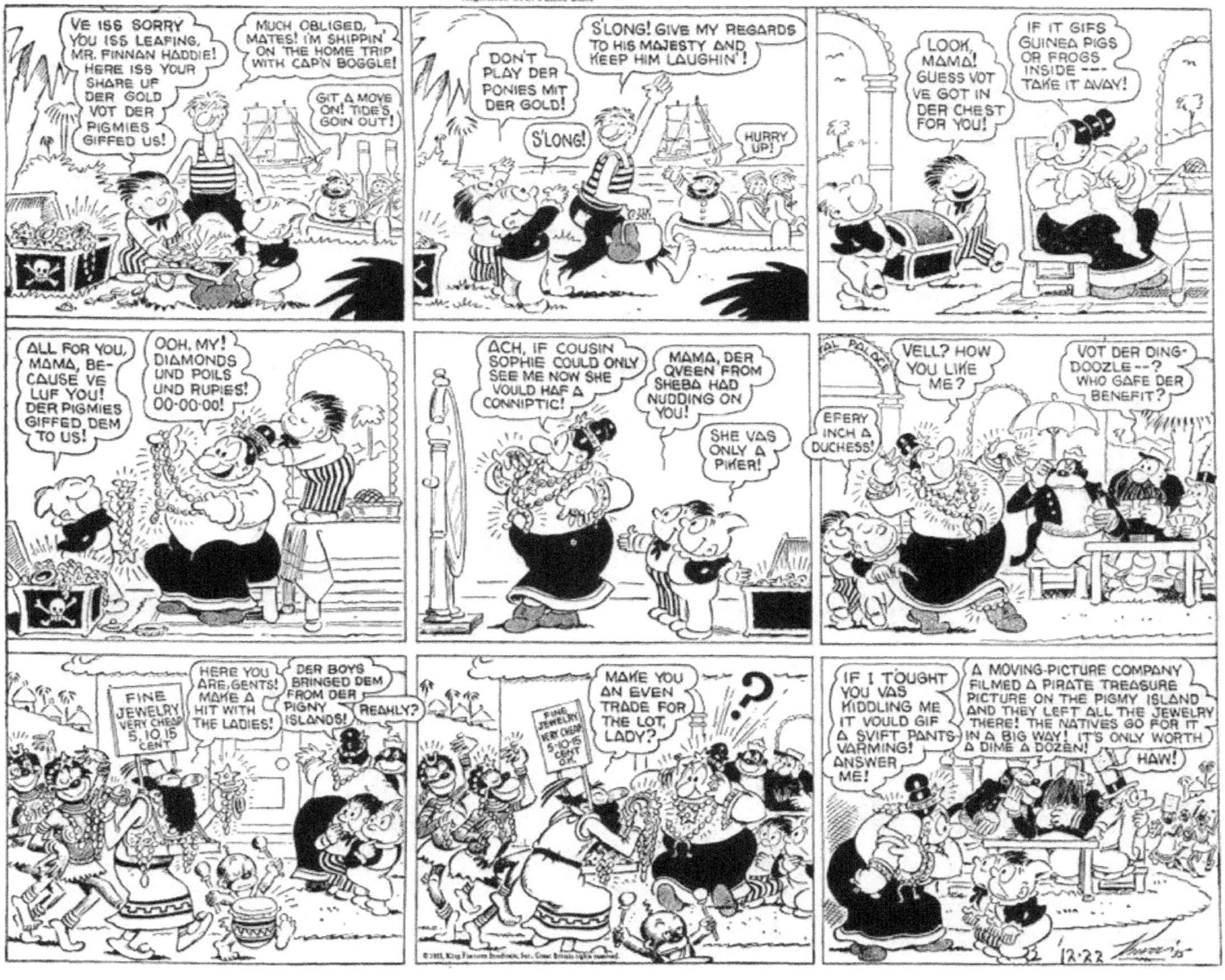
VE ISS SORRY YOU ISS LEAFING, MR. FINNAN HADDIE! HERE ISS YOUR SHARE UF DER GOLD VOT DER PIGMIES GIFFED US!
MUCH OBLIGED, MATES! I'M SHIPPIN' ON THE HOME TRIP WITH CAP'N BOGGLE!
GIT A MOVE ON! TIDE'S GOIN OUT!
S'LONG! GIVE MY REGARDS TO HIS MAJESTY AND KEEP HIM LAUGHIN'!
DON'T PLAY DER PONIES MIT DER GOLD!
S'LONG!
HURRY UP!
LOOK, MAMA! GUESS VOT VE GOT IN DER CHEST FOR YOU!
IF IT GIFS GUINEA PIGS OR FROGS INSIDE --- TAKE IT AVAY!
ALL FOR YOU, MAMA, BECAUSE VE LUF YOU! DER PIGMIES GIFFED DEM TO US!
OOH, MY! DIAMONDS UND POILS UND RUPIES! OO-OO-OO!
ACH, IF COUSIN SOPHIE COULD ONLY SEE ME NOW SHE VOULD HAF A CONNIPTIC!
MAMA, DER QVEEN FROM SHEBA HAD NUDDING ON YOU!
SHE VAS ONLY A PIKER!
ROYAL PALACE
VELL? HOW YOU LIKE ME?
VOT DER DING-DOODLE--? WHO GAFE DER BENEFIT?
EFERY INCH A DUCHESS!
FINE JEWELRY VERY CHEAP 5, 10, 15 CENT
HERE YOU ARE, GENTS! MAKE A HIT WITH THE LADIES!
DER BOYS BRINGED DEM FROM DER PIGNY ISLANDS!
REAHLY?
FINE JEWELRY VERY CHEAP 5-10-15 CENT
MAKE YOU AN EVEN TRADE FOR THE LOT, LADY?
?
IF I TOUGHT YOU VAS KIDDLING ME IT VOULD GIF A SVIFT PANTS-VARMING! ANSWER ME!
A MOVING-PICTURE COMPANY FILMED A PIRATE TREASURE PICTURE ON THE PIGMY ISLAND AND THEY LEFT ALL THE JEWELRY THERE! THE NATIVES GO FOR IT IN A BIG WAY! IT'S ONLY WORTH A DIME A DOZEN!
HAW!
12-22

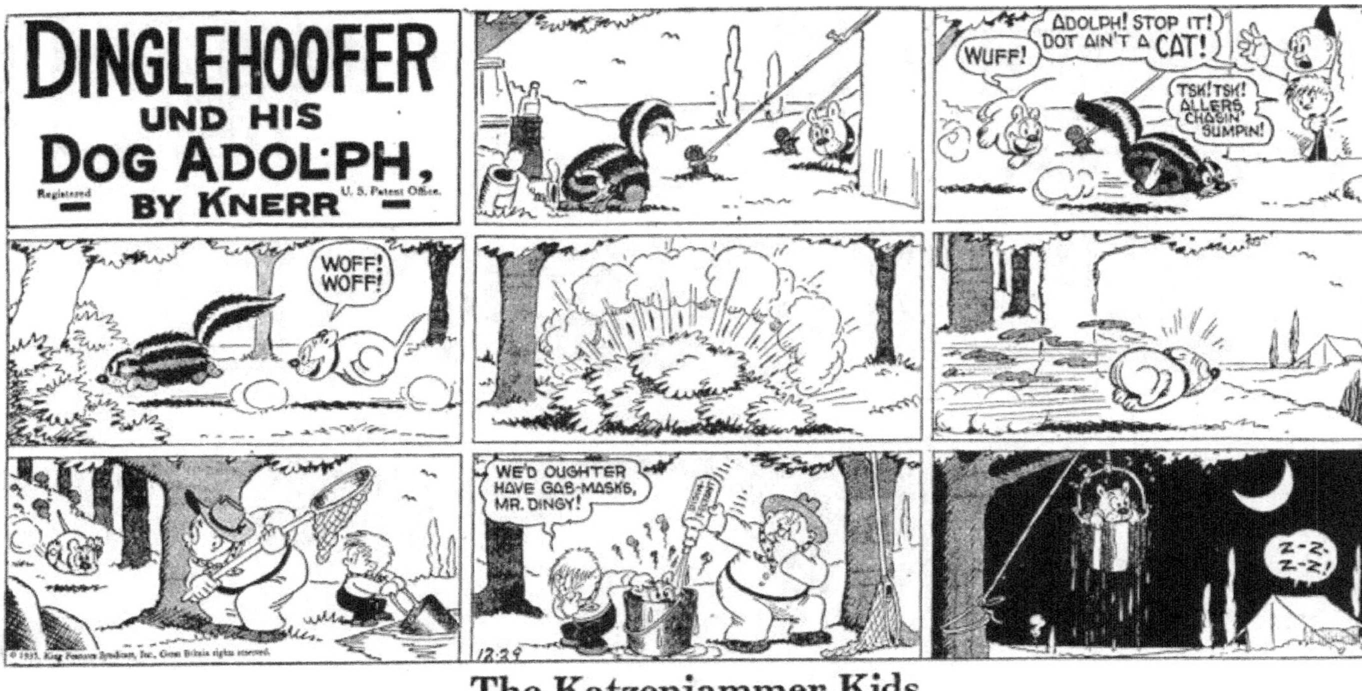
DINGLEHOOFER
UND HIS
DOG ADOLPH,
BY KNERR
Registered U. S. Patent Office.
WUFF!
ADOLPH! STOP IT! DOT AIN'T A CAT!
TSK! TSK! ALLERS CHASIN SUMPIN!
WOFF! WOFF!
WE'D OUGHTER HAVE GAS-MASKS, MR. DINGY!
Z-Z-Z-Z!
12-29

The Katzenjammer Kids

Registered U. S. Patent Office

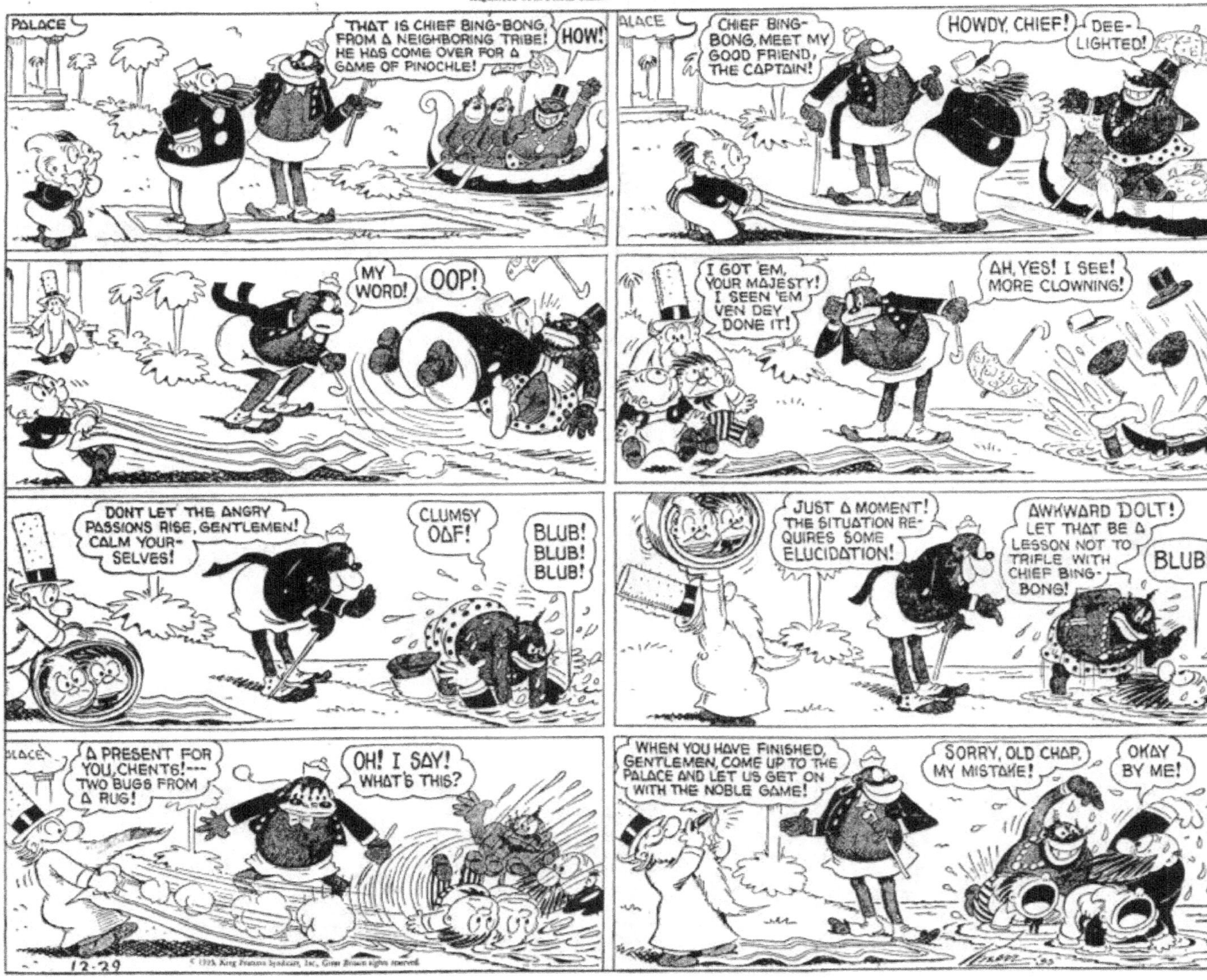
PALACE
THAT IS CHIEF BING-BONG, FROM A NEIGHBORING TRIBE! HE HAS COME OVER FOR A GAME OF PINOCHLE!
HOW!
PALACE
CHIEF BING-BONG, MEET MY GOOD FRIEND, THE CAPTAIN!
HOWDY, CHIEF!
DEE-LIGHTED!
MY WORD!
OOP!
I GOT 'EM, YOUR MAJESTY! I SEEN 'EM VEN DEY DONE IT!
AH, YES! I SEE! MORE CLOWNING!
DONT LET THE ANGRY PASSIONS RISE, GENTLEMEN! CALM YOURSELVES!
CLUMSY OAF!
BLUB! BLUB! BLUB!
JUST A MOMENT! THE SITUATION REQUIRES SOME ELUCIDATION!
AWKWARD DOLT! LET THAT BE A LESSON NOT TO TRIFLE WITH CHIEF BING-BONG!
BLUB!
PALACE
A PRESENT FOR YOU, CHENTS!--- TWO BUGS FROM A RUG!
OH! I SAY! WHAT'S THIS?
WHEN YOU HAVE FINISHED, GENTLEMEN, COME UP TO THE PALACE AND LET US GET ON WITH THE NOBLE GAME!
SORRY, OLD CHAP, MY MISTAKE!
OKAY BY ME!
12-29

PUBLISHER'S WORDS

ABOUT PUBLIC DOMAIN AND POLITICAL CORRECTNESS

The concept of public domain is not understood by a lot of people. Today when a book is created – or music, or art, or just about anything – the right to copy and sell it belongs to the person who created it. If you write a book tomorrow, those rights would belong to you, even if you don't take the time, money and effort to register it with the copyright office. Eventually that right would expire, though for most of us, we'd be long gone. Generations ago the copyright laws were more complicated and restrictive. The rights holder had to file certain papers at certain times, and place a notice is very specific ways in the publication or the book would become public domain. Public domain means that *everyone* owns the rights to it. Anyone can reproduce a book in the public domain, and sell or distribute it however he/she sees fit. Anything published before 1923 in in the public domain, and about 85% of everything from 1924-1963 are, too. It's difficult to know for sure, and finding out if a specific work is in public domain can be time-consuming and expensive, but to save you the trouble UP History and Hobby reprints many titles in the public domain, legally and properly. So enjoy!*

Comics reflect their times. Many of the ideas expressed in comics of the 40's and 50's contain racism, ethnocentrism, bigotry, sexism, and a whole list of other -isms that today people would find offensive and unacceptable. Part of the reason we leave these as they were is because they are a picture of the times, in many ways a historical document. It is a time that will never come again, so we should preserve what it was, even with its scars and wrinkles.

Kari Therrian - Publisher

* UP History and Hobby also publishes many books which are NOT in the public domain. Only those which specifically state they are public domain are copyright-free. The rest have all rights reserved.

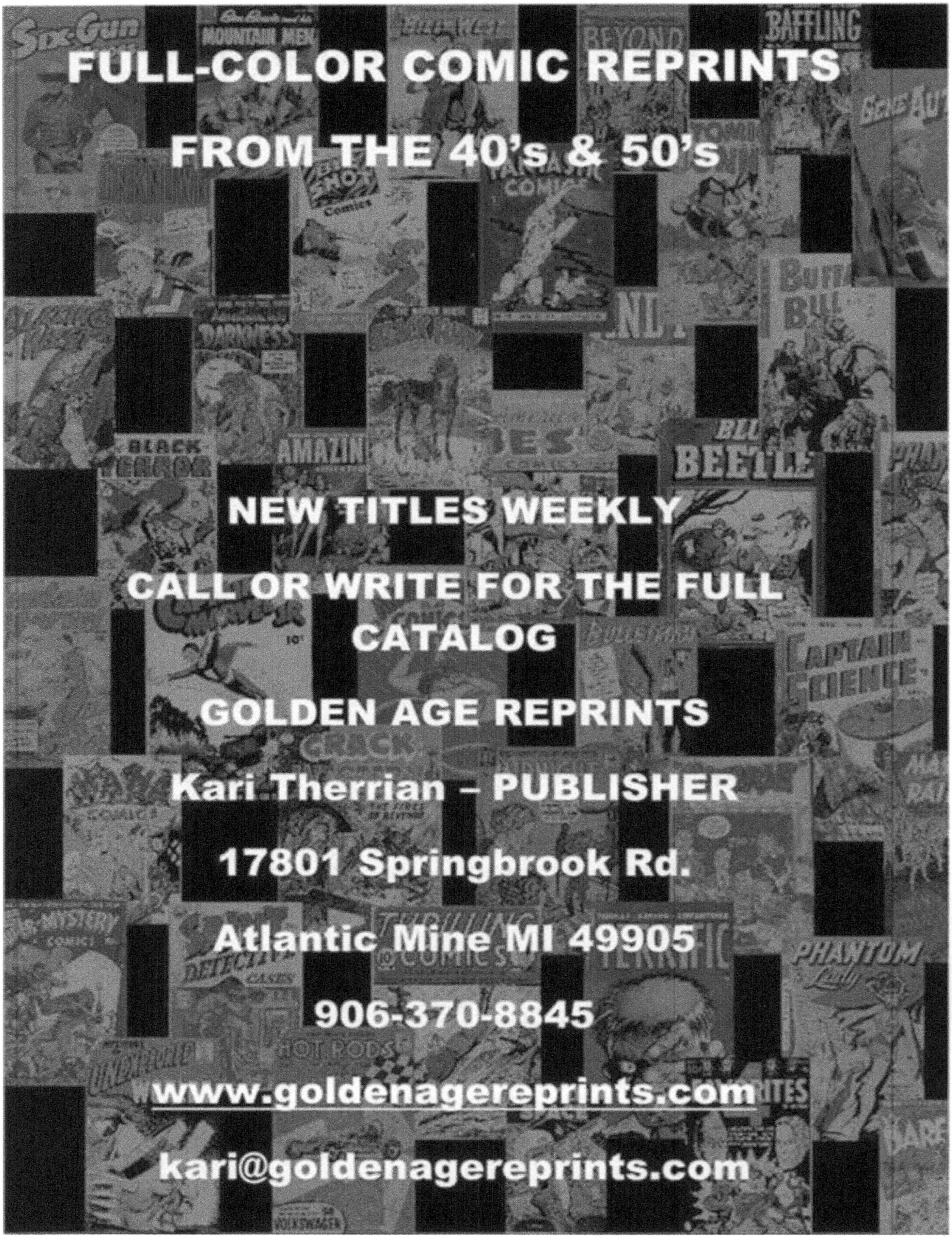
FULL-COLOR COMIC REPRINTS
FROM THE 40's & 50's
NEW TITLES WEEKLY
CALL OR WRITE FOR THE FULL CATALOG
GOLDEN AGE REPRINTS
Kari Therrian – PUBLISHER
17801 Springbrook Rd.
Atlantic Mine MI 49905
906-370-8845
www.goldenagereprints.com
kari@goldenagereprints.com

Made in the USA
Monee, IL
18 June 2022